OLD BOYS
NEW WOMEN

Joan Abramson

OLD BOYS
NEW WOMEN

The Politics of
Sex Discrimination

PRAEGER SPECIAL STUDIES • PRAEGER SCIENTIFIC

Library of Congress Cataloging in Publication Data

Abramson, Joan.
    Old boys--new women.

    Bibliography: p.
    Includes index.
    1. Sex discrimination in employment--Law and legis-
lation--United States. 2. Sex discrimination against
women--Law and legislation--United States. 3. Women--
Employment--United States. I. Title.
KF3467.A92   344'.73'014   79-65933
ISBN 0-03-049756-6

This work was supported in part by the Department of Health, Education and Welfare, U.S. Office of Education under the Women's Educational Equity Act. However, the opinions expressed herein do not necessarily reflect the position or policy of the U.S. Office of Education, and no official endorsement by the U.S. Office of Education should be inferred. Grant Number G007702857.

Published in 1979 by Praeger Publishers
A Division of Holt, Rinehart and Winston/CBS, Inc.
383 Madison Avenue, New York, New York 10017 U.S.A.

Printed in the United States of America

CONTENTS

INTRODUCTION

*"I consider this very much like a rape trial where the victim becomes the
perpetrator and the more the rape victim protests, the more the victim
has always been the perpetrator of the rape to begin with."*
Sharon Johnson, Complainant, 1978

Several years ago I presented a paper at a women's caucus session
held during the convention of a major professional organization. The
panel topic was the status of women in the profession and my talk was
sandwiched in between a presentation by a woman in the throes of a
bitter discrimination battle with her employer and a woman who had
won a similar, though less bitter, battle several years before.

When the panel ended I felt uneasy. I had provided an inadequate
and unsatisfying filling for the yeasty bread of the other two presentations. How could a straightforward exposition of the current status of sex
discrimination law in the courts compete with the high drama of a woman
fighting for her career or the exhilaration of a woman who had won such a
battle not long ago? But my dissatisfaction went beyond that immediate
contrast and I soon had to reluctantly admit to myself that I did not at all
like the talks of my two colleagues.

The woman currently embroiled with her employer could see no
further than her own victimization. She was appalled and surprised that
her employer and colleagues had treated her so abysmally when she was
so obviously well qualified to do her job. And it is true that what was
happening to her was appalling; but it was hardly surprising. She seemed
to be asking again and again, "How could this happen to *me?*" She
insisted that her case was vitally important, singular, and precedent
setting and closed her talk by asking the sizable audience to fill in
mimeographed forms she had distributed pledging contributions to her
defense fund. What disturbed me was that she could not get beyond her
own outrage: what had happened to her was wrong and it happened only
to her. I sensed no general outrage; she projected no understanding of the
system that had caused her so much pain, no sense of connection with the
overall problem of sex discrimination.

The woman who followed me presented an equally unsatisfying and
disturbing talk. She had successfully fought a discrimination battle. She
had achieved her goal and was secure in her job. Her talk consisted of a
set of "how to" guidelines for winning sex discrimination battles. She
went through her list of rules with eloquence and good humor. The
audience laughed in all the right places. She had clearly psyched out the
system for herself. And the impression I gained was that I, clod that I am,

and hundreds of other women, clods that they are, had lost our battles or were in the process of losing them because we did not play the game correctly. We had not been smart enough to learn the dos and don'ts. It was *our* fault. The victims were, after all, to blame.

I will admit that my impressions of my copanelists were formed on the slim evidence of half-hour presentations. But it was just these presentations and their tone that disturbed me. Had we learned nothing in all the years of struggle to achieve equity? On one side of me sat a woman who seemed incapable of understanding why the system had failed to accept her even though she was clearly worthy of acceptance. On the other side sat a woman who extended to the audience the wisdom of her own case: all women need do is learn how to manipulate the system. Neither seemed able to perceive or project the fact that there were larger points to be made: That a system that requires victims will continue to require victims, even if a few clever ones learn how to beat that system and join it. That such a system is inimical to the notion of merit. That the individual victim need not, indeed must not, blame herself or her own supposed shortcomings. That it is the system rather than the individual victim or even the victimizer that requires revamping and humanizing.

Over the years I had talked with dozens of discrimination complainants and most of them had learned these things. Most shared a perception of discrimination far broader than their own personal rejection by the employment system. Most learned that discrimination goes beyond their own personal victimization and beyond their own inability to play the system. They have been able to understand that they are not necessarily responsible for their failures in the employment system or in the complaint and court systems to which they have turned. The learning process has not been an easy one but it is precisely this broader view of discrimination that needs to be understood by all women who expect to pursue a profession. If we fail to understand it then we, too, are left with no other explanation than that we, as the victims of discrimination, are at fault for what has happened to us. Helping to achieve the broader perspective is the purpose of this book.

The book has of necessity been limited to professional employment, particularly in government and in education. The limitation has not been set because other areas of employment discrimination are not equally significant. It is self-imposed because I can write only one book at a time, because the professional area is one I am best equipped by my own experience to handle, and because it is my belief that as women attempt to move up the ladder professionally and economically, the barriers to their acceptance become more rigid.

The approach I have used is that of the journalist, not the sociologist. The approach, like the scope, was chosen for practical reasons: I am a journalist, not a sociologist. While collecting materials for this book I interviewed about 150 people—women who had filed discrimination complaints in the courts and with antidiscrimination agencies, affirmative action officers, employers, coworkers of complainants, university presidents, agency workers and agency heads, lawyers, statisticians, supervisors, deans, computer experts, and public interest agency workers.

The form of the book was dictated by the materials and by my own training. I have used a number of case histories of women who have filed discrimination complaints. Each is unique in its particular facts and in the particular pain of the woman involved. Yet all seem familiar because each of the women has experienced the same kind of obstacles, the same kind of excuses, and the same kind of harassment in response to her complaint. The case histories graphically illustrate the meaning of discrimination, the difficulties a woman is likely to encounter in the complaint process, or the major judicial obstacles currently standing between women and employment equity. They answer, very concretely and personally, such questions as: How have women first encountered employment discrimination? What happens when a woman decides to file a complaint with federal or state agencies? What can women expect from the peer review system currently in use in colleges and universities? What is the federal employee grievance system likely to produce in the way of results? What happens when a complainant actually wins a case? To what extent have complainants experienced harassment and reprisal?

I have also used the equally direct techniques of the investigative reporter. Innumerable volumes of federal self-assessment, innumerable outside assessments, innumerable court findings, and innumerable interviews with officials of various agencies have been tapped to produce what I hope will be a valuable assessment of the current state of antidiscrimination agency enforcement and the current state of judicial thinking, along with a few historical insights that may help to explain how we arrived at the current state of affairs. Through these means I have attempted to answer such questions as: How did we arrive at our current notions of employment discrimination? What have the federal agencies accomplished? What can we expect from the newly reorganized agencies under the Carter administration? What have the courts done with current antidiscrimination laws? And what can we expect the courts to do in the future?

When I began looking for funds to help underwrite the research for this project I discovered they were not easy to come by. The response to my proposals was quite often a sense of surprise that I considered sex discrimination in employment still a live issue; after all, hadn't we made it illegal over a decade ago? Nor was it an issue that could possibly interest anyone any longer—yesterday's headlines are hardly worth reading today. I was met, time and again, with a kind of television mentality: we have dealt with this issue in the law and in enforcement agencies for over ten years, *ergo*, we must have solved it. The program is over. The denouement never occurs after the last commercial.

The attitude is unfortunately not peculiar to those who grant research funds. It is shared by at least some of the nation's top level advisors on domestic affairs. During the recent study that preceded President Carter's plans to reorganize the federal antidiscrimination agencies, high-level advisors in the executive branch were insisting that civil rights enforcement was a creature of the past: the decade of enforcement was over, the task had been completed as well as could be expected. Now it was time to move on to new programs of economic incentives to encourage women and minorities to join the mainstream of the American economy. In America, they would have us believe, if we have dealt with a problem for ten years or so, we must have solved it.

Well, the problem hasn't been solved. It won't go away. And even those people who are involved in it, in their pain and isolation, or in their all too rare triumph, sometimes fail to perceive it in its full dimensions. This book, then, is still necessary and after some hard searching it was possible to find some funding agencies that agreed. Seed money from The Fund for Investigative Journalism in Washington, D.C., launched this project and a grant from the Women's Educational Equity Act Program helped it through some of the research stage. Those funds helped make it possible for me to travel around the country to conduct interviews.

But I am indebted to a far greater degree to the women complainants who generously gave me their time, shared their files with me, relived their painful experiences with me, and often chauffeured me around and fed me. Government officials, we often forget, are supposed to be working for us and therefore should make themselves available to members of the public who seek interviews and information. Nonetheless, I am indebted to these officials for the generosity with which they gave their time—sometimes, but not always, that generosity was inversely proportional to the zeal with which they were willing to pursue discrimination complaints: those with the most reasons to offer why it was not possible for the government to do this or that were the most free with their interview time. I am also indebted to the many supervisors, employers, and university administrators who didn't have to see me at all but were willing to share with me their reasons for believing that, in the particular case I asked about, there was (always) absolutely no discrimination involved. I had a hard time agreeing with any of them—generally they told me that the woman involved was incompetent or merely venting spleen at not being retained or promoted, even though she did not deserve to be retained or promoted, and generally they told me that they would love to hire more qualified women but there just were none to be found since federal regulations had made the competition for such women so intense—but I appreciate the fact that they took the time to talk with me. I also owe a debt of gratitude to Senator Spark Matsunaga and his staff, particularly Jerry Comcowich, for aiding me in the collection of materials and setting up appointments in Washington, D.C., and to Joan Duval, Joan Thompson, and the rest of the staff of the Women's Educational Equity Act Program for their support and cooperation. I am especially indebted to Nancy Stearns, who helped shape my perceptions about current judicial thinking on sex discrimination, to Terry Day, who helped in the chore of wading through legal books, to Howard Bray of the Fund for Investigative Journalism, who supported and encouraged this project, and to Dorothy Stein, who read the draft of this book and provided valuable suggestions for its improvement.

Not all of the people I interviewed chose to be named. Some, particularly women whose complaints were in critical stages and women in vulnerable government posts, understandably felt that their positions would be worsened if they made their opinions public. Two in particular, whose cases are outlined in this book, have asked that their identities not be revealed. Their complaints are presented here using the pseudonyms "Marcia James" and "Barbara Jackson." Those who have allowed me to use their names are listed in the bibliography at the back of this book. If I have left anybody out, I hope they will forgive me. But to all, alike, I would like to express my warmest thanks. The information you provided, in interviews and in documents and your own papers on your complaints, made this book possible.

Chapter One

WHAT'S GOING ON HERE?

"We get memos all the time on equal employment opportunity, on how equally we should be treated and if we're not then management will be called down. I don't believe them any more."
Marcia James, Complainant, 1977

Captain Phoebe Spinrad served as director of administration and as an equal opportunity and treatment officer at the U.S. Clark Air Force Base in the Philippines in 1975. In early 1976 she began receiving complaints from women who were in the military as well as from military wives and civilian women employed on the base. The complaints concerned a "rent-a-girl" system in operation at Clark's club for enlisted personnel.

Under the system, 118 Filipino women were brought to the base each evening on air force owned buses. They were deposited at the enlisted personnel club and made their living, Spinrad says, by "hustling GI's . . . women were being rented out like pieces of equipment." Officially, the Filipino women worked only in the club, where airmen paid for their company and drinks. Prostitution, says Spinrad, was never proven, although it was widely acknowledged to be part of the "rent-a-girl" program.

The source of discontent among the American women who used the club was that competition among the "rent-a-girl" contingency had become so animated it intruded upon their right to make use of the facility. The Filipino women resented the presence of the American women, Spinrad says, since they believed it detracted from their own business. Military wives who left their husbands in the bar to use the bathroom would return to find a "rent-a-girl" had moved in. Military and civilian women using the club were subjected to name calling and harassment by the Filipino women and very soon the club atmosphere became unpleasant for the American women stationed at the base.

What is more, the American women resented the use of air force funds to bring in women for the entertainment of airmen. No similar financial arrangement was contemplated for the entertainment of the women on the base.

While there was no proof of any kickback to base personnel, it seemed clear from subsequent events that someone on the base had an interest in the continuation of the "rent-a-girl" program and deeply resented anything being done to bring it to an end.

In the line of duty as equal opportunity and treatment officer, and in the face of mounting complaints, Spinrad finally filed an official complaint on behalf of the base women. The single copy, hand written complaint was submitted on April 6, 1976. The form, says Spinrad, was privileged and restricted to air force channels. But on May 10, 1976, when she inquired about the complaint, Spinrad was told that she could be sued for oral defamation by the Filipino women. She was also informed that there would be no cancellation of the "rent-a-girl" contract and that her own career in the military could be harmed by the complaint.

Spinrad, still "trusting in the system," next took a single, hand written copy of the complaint to the inspector general's office. Three days later she was confronted by three air force legal captains and told that she would, indeed, be sued by some of the Filipino women. The officers refused to tell Spinrad how the complaint was leaked. Moreover, they made it clear to her that she, not the "rent-a-girl" program, was responsible for creating a potentially serious international incident.

When American military personnel in foreign countries take action in the line of duty, they are generally protected under agreements with foreign governments from prosecution under foreign law. Such protection can be confirmed when commanding officers write out "duty certificates" testifying to the fact that the person involved was acting in the line of duty. But the protection can also be withdrawn when someone in the military has broken a local law and has clearly not been acting in the line of duty. In that situation, the individual is placed on international hold, cannot leave the foreign country, and is subject to prosecution under foreign law.

Spinrad was clearly acting in the line of duty as a base equal opportunity and treatment officer. Moreover, she had treated the complaint discreetly, making sure that only one copy existed and that it was kept within official channels. Nonetheless, articles about her complaint began to appear in Philippine newspapers and in Stars and Stripes, and Spinrad's commanders placed her on international hold. Seventy-four Filipino women sued her for libel—an offense that if proven under

Philippine law can place the perpetrator in prison. Attached to each charge of libel was a xeroxed copy of Spinrad's hand written air force complaint.

Even though Spinrad maintained the support of the lower-level and civilian personnel who worked for her—Filipinos among them—harassment from some of her air force colleagues soon began in earnest. She received threatening phone calls. Fellow officers took every opportunity to scream their displeasure at her. Her appearance, motives, and even her marital status became the subject of public criticism and ridicule. Her superior officers offered no comfort and no support. Even the duty certificate she needed to protect her from prosecution in the Philippine courts was withheld. Meanwhile, the inspector general reported that there were no grounds for Spinrad's complaint about the "rent-a-girl" system.

In July 1976 the "rent-a-girl" program was cancelled, the inevitable result of the publicity some people in the air force had apparently brought upon the program without thinking of all the possible consequences. And in late September 1976, after months of harassment and threats, the air force finally released a duty certificate to Spinrad and transferred her to Carswell Air Force Base in Texas with a promise that the incident would not hurt her career.

Spinrad had also been promised that her Carswell assignment would be a choice one; her record of past excellence entitled her to the best. But she discovered at Carswell that she would be assigned duties as an executive officer in a field maintenance squadron, an assignment three levels below her Clark duties. Her acting commander at Carswell held the same rank as Spinrad, but he used his position to persistently berate her. Often with enlisted men looking on, says Spinrad, he threw things at her, yelled at her, and called her a "mop squeezer."

When Spinrad was able to examine her personnel file, she discovered that the promise made at Clark Air Base that her career would not be damaged by the "rent-a-girl" complaint had not been fulfilled. The narrative report, says Spinrad, was excellent, but the numerical rating of her effectiveness put her below 50 percent of her peer group. A discrepancy between the narrative and numerical ratings in a military record can be highly significant, she explains. It provides an instant clue that something is wrong. The officer effectiveness report is the one document that determines an individual's career in the military: one cannot gain promotion or prime assignments if the report is not high in both the narrative and numerical ratings. Until that time, Spinrad had nothing but high ratings in her file. The discrepancy that now appeared was, she says, "a subtle way of nailing someone to the cross."

At Carswell Spinrad met another career officer, Lieutenant Barbara Pawlowski, who was at that time a maintenance officer at the base. Both women were assigned to the same commanding officer and Pawlowski, too, had been publicly called a "mop squeezer," a term that was apparently their commanding officer's choice means of ridiculing women in the military.

Pawlowski ordinarily rotated her duty shift so that every few months she was required to work at night. But in December 1976 she became pregnant and her civilian doctor recommended a temporary shift to more regular daytime hours. Pawlowski's commanding officer disagreed: he pulled a rubber stamp out of his desk and stamped "bullshit" on the doctor's letter and her own cover letter.

Pawlowski next went to a military nurse-midwife who wrote an identical request. This request, too, was stamped "bullshit" and was, says Pawlowski, "flung around the office and discussed publicly in front of enlisted men." Her commanding officer insisted that her husband must have put her up to making the request and that she had ordered the midwife to write the letter. It apparently did not occur to him that Pawlowski could think for herself, even in causing what he considered to be a problem. The commanding officer also informed Pawlowski that he had no use for a pregnant officer and that she clearly did not belong in the military.

At that point, says Pawlowski, she felt her career was at an end. Although she had been warned about filing complaints in the military, she saw no alternative. She went to the office of the inspector general.

Meanwhile, Spinrad's and Pawlowski's commander had decided that it was Spinrad, with her suspect background gained in the Philippines, who was really to blame for his problems. He informed her that he did not trust her, removed her from all her duties, and eventually saw to it that she was transferred. On February 1, 1977, after six and one-half years as a career officer, Spinrad was assigned to a civil engineering squadron at Carswell. While she still retained the title "executive officer," her office contained only two clerks, neither of whom she supervised, and her own duties were limited to clerical work. Spinrad attempted to discuss the matter with her commanding officer but eventually she, too, had no recourse but to file a complaint with the inspector general.

In time, both complaints were returned with the notation that the facts in each case were essentially accurate and that the commander had been "counseled on the seriousness of perceived discrimination." The inspector general insisted that the commander had improved. But Pawlowski insisted that he was worse than ever and that his sexist remarks and behavior continued unabated.

Spinrad noted on the complaint form that she was not happy with the outcome of the investigation but would not request further review. Pawlowski amended her complaint and asked that the commanding officer be disciplined. Spinrad's request that the complaint be dropped was ignored and both complaints were sent to another investigating officer. From that time on, the complaint kept being "upchanneled and then tossed back to the division." The one hope that remained rested with the man who had served as inspector general when the complaints had first been filed. He had been sympathetic and he was in line for promotion to wing commander. Things would be better when the promotion came, he insisted. But instead of getting better, matters got worse. On taking over as wing commander, the former inspector general relieved Pawlowski of her duties, noting as his reason that she was pregnant. Spinrad, meanwhile, was left to her clerk's duties.

After the complaint had been investigated once again, a new report was issued. There had been nothing amiss in the wing, it concluded, beyond minor errors in judgment. As the complaint moved up the ranks, Pawlowski says, it was made to appear less and less serious, almost to the point where the complained of activities were deemed admirable. In the new report she was characterized as a "young, impressionable, pregnant female."

Spinrad had by then undergone a new round of officer effectiveness evaluation and was found to be "untrustworthy" and ill suited to her surroundings. The evaluation, says Spinrad, was "the kiss of death." Pawlowski, too, had received an evaluation that implied she barely met minimum military standards.

Spinrad submitted another complaint to the inspector general about her evaluation. The reply from that office was only that there had been no reprisal against her. She then wrote to President Jimmy Carter. The response from Washington informed her that the president had sent her complaint to the office of the inspector general.

At that point Spinrad and Pawlowski felt they had no remaining options within the military. Their careers were ruined. The system had struck back at them because they are women. They went to the American Civil Liberties Union and, with the help of attorneys from that organization, they have filed a class complaint against the air force under the equal protection clauses of the constitution.

❋   ❋   ❋   ❋   ❋   ❋   ❋   ❋

In May 1969 Mary Lou McEver was hired by the Department of Rehabilitation and Counseling at the University of Florida to work on a federal research project. McEver had almost completed her Ed.D. in special education and counseling and had 19 years of experience in the field, including serving as a consultant with the Special Education Department of the State of Florida on programs for the retarded and eight years of work as a vocational rehabilitation counselor. Her new job was to train counselors in working with the retarded.

But McEver did not have much of an opportunity to concentrate on the federal grant work. Within two months of her hire, two members of the small department left and she was asked to take on the additional work of supervising all department interns, supervising students in practica, teaching seminars, and supervising research projects. During one six-week period she was also asked to serve as department chair.

When McEver obtained her doctorate, her rank at the University of Florida was changed from instructor to assistant professor. Since the department was small, she was continually asked to fill in. The pattern that was set during her first few months continued throughout her university career. Her ability to be flexible and her broad knowledge of her field was acknowledged through continued requests to fill in in every possible capacity within the department. Male faculty, says McEver, had assigned and delineated roles but she never knew from one semester to the next what her duties would be: "I didn't reject any assignments as my previous experiences had been in state agency work where program needs and client service are the basis for work assignments, not individual prestige. The program needed me to do these things, so I did them."

The department chair seemed pleased with McEver's work and took every opportunity to point out to others that she was the first woman employed by the Florida vocational rehabilitation program as well as being the first woman faculty member in the rehabilitation field in Florida and in the entire South. Nevertheless, men with less experience than McEver were hired after her at higher salaries and on secure state employment lines. McEver remained on the more tenuous federal grant line.

The value of state lines to a department, says McEver, is that they make possible stable program planning and growth. If a department is paying most of its personnel from federal grant funds that may be discontinued, it cannot maintain a stable program or predict what its faculty resources may be in the future. The value to the individual is that time spent in a state funded position counts toward tenure. Federally funded positions are generally not considered to be tenure track positions and time spent in them does not usually count toward gaining permanent academic security. McEver points out, however, that at the University of Florida, when she was first employed, federal lines were considered tenurable. This fact produced some problems for McEver later, when the university discovered it had fewer secure state lines than it needed for her department. The federal agency that was funding her department's training program had for several years been critical of the university's reliance on federal funds for faculty lines and warned that funds were going to be phased out. It seemed critical for department survival that some state lines be assigned to it.

At the beginning of her fourth year at the University of Florida, McEver was finally transferred to a state salary line. But by then retrenchment had hit the university and the dean, with only one state line available for allocation to the health related departments, apparently resented having to assign the position to McEver's department. One year later that resentment took its toll. The University of Florida had begun examining salary inequities between male and female faculty members during the 1972–73 year and, as part of that examination, McEver's department chair requested a salary increase large enough to bring her up to the level of the lowest paid male in the department. In his memo the chair pointed out that McEver, although she was the lowest paid faculty member in the department, had more experience both in teaching and in rehabilitation work than the lowest paid male. Moreover, she had been at the University of Florida for almost four years, while her male colleague had completed but one year on the campus. "Dr. McEver's salary should be at least equivalent . . . if not slightly greater, due to her years of University of Florida involvement and to her greater number of years of total experience," he concluded in his memo to the dean.

McEver should have been reviewed for academic tenure and possibly for promotion during the 1973–74 academic year, which was to be her fifth year at the University of Florida. Such review was normal for all fifth year faculty in tenure track positions. Instead, the dean responded to the request for a salary increase for McEver by informing her that she would be dismissed at the end of the 1973–74 academic year.

The dean said he could not retain someone who had done only field instruction on a training project and no other teaching. McEver countered with her record: She was working in areas beyond the training project. She had done clinical supervision of students—something that is, for others, considered part of their teaching—and she had also regularly been teaching departmental core courses. Indeed, the dean should have been well aware of this, for in his memo requesting a salary increase for McEver, the department chair had noted that she was "handling didactic course work similar to any other member of the department." The dean then informed her that she had been warned that she must publish her doctorate thesis. Her thesis, she pointed out, had been published in part by the State of Florida and was in use, as well, in workshops for teachers of the handicapped. Finally the dean came to what seemed the real point: he needed the state pay line for people with "higher credentials" who were currently salaried on federal grant funds that would not be available any longer. At that point, says McEver, "I crumbled, as anyone would when they see that a decision has already been made. Anything I said made no difference."

McEver was painfully aware that her teaching, apart from the narrowly focused federal field instruction project, was being ignored. Her position was being sacrificed to accomodate a man who had been given the promise of permanent employment while on a temporary, federally funded job line. Nonetheless, she reacted as she had in the past by filling in where she was needed to keep the department going. At about the same time that McEver received her termination notice, the department chair resigned his administrative duties and an untenured colleague took over as acting chair. McEver picked up the extra teaching burden and handled all the department's core courses. This time, however, she assumed that by doing so she would somehow be able to salvage her job. Yet the new chair was in no position to help her. As an untenured faculty member his future depended upon the same dean who had sent McEver her termination notice. He could not be counted on to argue in favor of retaining McEver. The outgoing chair, although he undoubtedly was in a position to help, did nothing.

McEver's appeals within the university system proved fruitless. She assumed that the 1974 summer quarter would be her last. In June, just before the start of the quarter, she made one last effort to retain her job by writing the university vice-president. The letter did, indeed, focus attention on her case, but only on a technicality. University regulations required that employees receive a full year's notification before being terminated. McEver had been notified of her termination in August 1973. Since she normally taught during the summer quarter, both she and the university officials who had issued her notice of termination assumed her contract would expire in August 1974. But the administration now noticed that her contract year ended in June 1974. The termination letter sent the previous August had failed to meet university requirements: it had been two months late. She was entitled to work until June 30, 1975. What is more, if all speed were not used to send her a new termination notice before June 30, 1974, she would be entitled to yet another year, through June 30, 1976.

A frantic search for McEver began so that she could be served in good time. Her own effort to obtain a review of her academic credentials had brought her case to the attention of administrators. Their response had been only to make sure that a new termination was legally correct.

During the 1973-74 academic year, McEver had been denied the standard academic review of her records for possible tenure and promotion. The review had been denied because McEver was supposedly in her terminal year of employment. But the sixth year contract opened the issue: if termination at the end of the 1973-74 academic year had been untimely and therefore illegal, academic review had been improperly denied. She therefore requested that the review be conducted immediately. But once again the review was denied since she was once more in her terminal year.

Not once during her six years at the university had McEver been reviewed on her academic record. "Many times," says McEver, "I commented to friends that five minutes in an objective review of records would have settled my case." But no such objective review was forthcoming. A last minute offer to hold hearings was extended to McEver by the administration just before her contract expired; but the administration had already made it clear that it would support the dean and would insist that the dean's original termination decision had been based on a proper review. Moreover, McEver's untenured department chair had become so unsettled by her appeal efforts that he informed her "he couldn't help nor would he supply information." The university administration had adopted an adversary stance by this time and had even begun assigning an attorney to attend all its meetings with McEver. At one such meeting, McEver recalls, she finally persuaded a university vice-president to make some inquiries on her behalf. The lawyer stopped him just as he picked up the telephone to begin his inquiries and told him, "You can't do that, she's on the other side."

In June 1975 McEver's position at the University of Florida came to an end. Her appeal continued to float through the university committee structure. A complaint to the Equal Employment Opportunity Commission made shortly after her termination brought promise of an investigation but the investigation never materialized. And McEver, shadowed by unanswered questions concerning her termination, has managed to find only minimal employment.

❀   ❀   ❀   ❀   ❀   ❀   ❀   ❀

"Marcia James (a pseudonym) worked as GS 9-level investigator for one of the federal government's many regulatory agencies. She became a government employee in 1973 in an area office that was, according to James, not a pleasant one for women. She recalls, for example, one of her colleagues telling her, "The largest decision a woman should ever make is what color her appliances should be." That remark, says James, characterized "the attitude of all the men I worked with. They are all from small towns. Most of them truly and honestly believe that. They don't see it as discrimination."

James also reports that she was "detailed" more often than any of the men in her office (details are temporary assignments to some other place or duty than would be normal). Her details, she explains, were usually to lower grade level work, thus she could not accumulate credit toward promotion while on such temporary assignments.

> For instance, you work a whole case and you get to the point where you are just about ready to complete it and they say, oh, no, we need to detail you here or there or we need you to do such and such. Well, if you say no, you know what happens. So you say yes. Then they give the

work to some guy, especially a guy who is eligible for promotion in the near future. Then he closes out—by close out I mean he goes and talks to the company . . . and tries to get an agreement with the company. You're just kind of shuffled off. He gets credit for closing out that case which also means that indirectly he gets credit for working that case.

In spite of the difficulties, James remained determined to progress up the career ladder. She enrolled in a graduate program and began working toward a master's degree in business administration. On the advice of her supervisor, however, she did not bother earning credits in accounting—he informed her that they would not be necessary for promotion.

Compliance work at James' agency was performed by persons whose job titles were either audit specialist or accountant. The two jobs were identical, says James, but the accountant title was assigned to persons who had completed 12 college credits in accounting. But in December 1976, shortly before she was due for a promotion, James' agency announced that the audit specialist career ladder would be phased out and that only accountants would be hired in the future to do compliance reviews. While James was not in any immediate danger of losing her job, the change meant she could not be promoted within the audit specialist category; she would have to wait until she qualified as an accountant to move up the career ladder.

A month after the announcement was made, most of the men in the area office were converted to accountant positions. They had been informed of the planned change two years earlier, says James, and had no difficulty accumulating the 12 needed credits in accounting. But she had been discouraged from taking accounting. Soon James began comparing notes with a friend in a neighboring area office. Both had been deeply involved with their careers, both had completed half the requirements toward master's degrees in business administration, both were the only women in their offices working as audit specialists, and neither had been informed of the change until the last possible moment. "We looked at the way I was told about it, the way she was told and the way the men were told about this same move," James says, and discovered that they were the only ones caught by surprise.

The two women then began asking questions. Their inquiries went unanswered, but one was told, "People who ask questions don't go too far." The other was advised, "Sometimes when you fight for something, by the time the fight is over you are gone. You don't win anything."

The two women next decided to write to the agency director in Washington. They had nothing to lose, says James, "Because once they spot you as someone who asks questions you're in a category by yourself anyway. . . . Our training programs had been stymied, our promotions stymied, our work assignments stymied. There was discrimination in all the different areas of work."

The Washington office sent investigators to look into the allegations made by the women. "They agreed that the complaint was accurate," says James, "so of course those investigation reports have been shelved in Washington."

Meanwhile James' friend was subjected to more harassment. Her supervisor "was calling her in and swearing at her, being abusive front of other people, using every kind of psychological trick to harass her." Finally she left her government job.

In July 1977 James was told she would be detailed to Montana. The job, which required a two month stay away from her family, called for a GS 2 level clerk. Under civil service regulations, employees with a high grade level who are actually doing lower grade work can have their grade reduced and James understandably felt that this particular assignment was meant solely to harass her and threaten her grade level. In fact, she had only recently been told by a grade classification specialist examining her work that she would have qualified for a higher grade level except for the fact that she had spent so much time on low level details and, because of the details, had closed out so few cases on her own. The months of clerical work, away from her family and her MBA course work, if they did not make her vulnerable to reduction in grade would at the least set back her chances for promotion even further. James therefore declined the assignment and filed an official equal employment complaint through the agency grievance procedure.

Her supervisor responded by placing her on a one week suspension without pay. Such suspension, says James, is almost unheard of in federal employment. James therefore filed a second equal employment opportunity complaint in protest.

Following her suspension, James' supervisor once again ordered her to accept a detail outside the area. She asked that any such assignments be put off until her complaints had been resolved. But this time her supervisor responded by informing her he would immediately begin proceedings to remove her from her job permanently for insubordination. In December 1977 the proceedings were completed and James was unemployed.

The process for removal of a government employee who has job security is used only rarely, James says. "I've seen people with all sorts of questionable things happening as far as their work habits, their careers, and everything else, and they have never even been suspended. There are very few things that they can suspend you or fire you for and one of them is insubordination."

Male colleagues, says James, still do not understand her experience. "I don't know how they can look at me, as slow as I've gone up compared to men. I had to start as a GS 3 to get in because of veterans' preference points. I had to start as a three (GS 3) secretary. But these guys honestly thought I was well off. So there's no reaching them."

When James' friend quit her job, she wrote on the required government separation form that she was leaving because she had been harassed beyond endurance. On the bottom of the form a supervisor wrote that if she had been harassed she should have filed a complaint instead of quitting. Marcia James did file a complaint. Now she says, "If you file a complaint, you may as well quite because if you don't quit you'll be fired."

❖   ❖   ❖   ❖   ❖   ❖   ❖   ❖

In 1973 Iris Carter applied for a post as an elementary school principal in the Dayton (Ohio) City School District. Five such positions were open that year. All five were filled by white males. Three years later, Carter's job as a curriculum supervisor had disappeared, she had been demoted to fifth grade classroom teaching, and her salary had been cut $5,000. Was all of this coincidence?

Carter had been working as a curriculum supervisor in January 1973, when she was asked to fill in as an acting principal. At the end of that school year her supervisor praised her work and recommended her for a position as a permanent principal. Carter, encouraged by her successful experience and hearing that a number of posts had opened up, applied. During the summer she placed repeated calls to the district office to find out the status of her application. Each time she was assured that she was under consideration, although later school district officials insisted that, while she was eligible, she had not been recommended and was therefore not even in the running.

Two weeks before the start of the 1973–74 school year she discovered that the positions had all been filled and that somehow she had been "lost in the shuffle" and her old job as a curriculum supervisor was no longer available. The assistant superintendent for instruction was asked to take her on as a "curriculum facilitator," a less responsible post than the job she had held six months earlier before being drafted to fill in as an acting principal.

During her year as a facilitator, according to Carter, she was not even given office space. Instead, she was forced to operate out of the trunk of her car and to borrow temporarily vacated desks in the division office at the end of the school day when the elementary schools she served were closed but when she was still expected to be on duty.

A lot of things "started clicking" at that point, says Carter. She decided it was time to check her personnel file and found that most of her evaluations she believed were in the file were nowhere to be found. At that point Carter had five years of teaching background. Her administrative work, in addition to her half year as acting principal and 18 months as a curriculum supervisor, included two years' work as an assistant principal. Yet the only evaluation of her work in the file was a years-old assessment of her classroom teaching.

Carter next began to assess the recent appointments made in the district—a district that in students as well as teachers has a high proportion of blacks. All five of the assistant superintendents appointed by the superintendent in 1973 were males and four of the five were white. At the next level all but one of the district's division directors were white males. Of a total of 56 principalships in Dayton elementary schools during the 1973-74 year, 35 were held by white males, nine by black males, eight by black females, and only two by white females. The number of female elementary school principals had decreased by more than 50 percent: In 1967-68 one of every three such posts had been held by a woman.

> I had always been an independent person [says Carter], I never felt discriminated against before. I just did what I wanted to do and I thought the world was fair. I thought if you worked hard and you were competent, if you got your degrees and had your head on right, you could go where you wanted to go and get what you wanted. And it became clear to me that I wasn't going to get that no matter how many degrees I had and no matter how competent I was. . . . I had a wider breadth of experience than any men appointed to those principalships.

After a year of traveling between the three elementary schools whose curriculum she supervised with her office in her trunk, Carter again applied for a principalship. She was told, says Carter, that she was "the wrong color"—Carter is white. However, the one new principal who did receive an appointment that year was also white, but male.

Following her second effort to gain a principalship, Carter found her position reduced still further. Instead of supervising curriculum for three schools she was assigned as a school services advisor at one elementary school. At the same time her salary was reduced by $5,000.

The Dayton school district had no grievance system Carter could use beyond the informal inquiries she had made to discover why she was gradually being pushed further from administrative work or why her personnel file was so sparse. Carter therefore filed a complaint with the Ohio Civil Rights Commission, with the Equal Employment Opportunity Commission (EEOC), and, later, with the Department of Health, Education and Welfare's (HEW) Office for Civil Rights.

It took 18 months for the Ohio commission to rule and in the meantime Carter's position as a school services advisor had also disappeared. During the 1976-77 year she was returned to classroom teaching, a position she had left six years earlier for administrative work.

The Ohio commission ruled in Carter's favor and EEOC later adopted and endorsed the ruling. But neither agency was able to negotiate a settlement with the Dayton district. The EEOC findings were forwarded to the Department of Justice and, after holding the file for several months, Justice gave Carter her right-to-sue letter—the letter required before one can bring a private Title VII discrimination action in federal court. Carter is a single parent and the sole support of three teen-aged children. Similar cases have cost upwards of $100,000. Nevertheless, with the help of lawyers from the Women's Law Fund of Cleveland, Ohio, Carter did take the case to court in 1978.

In December 1978, following the court hearing but before any ruling had been made, HEW belatedly released a finding in Carter's favor. The agency noted that several of the men who received principalships over Carter did not even meet the district's own written criteria for such jobs. "In terms of total administrative experience," HEW reported, "none of the 5 appointees had more than the Complainant." The agency also found Carter's experience exceeded that of nine out of ten principals appointed in the district between 1973 and 1978. And it found that of 27 elementary principals appointed between 1969 and 1977, 15 were white males, 10 were black males, and only two were women, one black and one white. "There has not been a female appointed to an elementary principalship since the 1971–72 school year at Dayton. In fact, in the past four years white males have been the only persons appointed to elementary principalships," wrote HEW. Where one of every three principals had been female in the late 1960s, HEW now noted that "only one out of every six elementary school principals is female."

Black males, while still underrepresented, had increased at the expense of white women, said HEW. "In order to maintain white male dominance and in order to appear to comply with affirmative action in the appointment of blacks, white females have been virtually eliminated from the position of elementary principal in Dayton Public Schools."

Among the actions ordered by HEW were the immediate promotion of Carter to "the job classification, title, and salary of elementary principal." In addition, the agency ordered back pay with interest, retroactive administrative seniority, appointment of Carter to the first available elementary school principal opening, and "pecuniary compensation" for losses Carter incurred while she was attempting to gain a remedy.

The school district, however, declined to follow HEW's orders. Instead, it responded with a letter from its attorneys that even questioned HEW's authority to examine the issue of sex discrimination in its employment practices.

Chapter Two

WHAT IS DISCRIMINATION?

"Congress didn't pass a law to continue things as they were."
Peter Robertson, EEOC official, 1978

In its finding of discrimination by the Dayton school district against Iris Carter, the Office for Civil Rights of HEW seemed to be following the disparate impact notion of discrimination that was underwritten by the Supreme Court in its 1971 decision in *Griggs v. Duke Power Company* (401 U.S. 424). In that case, brought by black workers who complained that Duke Power maintained testing policies that screened out more blacks than whites as potential employees, the Court concluded that the law "proscribes not only overt discrimination but also practices that are fair in form, but discriminatory in operation. The touchstone is business necessity. If an employment practice which operates to exclude Negroes cannot be shown to be related to job performance, the practice is prohibited" (at 431).

But the Dayton school board begged to differ. In its response to HEW it noted:

the HEW determination relies heavily upon the disproportionate impact theory (that is relationship of positions held by males to those held by females). In past dealings your office has steadfastly taken the position (to which we subscribe) that administrative appointments should be made on the basis of qualification for the position irrespective of race, sex or creed. If the Dayton Board continues to follow this qualification procedure, it will undoubtedly run afoul of the disproportionate impact theory. Certainly, it is foreseeable that the selection of the best qualified person could result in a substantially disproportionate representation of males or females on the administrative staff.

Quite aside from the implied assumption that a merit system was at work and that it was no surprise white males came out ahead, the board's response to HEW confidently ignored legal precedents that had taken a decade to develop. Even the Supreme Court's disparate impact theory, the Dayton board insists, is open to debate.

Is there, then, any bottom line definition of employment discrimination upon which a potential complainant can rely? Is there any definition enforcement agencies accept as the standard against which to conduct investigations and courts accept as the measure against which to try facts? For some clue we will look first at the law itself, then at the genesis of that law and the administrative structure set up to enforce it, and last at some of the present thinking of agency officials who have attempted to define discrimination.

Before we begin, it would be helpful to sketch out the framework for government antidiscrimination enforcement in the employment area and to mention the changes that were brought about in 1978 under a presidential reorganization of civil rights enforcement agencies. It is useful to remember that there has always been a basic division between congressionally enacted laws forbidding discrimination in employment and presidential "executive orders" that require businesses engaged in selling goods and services to the federal government to refrain from discriminating against their employees. Both types of regulation have their elements of confusion. Congressional legislation has sometimes been quite broad and comprehensive and has, at other times, been limited to specific fields such as education or finance, or to limited types of discrimination such as salary discrimination. Thus there has developed over the years a patchwork of confusing and sometimes conflicting antidiscrimination laws. Executive order regulation has been equally confusing, both because of the difficulty of ascertaining whether or not an employer is in fact a federal contractor and therefore covered by such regulation, and because in the past the government has assigned enforcement of the executive order to numerous federal agencies.

The basic pattern for congressionally enacted antidiscrimination prohibitions before 1978 was that the Equal Employment Opportunity Commission handled Title VII of the Civil Rights Act of 1964, the major antidiscrimination in employment law, for all private employers and for state and local government. The agency often worked in conjunction with state equal employment offices to which it assigned part of its complaint case load. Title VII enforcement for federal government employees was handled by the Civil Service Commission. Other laws, less comprehensive in coverage or scope, were parceled out to other federal agencies such as the Wage and Hour Division of the Department of Labor, the Office for Civil Rights (OCR) in the Department of Health, Education and Welfare, or the Compliance Division of the Office of Revenue Sharing in the Department of Treasury. Some of these offices were created to handle single laws. Others, like HEW's OCR, eventually were charged with the enforcement of a variety of antidiscrimination laws.

The basic pattern for executive order enforcement was that the Office of Federal Contract Compliance Programs (OFCCP) handled rulemaking and administrative oversight while government departments close to various contract and procurement areas handled enforcement.

In an effort to simplify and consolidate the enforcement of these many laws and orders, President Carter set about to reorganize the structure in 1978. EEOC became the major unit in charge of congressionally enacted prohibitions while all executive order compliance was removed from enforcement agencies and consolidated within the OFCCP. The details of presidential consolidation can be found in Chapter 14.

There were some loose ends left by the consolidation and we cannot hope to discuss them all in this book. What we have done, instead, is to concentrate our discussion in two major areas of enforcement: Title VII of the Civil Rights Act of 1964, as enforced by the EEOC, and Executive Orders 11246 and 11375, as enforced by the OFCCP, because these laws are more comprehensive in both the kind of coverage they offer and the number of individuals covered and because the two agencies were the major ones charged with enforcement following the presidential reorganization in 1978. We have, however, paid some attention to the Office for Civil Rights of HEW and to the Civil Service Commission since, after the 1978 reorganization, both agencies continued to retain some authority over sex discrimination in employment in areas that affect a significant proportion of women in professional work.

It should also be noted that in this chapter we deal with the law and the structure in the ideal. The actual functioning of the agencies charged with enforcement will be a subject of consuming attention in the chapters that follow.

    ✿   ✿   ✿   ✿   ✿   ✿   ✿   ✿

Surprisingly, neither Title VII of the Civil Rights Act of 1964 nor the executive orders, the two major federal prohibitions against discrimination in employment, give a formal definition of discrimination. Instead they list specific kinds of employment practices that are prohibited.

Title VII begins with a series of definitions. They include the terms "person," "employment agency," "labor organization," "employee," "commerce," "industry affecting commerce," and "religion," but not discrimination. Nonetheless, the practices prohibited by the law seem clear:

It shall be an unlawful employment practice for an employer—(1) to fail or refuse to hire or to discharge any individual, or otherwise to discriminate against any individual with respect to his compensation, terms, conditions, or privileges of employment, because of such individual's race, color, religion, sex, or national origin; or (2) to limit, segregate, or classify his employees or applicants for employment in any way which would deprive or tend to deprive any individual of employment opportunities or otherwise adversely affect his status as an employee, because of such individual's race, color, religion, sex, or national origin [Section 703(a), 42 U.S.C. § 2000e-2 (1972)].

Title VII does, however, allow for one exception to the rule: there is an exemption when the sex, national origin, or religion (but interestingly enough not the race or color) of an individual is a bona fide occupational qualification (BFOQ). The BFOQ has generally been interpreted in the narrowest way. It would, for example, be permissible to exclude males from employment as wet-nurses or females from employment as sperm donors. As we shall see, however, the BFOQ exemption has not always been quite so clear cut.

Executive Order 11246, like Title VII, contains no specific definition of discrimination. Its key provision requires that all government contracts contain a lengthy section including the following statement:

During the performance of this contract, the contractor agrees as follows:

(1) The contractor will not discriminate against any employee or applicant for employment because of race, color, religion, sex or national origin. The contractor will take affirmative action to ensure that applicants are employed, and that employees are treated during employment, without regard to their race, color, religion, sex or national origin. Such action shall include, but not be limited to the following: employment, upgrading, demotion, or transfer; recruitment or recruitment advertising; layoff or termination; rates of pay or other forms of compensation; and selection for training, including apprenticeship.

The first provision is basically passive: it requires a commitment on the part of federal contractors to refrain from taking discriminatory actions. The second provision requires federal contractors to do more. It calls for "affirmative action" to overcome the effects of past discrimination and to ensure that all employees and potential employees are treated equitably.

Perhaps an examination of the genesis of the two major provisions will provide further insight. What, after all, were elected officials claiming they wished to accomplish with their demands on employers and how did they anticipate achieving their goals?

The two major employment discrimination regulations differ considerably in their origins, in their approach to enforcement, and in their administrative structure. The first to be developed was executive order enforcement. In fact, the use of the federal government's buying power and contract authority as a means of bringing about equal employment opportunity predates the use of legislation such as Title VII by several decades.

President Franklin D. Roosevelt organized the first committee on fair employment practices for federal contractors in June 1941. The committee was established under Executive Order 8802. It was housed in the Office of Production Management and was supposed to enforce nondiscrimination in defense contracts (OFCCP 1977). With defense contractors still primarily in mind, Roosevelt created a second, temporary committee on fair employment practices in 1943, with authority that expired in 1946.

In 1951 President Harry S. Truman created a President's Committee on Government Contract Compliance under Executive Order 10308, and in 1953 President Dwight D. Eisenhower created a President's Committee on Government Contracts through Executive Order 10479, with the vice-president serving as chair and the secretary of labor as vice-chair.

The early executive orders were little more than statements of public policy given status by committees that had no enforcement powers. Roosevelt's initial order came in response to a threatened march on Washington by blacks seeking a share of defense industry jobs. What little financing the committee had came from presidential contingency funds. Opposition to the early orders was led by Senator Richard B. Russell of Georgia and in 1944 that opposition took the form of a legislative amendment that prohibited funding for agencies created by presidential orders lasting more than one year. His successful move produced a six year hiatus in executive order enforcement.

Even though normal congressional financing was still politically unfeasible, the groundwork for a viable contract compliance system was laid by then Vice-President Johnson, who headed the Committee on Employment Opportunity set up by President John F. Kennedy in 1961 under Executive Order 10925. Kennedy's order had apparently been accompanied by some political bargaining behind the scenes that resulted in a commitment from various government agencies to assign some of their funds for compliance tasks. The order limited the responsibilities of the president's committee to policy making, program oversight, and evaluation and assigned compliance and enforcement to executive agencies that administered federal contracts. Politically, visible budgets for compliance in these agencies were not feasible and the executive order provided that the agencies select compliance officers from among their existing personnel.

In 1965 President Lyndon B. Johnson, through Executive Order 11246, transferred the functions of the earlier committee to the Department of Labor and gave the secretary of labor the right to create a compliance office and to promulgate rules and regulations for the enforcement of the order. By 1967 the political mood had changed sufficiently to allow for financing of the program on a line item basis through the congressional appropriations system.

Until 1968 the executive order had no provision to prohibit sex discrimination. But during that year President Johnson issued Executive Order 11375, which amended the earlier order and extended the contract compliance system to cover sex discrimination.

By the time the contract compliance system had gained sufficient respectability to attract congressional funding, the administrative structure for enforcement had become fixed. The Office of Federal Contract Compliance in the Department of Labor administered the program while compliance agancies in some 16 federal agencies and departments were responsible for enforcement in areas tied to the contracting done in each agency. Thus the Department of Defense was charged with enforcement for defense contractors, the Maritime Commission enforced among shipbuilders, and so forth. This structure continued without change, except in the number of compliance agencies, until October 1978, when all contract compliance activity was transferred to the OFCCP.

Direct congressional lawmaking prohibiting discrimination in employment would have been unpopular in an era where even the funding of a contract compliance program could not be managed. But by the early 1960s there was a sufficient change of mood in Congress to enable such legislation to gain a hearing. The first law forbidding discrimination against women in employment was the Equal Pay Act of 1963, which amended the Fair Employment Standards Act of 1934 and which forbade employers from paying unequal wages for work that required equal skill, effort, and responsibility. The Equal Pay Act was assigned to the Wage and Hour Division of the Department of Labor to enforce.

A mood favorable to antidiscrimination legislation carried over into 1964 and during that year Congress passed Title VII as part of its comprehensive Civil Rights Act. The inclusion of women as a class of persons employers could not discriminate against was the work of Representative Howard Smith of Virginia, who opposed the entire package and who quaintly believed that he was illustrating the inanity of the law by adding a far fetched notion such as a phohibition against sex discrimination into Title VII.

The administrative structure created to handle Title VII differs considerably from that set up to handle the executive order. When Title VII was passed, it included a provision establishing the Equal Employment Opportunity Commission as a separate government agency outside any cabinet department and with sole responsibility for implementing Title VII up to the point where litigation might be required. At that point Title VII became the province of the Justice Department, which had discretion over whether or not to bring suit against employers who refused to settle voluntarily. Private individuals retained the right to go to court on their own behalf or to bring class action suits.

In 1972 Congress amended Title VII in two major ways. First, coverage was extended to previously excluded public employees and faculty employees of educational institutions. With the exception of federal employees, whose Title VII claims were processed through the Civil Service Commission, the newly covered employees were placed under the jurisdiction of the EEOC. Second, EEOC was given the right to litigate cases against private employers. Justice, however, maintained the right to litigate cases against public sector employers.

The EEOC has functioned primarily as a complaint investigation agency rather than a law enforcement agency. Investigations of illegal employment practices are triggered, for the most part, by complaints of discrimination filed by individuals or groups. Comissioner initiated investigations, however, play a role in enabling the EEOC to develop key legal precedents.

Executive order enforcement activity can be triggered in three separate ways. Complaints of discrimination by individuals and groups are one means. But the compliance agencies were also required to conduct preaward compliance reviews to see if potential federal contractors were capable of fulfilling their employment obligations under the executive order. Agencies were also required to keep all current federal contractors under periodic review to see if they continued to be in compliance with the law. Administrative law hearings under the executive order can be initiated following investigative findings that a contractor is out of compliance.

Under the executive order, the penalty for failure to live up to the contract provisions on nondiscrimination and affirmative action is written into the contract along with those provisions: "In the event of the contractor's noncompliance with the nondiscrimination clauses of this contract or with any of such rules, regulations, or orders, this contract may be cancelled, terminated, or suspended in whole or in part and the contractor may be declared ineligible for further Government contracts. . . ."

The penalty for failure to treat employees or potential employees in compliance with Title VII is more remote. An employee, a group of employees, or the EEOC may file a complaint of discrimination. The complaint may be investigated and, if there is a finding that discrimination was likely, the EEOC will attempt to negotiate a settlement. If negotiation fails, an employer may be taken to federal court and if the court agrees with EEOC or makes an independent determination of discrimination the court may require the same kinds of remedies as EEOC attempted to negotiate or may impose more severe penalties such as quotas for hiring women and minority group members. In addition, the court can rule that defendant employers—or plaintiff employees, if it is judged they have brought a frivolous suit—should be required to pay court costs and attorney's fees for the prevailing party.

Under Title VII the agency must depend upon the federal courts for its ultimate enforcement authority. Under the executive order, the federal compliance agency, through an administrative law judge, has the final authority and need not use the federal courts. In terms of immediate and direct clout, the executive order clearly has an advantage over Title VII. It writes employment equity into the contract of those industries and institutions wishing to do business with the government. It theoretically withdraws that business if the contractor breaks the contract by failing to fulfill his employment equity obligations. In terms of accessibility to women and minorities, however, Title VII has the advantage. It gives individuals and groups a direct legal right to be free from discrimination and thus to go to court to seek enforcement of the law. They need not even wait for EEOC to take action on their complaints: if the agency exceeds its legal time limit of 180 days for handling a complaint without taking action, individuals have the right to file their discrimination complaints in federal court. Under the executive order, the individual or group seeking redress of employment discrimination enters the picture as a third party not involved in the contract. The legal standing they may have is not clear in relation to the executive order: they are asking that the obligations of a contract be met, even though they are not parties to the contract. To date most courts have held that such individuals have no right to bring suit under the executive order, though there have been cases brought successfully in an oblique manner, against the government, not the employer, by persons seeking court orders forcing the government to enforce the executive order.

Although the mechanisms for enforcing the two regulations differ, the initial step is the same: it involves an investigation of employment practices triggered by either a complaint of discrimination or a routine compliance or preaward review.

Over the years there have been a number of other laws passed that forbid sex discrimination in employment in more limited ways. Title IX of the Education Amendments of 1972, for example, requires that "(n)o person in the United States shall, on the basis of sex, be excluded from participation in, be denied the benefits of, or be subjected to discrimination under any education program or activity receiving Federal financial assistance. . . ."

Title IX was designed to parallel Title VI of the Civil Rights Act of 1964, which forbids discrimination on the basis of race in school systems receiving federal funds. While Title VI specifically excluded the coverage of employment, except where it was directly related to the purpose of the federal funds, Title IX was passed without any language exempting employment. Nonetheless, federal courts have interpreted Title VI's limited employment coverage quite broadly while, in almost every ruling on the issue to date, federal courts have insisted that Title IX does not extend to employment. Title IX has thus added a certain amount of confusion to the enforcement mechanism for women employed in education.

Another more limited law is the Equal Pay Act of 1963, the first law passed by Congress affecting sex discrimination in employment. The law has generally not been interpreted as covering issues other than salary. Equal pay is required, as well, under both the executive order and Title VII. The Equal Pay Act, however, has stronger penalties associated with violation of the law. Under the executive order and Title VII, a finding of unequal pay can produce an "equitable" remedy of back pay and a salary increase to bring a woman into line with the salaries of male peers. The Equal Pay Act can provide, in addition, double back pay to the victims of "willful" violation of the law and a six month jail sentence for the employer who has been found in willful violation more than once.

❋ ❋ ❋ ❋ ❋ ❋ ❋ ❋

In light of the many complications in the structure of enforcement, it would seem that some clear definition of employment discrimination would seem to be invaluable to potential complainants, employers, and law enforcement officials alike. However, until recently, little was done by any of the agencies to arrive at a simple working definition of discrimination and to lay out approaches for measuring it. Indeed, one of the most frequent complaints of people who have filed discrimination charges is that they have great difficulty explaining the discrimination they allege to government investigators whose job it is to recognize discrimination.

Among the few helpful analyses of discrimination by agency officials is one formulated by Peter Robertson, who until recently headed the EEOC Office of Program Planning and Review. According to Robertson, the definition of discrimination has evolved through three stages. Each stage involves a progressively broader perception of acts that are considered discriminatory.

In the first stage, which Robertson has labeled "motivation" or "ill-will" discrimination, employment discrimination meant only overt, intentional discrimination. Thus an employer who maintained a policy that no blacks need apply for jobs or one who told female employees that they could never be promoted because he did not believe women could be good managers could be found guilty of employment discrimination. Indeed, he had admitted such discrimination with his announced policy. In the early days, says Robertson, "employment discrimination tended to be viewed as a series of isolated and distinguishable events . . . due to ill-will on the part of some identifiable individual or organization" (Robertson 1978, p. 12).

Robertson has labeled stage two unequal treatment discrimination.

"At this stage discrimination was defined by reference to the *actions* (not *motivation*) of an employer or labor union but focused on identifying only those actions in which blacks and whites similarly situated were treated *differently*; males and females similarly situated were treated *differently*; or anglos and chicanos similarly situated were treated *differently*, etc. Government investigators and compliance mechanisms focused only on investigations designed to establish fact patterns showing that specific identifiable individuals were treated differently than other specific identifiable individuals of a different racial, sexual, religious or ethnic group (1978, p. 12).

Robertson acknowledges that it is possible to conceptualize the two types of discrimination in the same way: "There is some support for the theory that Stage #1 (intent) and Stage #2 (unequal or 'disparate' treatment) are really the same." In fact, he admits that investigators originally used disparate treatment merely as a more convenient means of proving intent (1978, p. 13). If, for example, black workers are required to use a single washroom located at a distance from their work while white workers have several close by washrooms for their use, one can assume that the employer is intentionally discriminating against blacks, even if he does not openly admit that this is so.

Stage three or "Griggs" discrimination, says Robertson, focuses on the consequences or the effects of an employment practice. It takes its name from the Supreme Court decision in *Griggs v. Duke Power Company* in which the justices declared that even employment practices that appeared to be neutral on their face in terms of equal treatment and even in terms of their overt intent could be discriminatory if they had a disparate effect on women or members of minority groups.

The *Griggs* case, says Robertson, requires a kind of systemic thinking:

it basically stands for the proposition that the inquiry for the government in determining whether a system is discriminatory is to look at its effect in terms of race, sex, national origin and religion. It is a statistical examination and if the statistics show that an employment practice or system "operates to exclude," and if the practice or system in question "cannot be shown" by the employer to be job related *and* a business necessity then "the practice is prohibited" (1978, p. 14).

Stage three discrimination can be proved by the agency by showing that women or members of minority groups are adversely affected by a seemingly neutral employment policy. Theoretically it does not even require identifiable victims. Nor does it require any proof of intent to discriminate—proof that for most discrimination victims is all but impossible to obtain. Theoretically, it matters not at all whether the employer is covertly using the employment practice to keep out blacks and women or whether he believes it is neutral and merely for the good of the business. Indeed, the only defense available to the employer would be to *prove* beyond doubt that the questionable practice was both necessary for the operation of the business and that it was in fact related to job performance. Even if the employer could prove this, the practice might still be prohibited if another practice (or test) could be found that would satisfy the employer's "business necessity," prove equally related to job performance, but have a less discriminatory impact on minorities or women.

If, for example, an employer required that all potential employees be at least five feet, six inches tall, that employer might be found to be discriminating against women and possibly against Orientals and Hispanic Americans. His only defense would be that the height requirement was essential to job performance and that the business could not be maintained if the requirement were dropped—in other words, that there was no other possible substitute requirement that was equally predictive of job performance but less deleterious in its effects on women, Orientals, and Hispanics. If an employer required all employees to have a high school diploma, as was the case in *Griggs*, he would have to show that the possession of a diploma was clearly required for job performance and that the business would be severely adversely affected if the requirement were dropped.

The three stage view of discrimination presented by Robertson is certainly useful. It is appealingly neat and well organized and it assumes a logical historical development of discrimination definitions by Congress, by the agencies, and by the courts. But while it is a useful aid to thinking about discrimination, in reality the perception of discrimination has not been nearly so sequential in its development.

The historical development of the perception of discrimination has been and remains spasmodic. Even Supreme Court decisions have shown no logical development toward stage three or a "Griggs" perception of discrimination. Nor has the Court, having reached stage three, felt obligated to remain there. As early as 1970, EEOC released guidelines in which "stage three" discrimination was clearly laid out. Indeed, the Supreme Court leaned heavily on these guidelines in shaping its decision in *Griggs*. But as late as 1977 the Supreme Court released a ruling that seems a throwback to the narrowest possible definition of discrimination.

The case was brought by a woman seeking employment as a prison guard in maximum security units for men in Alabama. The woman was initially rejected because she failed to meet the 120 pound minimum weight requirement. She also failed to meet a requirement imposed after she applied that excluded guards from working in state institutions where they would be in "contact positions" with prisoners of the opposite gender (*Dothard v. Rawlinson*, 97 S. Ct. 2720 [1977]).

Justice Potter Stewart, writing for the majority, said that the bona fide occupational qualification exemption permitted under Title VII, even though it had previously been applied extremely narrowly, could legitimately be expanded in this set of circumstances. His reason was that the environment in Alabama's maximum security prisons was a "peculiarly inhospitable one for human beings of whatever sex." He pointed out that federal courts had already characterized conditions in the state's prison system as "constitutionally intolerable." He further insisted that the presence of women in an institution that included a population of sex offenders and where all inmates were deprived of heterosexual contacts would pose a real risk.

Justice Thurgood Marshall, writing the dissent, pointed out that the court's majority opinion had sanctioned discrimination against women because of "barbaric and inhumane" conditions that Alabama state officials had already admitted were in violation of the Constitution. "A prison system operating in blatant violation of the Eighth Amendment is an exception that should be remedied with all possible speed. . . . In the meantime, the existence of such violations should not be legitimized by calling them 'normal.' Nor should the Court accept them as justifying conduct that would otherwise violate a statute intended to remedy age-old discrimination."

Even more objectionable than using an unconstitutionally barbaric situation to excuse discrimination against women, according to Marshall, was the attitude expressed by the Court majority that women constituted a threat to prison security.

> In short, the fundamental justification for the decision is that women as guards will generate sexual assaults. With all respect, this rationale regrettably perpetrates one of the most insidious of the old myths about women—that women, wittingly or not, are seductive sexual objects. The effect of the decision, made I am sure with the best of intentions, is

to punish women because their very presence might provoke sexual assaults. It is women who are made to pay the price in lost job opportunities for the threat of depraved conduct by prison inmates.

In another 1977 action the Court affirmed without comment the decision of the third circuit in *Vorchheimer v. School District of Philadelphia* (97 S. Ct. 1671). The case had been brought by a female high school student seeking admittance to all-male Central High School because she believed the school offered the finest academic program in the city. The circuit judge, in denying her claim that separate sex admission to public high schools was discriminatory, found that Vorchheimer could have attended an academic high school for girls. "The courses offered by the two schools are similar and of equal quality. The academic facilities are comparable, with the exception of those in the scientific field where Central's are superior" (532 F. 2d 880).

The court therefore acknowledged that the schools were *not* equal. But the judge's argument is based on the assumption that separate but equal school facilities are appropriate for girls and boys. The line of reasoning would clearly have been thrown out had the case involved separate schools for black and white children. The judge even acknowledged that his decision would have been different were the case brought by a black: "We are committed to the concept that there is no fundamental difference between races and therefore, in justice, there can be no dissimilar treatment. But there are differences between the sexes which may, in limited circumstances, justify disparity in law." One such acceptable disparity, the judge found, was separate but equal (or even somewhat unequal) education for girls. He insisted that if Vorchheimer "were to prevail, then all public single-sex schools would have to be abolished. The absence of these schools would stifle the ability of the local school board to continue with a respected educational methodology. It follows that those students and parents who prefer an education in a public, single-sex school would be denied their freedom of choice." One need not imagine what would happen if the same argument concerning the freedom of choice of white parents to have single-race schools were brought before the court today. The argument was used and rejected in 1954 when the Supreme Court, in *Brown v. Board of Education* (347 U.S. 483) ruled that separate but equal schooling for black and white children was inherently unequal, even in circumstances where programs, facilities, and quality were identical.

While Robertson's theory of an ever broadening perception of discrimination is useful in thinking about the nature of discrimination, it is clear that the development of that perception, at least in relation to sex discrimination, has been far from tidy or complete. We cannot assume that every employer or everybody in the agencies and the courts who might be in a position to rule on a discrimination complaint shares the broadest perception of discrimination. Nor should we confuse the broadening perception of what is included in the legal or enforcement agency definition of discrimination with the basic phenomenon itself. The three stages are a convenient means of looking at a single phenomenon.

That phenomenon can be viewed best in terms of its outcome rather than the means through which the outcome is accomplished or the ease with which one can attribute intent to the employer or to the people in the decision making process. It matters not at all whether an employer wants to discriminate or has buried his prejudices so deeply that he innocently believes there is no discrimination whatever in his employment practices or even if he sincerely and honestly has no discriminatory intentions. What matters is whether women and minorities are somehow victimized by those employment practices.

Discrimination, in all its "stages," is nothing more nor less than disparate treatment on the basis of some irrelevant characteristic such as sex. Even "disparate impact" is simply a more sophisticated means of talking about disparate treatment. It means, after all, that women or minority group members go without the jobs, salaries, promotion, or tenure status that white men enjoy: they are being treated differently on the basis of characteristics irrelevant to job performance.

It will be useful to keep this simple definition in mind in reading the case histories in this book and in approaching the bewildering maze of complications appended to the concept of discrimination by the agencies and the courts, for without it one can easily lose track of the very personal damage and the very specific pain that discrimination involves for the individual victim.

—— *Chapter Three* ——

EQUAL EMPLOYMENT
OPPORTUNITY IS THE LAW

*"If people want to talk about a bureaucratic foul-up it has been in civil
rights. And it has been a way to keep civil rights from being enforced."*
Mary Lepper, former director Higher Education Division,
HEW Office for Civil Rights, 1976

Among the requirements employers must meet in order to comply
with equal employment opportunity laws is the requirement that they
inform workers and potential workers that discrimination is illegal.
Generally employers are able to meet the requirement by exhibiting
government-provided posters in public places around their business
establishment. The posters give the potential complainant a sense of
urgency and a choice of two possible agencies with which to file:

FEDERAL LAW PROHIBITS job discrimination because of RACE,
COLOR, RELIGION, SEX or NATIONAL ORIGIN.... ANY PER-
SON who believes he or she has been discriminated against should
contact immediately THE U.S. EQUAL EMPLOYMENT OPPORTU-
NITY COMMISSION or ... THE OFFICE OF FEDERAL CON-
TRACT COMPLIANCE.

If the potential complainant is familiar with the law she may want to
ascertain whether or not her employer is a federal contractor. If she
discovers that her employer does receive federal contract funds, she may
next weigh the advantages and disadvantages of seeking Title VII or
executive order compliance. She may decide that her own standing as a
complainant is clear under Title VII but clouded under the executive
order and she should therefore file with EEOC. Or she may decide that
the advantage lies with the executive order mechanism since the threat of

withholding federal funds would be far more effective with her employer than the threat of a Title VII court action. But no matter how well she goes about her task of understanding the laws and the administrative structures set up to enforce them, she has little chance of finding out what may actually happen to her complaint once it has been filed, since what happens in most instances has little relationship to what the law says should happen. A few examples will suffice.

❖   ❖   ❖   ❖   ❖   ❖   ❖   ❖

Shirley Lilge teaches mathematics at Cleveland State University. Her teaching career began in 1960 when she was employed as a math instructor at Fenn College in Cleveland. In 1964 she was promoted to the rank of assistant professor and in 1965 she was granted tenure. That same year Fenn College and its faculty were absorbed into the newly created Cleveland State. All Fenn tenures were honored by the new college and tenured faculty members retained the rank they had held at Fenn.

During the 1970-71 academic year a committee of the Cleveland State chapter of the American Association of University Professors released a study of salaries at the institution. It revealed that women were paid far less than men in the same fields and with the same length of service at the institution. The report did not deal with relative research productivity. Fenn College had been primarily a teaching college and it was some years before Cleveland State developed an emphasis on research. The study revealed a $2,000 a year gap between the salary Lilge earned and that earned by similarly situated men.

After reading the study Lilge went to her department chair. He insisted that he had no control over her salary since he only made recommendations to the dean. She should take the matter up with the dean, said he. Lilge then went to the dean. He indicated that her salary was probably $1,000 below where it should be. However, he also insisted that the matter belonged with the department chair since he simply approved departmental recommendations. She should take the matter up with the department chair. But in the summer of 1971 the math department acquired a new chair and the salary inequity was continued.

In 1976 Lilge applied for a long overdue promotion to associate professor. She had been at assistant professor rank for 12 years, longer than anyone in the math department and possibly longer than anyone at the university. Yet her department chair had never initiated a promotion recommendation for her.

The department promotion committee approved Lilge's application unanimously but the department chair recommended against promotion and the university concurred. When university officials wish to deny promotion, Lilge points out, they can always find some reason: "They don't look at what you have done, they look at what you haven't done and they can make a strong case against anyone. . . . Einstein probably didn't do any community service."

Lilge attempted to take her case on appeal through normal university grievance procedures. Although one faculty committee found that "a presumption of discrimination existed," they recommended only that a university vice-president look into the matter. After months of delay, the vice-president finally concluded that no discrimination could be found.

During the long weeks of waiting for the vice-president to decide on her complaint, Lilge filed charges with the EEOC, the Wage and Hour Division of the Department of Labor, and HEW's Office for Civil Rights. Her EEOC charge was quickly deferred to the Ohio Civil Rights Commission. A preliminary investigation was made with remarkable speed and a full investigation followed immediately. In December 1977 Lilge received notice that the agency had found sex discrimination. A conciliation meeting would be held as soon as possible, she was told. But Lilge heard nothing more from the agency.

The pattern at HEW was similar. HEW's Office for Civil Rights maintains an office in Cleveland and, perhaps because of its proximity to the campus, the agency was able to begin its investigation within ten days of receiving the complaint, something of an all-time record for the agency. At that time, says Lilge, the university had developed a policy that was supposed to normalize work load for teachers. The maximum load any teacher was to have was 1,400 student credit hours per year. Student credit hours were ascertained by multiplying the number of students enrolled each quarter by the number of hours of class per week. But Lilge had taught double the number of credit hours allowed while one man in the math department had a total of 13 students in all of his classes for a year.

HEW investigators fastened their attention on the credit hour difference. But they also expanded their study beyond Lilge and her colleagues in the math department. They asked the university to supply records of all credit hours taught by all Cleveland State faculty members for each year since the institution had been in operation. The request was made in early 1977. Since then Lilge has heard nothing from HEW. HEW, however, maintains a computerized case following system and while the system does not reveal the names of complainants, it does log complaints by the date on which they were submitted, the name of the institution, and the nature of the complaint. Thus it is possible to compare Lilge's story with the case log. The log reveals that all investigative activity on her complaint took place within the first six weeks after the complaint was filed. As of year's end 1977, no further activity appears on the computer printout.

Lilge's experience with the Wage and Hour Division differs in form but not in outcome. Although her complaint was filed early in 1977, her inquiries in March 1978 revealed only that the agency planned to begin its investigation "soon."

❈   ❈   ❈   ❈   ❈   ❈   ❈   ❈

Margaret Dobbyn began working at the Kansas State University library in 1970. She came to her job with considerable experience both as a university librarian and as a graduate instructor in library science. Her credentials were superior to those of at least one-third of the professional library staff who did not even have degrees in library science, though a master's in library work has been the minimum qualification set by the National Librarian's Association since 1951. Dobbyn became head of the social science division of the library and for several years her work went smoothly. Her only conflicts occurred as a result of her constant effort to encourage upgrading of the library staff to meet the standards set by the library association.

In February 1973 a new library director came to Kansas State and, from that time on, Dobbyn's position seemed in jeopardy. The reason, apparently, was that the new director wished to free positions so that he could reorganize the library staff to suit his own plans. But Dobbyn also acknowledges that she may have lost supporters both because of her efforts to upgrade the library staff and because of efforts she made during 1973 while working with a campus committee on the status of women.

During the 1973–74 academic year several high-level positions were created by the new library director and filled by him with no search for candidates and no competitive evaluation. At the same time, the library director wrote a negative evaluation of Dobbyn's work that was based largely on "gossipy remarks." Her efforts to gain a hearing through campus grievance procedures proved fruitless. Says Dobbyn, "I didn't get any due process." So in August 1974 Dobbyn filed a complaint with the Washington office of the EEOC. The complaint charged the library with salary discrimination. Dobbyn says that men with comparable jobs held higher ranks and received larger salaries than did she. She also charged the library director with failing to open two new administrative jobs to competition.

The library staff at that time, Dobbyn recalls, was two-thirds female. The library director was male, as were two assistant directors. Nonetheless, the director planned to name a third male to another assistant director position in 1974. However, to satisfy the university affirmative action office, he instead appointed one male and one female to two newly created positions of assistant to the director. Five of the six library division heads were male at that point. What is more, the salary gap between male and frmale librarians was rapidly widening. During the 1971–72 academic year, according to Dobbyn's statistics, the average salary of male librarians was $1,992 larger than the average for female librarians. By 1973-74 the gap was $3,054, and by the 1976-77 academic year it had grown to $4,295. The figures, Dobbyn points out, are available each year in the preliminary budget of the university.

Word of Dobbyn's complaint reached the library administration early in 1974. By July 1974 her position was made subordinate to that of an assistant to the director who had far less experience and lower qualifications than Dobbyn. And following the news of her EEOC complaint, Dobbyn received a second and worse evaluation of her work, one that placed her at the bottom of the library staff. "I was horrified, angry, sad . . ." says Dobbyn. "They can say anything they want to, write it down on a little note, stick it in your file and pull it out any time they need it." The library administration complained that Dobbyn had caused problems, she says, but "of course the problem I caused was filing a complaint. . . . I couldn't believe that people could be as mean and petty and vicious as these people were." The path the library administration had taken seemed clear: the groundwork was being laid for her dismissal.

Meanwhile Dobbyn discovered that she could expect no help from EEOC. Her complaint was sent from the national office to the Kansas City office and from there to the Kansas State Commission on Civil Rights. The state commission, with 60 days in which to investigate, did nothing. And EEOC, which under law has six months in which to complete its work, did nothing. "I figured in a couple of years I would be out and gone before EEOC did anything, Dobbyn says. Thus in December 1974, believing that a court complaint would prove faster than an EEOC investigation, Dobbyn wrote the agency to request her right-to-sue letter, the letter that would certify to the courts that the agency was not going to handle the case and that she was therefore entitled to file suit as a private individual under Title VII of the Civil Rights Act of 1964.

In spring 1975 Dobbyn's fears concerning her future at the Kansas State library became a reality. She was denied tenure and notified that the 1975-76 year would be her last year of employment. "It scares you to death," she says, "especially somebody my age. What am I going to do if I live to be 75, 80, 90 years old? I lost my retirement . . . I lost my good name. It looks like I've lost my career."

❋　　　❋　　　❋　　　❋　　　❋　　　❋　　　❋　　　❋

Before the enactment of Title VII it was common practice to require that women take leaves of absence during pregnancy and to reemploy them with a loss of job seniority. Patricia MacDonald was one of the women affected by that practice. She began working for American Bridge, a division of United States Steel in Ambridge, Pennsylvania, in 1954 and was first required to take leave in 1960. When she was called back to work in January 1961, she had to start at the bottom once again.

Because of union seniority rules affecting cutbacks, it was not long before her job disappeared again. She was, she found, "bumped by a messenger boy."

The last hired, first fired pattern continued to affect MacDonald following her second forced maternity leave in 1962, despite the fact that she had continually taken courses to upgrade her skills, is working toward a business degree at Duquesne University, and has acquired an unusual degree of expertise in company computer usage. Had she been a man, MacDonald says, the education she has acquired on her own would have been company financed and she would, by now, have been moved into a management position. Instead, because of discriminatory practices, she remains at a relatively low pay rate while her responsibilities within the computer operation grow.

In 1971 an agreement that restored seniority for many women who had taken mandatory maternity leaves was made between American Bridge and the small union that then represented many of the clerical workers. MacDonald was left out of the agreement but union officials later said the exclusion was due to an error. She was included in an agreement reached in 1974, after the United Steelworkers took over as collective bargaining representative. (MacDonald believes her exclusion from the earlier agreement was undoubtedly deliberate. She had fought the takeover by the United Steelworkers because she believed women were better represented by the old union. But officials of the old union had fought *for* the takeover; they became local officials of the Steelworkers.)

But neither the 1971 agreement on seniority nor the 1974 agreement was satisfactory to MacDonald or to the other women involved. No effort had been made by either the union or the company to bring the women's salaries into line with their new seniority dates and no back pay awards were worked out. Following the 1971 seniority agreement, one of the affected women had filed a complaint with the EEOC. From that time on, both union and company officials insisted that the issue of back pay was out of their hands and could be resolved only by EEOC or by the Pennsylvania Human Relations Commission, which had taken over investigation of the complaint. The Pennsylvania Commission, the women were told, was handling the case on a classwide basis. Therefore, if back pay were to be awarded, it would be as a result of a favorable finding by the Commission and negotiations following the finding. Both union and company officials maintained the same position following the additional 1974 adjustments in seniority. But the Pennsylvania Human Relations Commission had still not ruled on the issue.

Following the 1974 seniority agreement, MacDonald and several other women attempted to file a grievance with the Steelworkers' Union, claiming that they should have been awarded back pay in line with the newly assigned seniority dates. The union refused to accept the grievance. Moreover, in the case of MacDonald and several other women who had fought the Steelworkers' takeover and who were not members of the union, officials also threatened that the women could lose their jobs if they did not authorize union membership deductions from their paychecks.

In June 1974 MacDonald filed a complaint with the National Labor Relations Board (NLRB), which, by law, has the obligation to consider discrimination complaints involving union activities. In her complaint to the NLRB, MacDonald charged that the United Steelworkers had violated the National Labor Relations Act "by its refusal to process [her] grievance concerning backpay" and "by its statements and actions concerning initiation fees."

In his initial findings, the NLRB regional director concluded: "it appears as a result of the investigation that further proceedings concerning those allegations are not warranted inasmuch as there is insufficient evidence of violation. More specifically, the evidence indicates that the union refused your grievance concerning backpay primarily because of its conclusion that the matter was essentially being resolved by a pending suit with the Human Relations Commission." The NLRB official then refused to issue a complaint against the union on the discrimination issues and on the refusal of the union to accept a grievance. He retained for further investigation only MacDonald's allegation that union officials had threatened "to attempt to cause the termination of certain employees."

MacDonald appealed the ruling and filed a complaint of discrimination with EEOC. The issues that were retained by the NLRB were assigned to an administrative law judge who eventually ruled in her favor. However, even this finding ignored the discrimination issue. Instead, the judge concluded that "in the final analysis agents of the Respondent [United Steelworkers] on repeated occasions in April and May, 1974 . . . threatened to seek the discharge of nonmember employees . . . unless they signed checkoff cards for the Respondent." He further concluded that "by restraining the employees in their rights guaranteed in Section 7 of the Act in threatening to and withholding representation, the Respondent has engaged in unfair labor practices within the meaning of . . . the Act."

The decision was rendered in January 1976. The remedy required the union to "cease and desist" from threatening to seek the discharge of employees who had refused to allow union payroll deductions and from withholding representation to those employees. The union was also required to post notices informing employees that it "will not threaten to seek the discharge of the Charging Party and other employees" and "will not restrain employees in the exercising of their rights." Nothing was decided about the substance of the discrimination grievance.

MacDonald's complaint to the EEOC (and to the Pennsylvania Commission to which it was deferred) fared even worse. The regional director of the Pennsylvania Commission told MacDonald the commission had spent a great deal of time and money on the case, but she adds, "to date they have done nothing but change personnel on the case." Her complaint was not the only one filed by American Bridge employees concerned with the back pay issue. MacDonald is aware of seven related individual charges that were filed with EEOC and eight others filed separately with the Human Relations Commission between 1971 and 1976. Most were filed against both the company and the union. All basically contend that the two operated together to defer back pay grievances and to prevent any negotiations on the issue.

But by 1978 only one of the cases had reached settlement. The woman who had filed the original complaint in 1971 was awarded $10,000 in back pay in 1976. The others, all of whom had been told by both the company and the union that they could not submit grievances since their complaint was being handled under the umbrella of the 1971 complaint to EEOC, have received nothing. Instead, they are now being told by the union that it is too late to submit a timely grievance. Further, says MacDonald, the Pennsylvania Commission is now expressing some doubts as to whether it will accept the complaints filed in recent years, after the women realized that they would not be included in the settlement of the 1971 complaint. Even though the commission has been aware of the problem since 1971 and even though it has established the precedent of back pay through its single ruling, the State Commission, too, is talking about the lack of "timeliness" of the recent back pay complaints.

❖   ❖   ❖   ❖   ❖   ❖   ❖   ❖

Alberta Gilinsky serves as a tenured professor of psychology at Bridgeport University in Connecticut. She graduated magna cum laude from Smith College, where she was awarded membership in Phi Beta Kappa, and she received her doctorate from Columbia University. After receiving her Ph.D., Gilinsky received postdoctoral training at Columbia. For four years, as a member of the Columbia scientific staff, she served as principal investigator on research in space perception under a U.S. Air Force contract. She also collaborated with other professors at Columbia on a number of other government research projects.

In 1968, when Gilinsky was an associate professor at Bridgeport, a member of the Columbia department of psychology suggested she write to the department's personnel committee since a teaching appointment had opened in experimental psychology. Since she was interested in returning to Columbia with its research oriented faculty, Gilinsky sent an inquiry.

In reply, Gilinsky was told that, due to student riots on the Columbia campus, there would be "no business as usual." But some months later she was encouraged to write again to the new department chair to "present her name" since, she was told, there was "a possible opening at Columbia." This time Gilinsky received no reply. Her only communication on the subject came from a professor at New York University who told her that he was being considered for a senior position in perception at Columbia.

In 1970 William J. McGill, who had headed the psychology department, was appointed president of Columbia. Gilinsky wrote to congratulate him and noted in her letter that the university was under fire for its failure to employ qualified women. To underscore her point, she enclosed a copy of an article that had appeared in the New York *Times* in which Columbia's dean of graduate faculties of pure science was quoted as saying that "a tenured university position . . . requires a tremendous amount of education and time that interferes with our normal idea of a woman's role in the family."

In February 1972 Gilinsky wrote once again to McGill. She was serving at that time as a visiting professor at Cambridge University in England and she wrote to express her interest in a temporary appointment during her 1972–73 sabbatical year, as well as in a permanent, tenured appointment.

In his 1972 reply McGill admitted that the university was under pressure from HEW to adhere to its own affirmative action guidelines. McGill also forwarded Gilinsky's letter and the vitae she had enclosed to the psychology department chair. But her application for employment both temporary and permanent—was rejected. Due process, says Gilinsky, "was scant." The department failed to follow Columbia's prescribed procedures for considering appointees and, instead, allowed the decision to reject Gilinsky to be made by the dean—the same dean who had been quoted in the *Times*. Says Gilinsky, "academic qualifications and the existence of authorized openings were never questioned by the department executive committee." The only issue was Gilinsky's sex and the need to find an acceptable excuse for rejecting her.

Between 1968, when she first applied at Columbia, and April 1972, when the school finally rejected her, five men were appointed to tenured posts and two others received untenured appointments. All seven had similar or less impressive qualifications than Gilinsky's. The reason given for rejecting Gilinsky was "no need," yet later, when another vacancy opened in a tenured slot, Columbia proceeded to promote to tenure a man whose field was sensation and perception—the same field in which

Gilinsky was a recognized expert. "Positions were open for men, not for a woman," says Gilinsky.

The faculty of pure science at Columbia during the time Gilinsky attempted to gain employment contained 85 tenured men and only one tenured woman, a physicist. The psychology department had no women on its tenured faculty. According to one sworn witness, President McGill, who had chaired the psychology department, admitted that "it was a non-written rule in the department that no woman would be hired."

In April 1972 Gilinsky filed a complaint of sex discrimination with the EEOC. The complaint was deferred to the New York State Division on Human Rights. And in September 1972 Gilinsky filed a second complaint with the State Division under a New York State law that has prohibited sex discrimination in employment since 1965.

After an initial investigation, the State Division found probable cause to believe that Columbia had discriminated against Gilinsky and recommended a full public hearing on the case. But the hearing was not held until one year after Gilinsky had filed with EEOC and the findings of the commissioner of the State Division were not released until March 1974. Although the findings held that Gilinsky was well recognized in her field and highly competent, they also held that there was no discrimination in the failure to hire her. In his final ruling the state commissioner gave two reasons for this decision: Columbia had been on a belt-tightening program and could not replace all tenured professors lost to the department of psychology over the years during which Gilinsky had applied. And the department already had sufficient strength in Gilinsky's areas of expertise.

Gilinsky appealed the decision to the State Human Rights Appeal Board and on February 14, 1975, by a three to one decision, that board ruled that there had in fact been sex discrimination in the failure to hire. The board remanded the issue back to the State Division and ordered the commissioner to take action "consistent with this decision. . . ." In its decision, the board noted the budgetary pleas that had impressed the State Commission were pretextual. In fact, the department had continued to hire white males rather freely over those years. It also observed that Gilinsky's "areas of expertise in research, publication and teaching were much broader than respondents here would have us believe." The seven men who had received tenured positions during the period "could be similarly identified with her background," said the board.

The State Division, however, was not given the opportunity to reshape its order. Instead, Columbia University appealed the decision of the State Human Rights Appeal Board to the state appellate court, charging that the Appeal Board had exceeded its authority in its reexamination of the evidence presented at the original hearing. But the appellate court in New York unamimously upheld the Appeal Board and the decision that there had been discrimination at Columbia. Columbia was still unwilling to back down. It petitioned the appellate court for a reargument or for the right to appeal to the New York State Court of Appeals. Reargument was denied but the university won the right to appeal the case still further. And on appeal the decision of the Appeal Board and the appellate court was reversed. The initial determination that there had been no discrimination at Columbia was upheld.

By this time four years had gone by since Gilinsky filed her initial complaint. The entire battle had been based on Gilinsky's original complaint to the State Division on Human Rights, filed under New York State Law. In all that time, no decision had been made on her Title VII rights. But EEOC, which had deferred to the State Division in 1972, came back into the picture in 1976. Without conducting any independent investigation, the agency decided to go along with the Court of Appeals and issued its own determination that there had been no discrimination in the failure of Columbia University to hire Gilinsky, or even to seriously consider hiring her, for a position in its department of psychology.

❋   ❋   ❋   ❋   ❋   ❋   ❋   ❋

One of the earliest class complaints of sex discrimination filed with HEW's Office for Civil Rights was a complaint against certain departments at Rutgers University's Newark, New Jersey, campus. The complaint was filed in 1971 and was deliberately limited by the complainants to two departments on the campus in the hope that the limited scope would encourage HEW to take on the investigative task. The complainants believed that once HEW had established a pattern for investigation on the campus, more comprehensive charges could be investigated.

The tactic was well informed: in the late 1960s and early 1970s hundreds of class complaints of sex discrimination had been lodged with HEW against universities, all of the campuses of Rutgers among them, by the Women's Equity Action League. Not one charge has been investigated and most were eventually dropped by the agency during 1975 and 1976.

The limited charge was filed on behalf of all women in the Rutgers Newark campus zoology department and the school's combined psychology-physiology department. Faculty of the two departments worked closely together and the three fields formed a working unit that was, according to one official familiar with the complaint, "ideal for comparison purposes." The complaint involved the standard academic sex discrimination issues—equal pay, promotion, and tenure—and it also involved the failure of the school to back a vital community action program.

The tactic of limiting the complaint to the two departments seemed at first to be welcomed by HEW. Regional officials in New York "accepted the complaint within the context in which it was filed—we were well within our rights to contain it within the context in which it was written." They began the investigation almost at once. A finding of discrimination was made and regional officials next began working toward a negotiated settlement.

It would be wrong to assume that the investigative stage went without a hitch. The women involved as complainants remember the experience as one that required constant pushing of agency personnel, but it was not half so difficult as the events that followed.

Regional OCR officials were, however, willing to consider several rather unconventional issues. One involved a woman psychologist who taught classes on the Newark campus and spent some of her working time in a child care center for welfare mothers. Rutgers had refused to credit the work done at the care center as part of the psychologist's university work and she had been paid only on a part-time basis. Regional OCR officials took the position that Rutgers, as a government contractor, had an obligation to help meet community needs. The woman's work was, in their view, as vital as research done by male psychologists at the university who were paid on a full-time basis though they carried no more teaching responsibility than did the woman. The view is not far fetched at all, considering that most universities, on paper at least, demand that faculty contribute in three ways in order to maintain their status: they are required to show excellence in teaching, research, and community service.

Another of the women involved in the complaint was a zoologist whose research required that she maintain a laboratory with a number of animals. The animals required attention all year and the woman therefore had to work during the summer months if she wished to continue her research. The university, however, had kept the woman on a 10 month contract year, although a number of men were kept on 12 month contracts on the grounds that they were engaged in research as well as teaching. Some, in fact, did their "research" off campus during the summer months. Regional OCR officials took the position that the woman should have been on a 12 month salary.

Both of these women had been placed in double bind situations. Advancement in the academic world could be achieved only if they demonstrated research accomplishment. Men in similar circumstances are sometimes given time off from teaching with no reduction in salary to facilitate their research efforts. The university, by refusing to support the research of these women, was telling them that their work was not valued and discouraging them, both financially and psychologically, from continuing it. Yet if they did not demonstrate research accomplishment, they could later be told that they had failed to qualify for advancement or even for continued employment.

Negotiations continued through January and in February 1974 Rutgers and OCR's New York office reached an agreement. Each proposed settlement was then sent to the woman involved for her final approval. In each case OCR acted as an intermediary. The separate approach gave each woman a chance to accept or reject the settlement for herself and a chance to control disclosure of the information.

Eight complainants were involved and all eight signed settlement agreements, although the agreements still left a number of issues unresolved. In March 1974 OCR and Rutgers officials took a last look at the settlement and signed.

OCR national officials had been present during the final negotiations, according to one regional official. In fact, the national director of the Higher Education Division, Dr. Mary Lepper, was present during the negotiations, had approved the final agreement, and was aware of everything that went into the agreement as well as the method of settlement. HEW's general counsel office had also approved the agreement.

But OCR has rarely been free from internal conflicts and the Rutgers agreement, though signed by all parties, soon became caught up in the conflict that was current at that time. Some national officials apparently had sufficient political power within OCR and with the then director of OCR, Peter Holmes, to prevent execution of the settlement. As an excuse for stepping in, according to one agency official, they used the fact that the women had been asked to sign separate agreements: one single conciliation agreement between Rutgers and OCR would have been proper, they claimed. They also complained of the effort to investigate and work out a settlement for a small, limited group rather than the whole university, although they could hardly have been ignorant of the manner in which the investigation was being conducted since it had been going on over a two year period. The tone taken by the officials who opposed the settlement was actually militant: all of Rutgers should have been investigated and all issues should have been covered. If discrimination was found against one woman, then the employment situation of every woman on the campus should have been studied and resolved before any settlement was reached.

The wider investigation that was used as a rationale for stopping the settlement was never begun. Instead, OCR officials in Washington debated for almost a year about what would be a proper scope for the investigation. Some insisted it had to be university wide, though OCR had never yet been able to complete a university wide investigation of discrimination. Some conceded that a unit such as the school's college of arts and sciences would do. According to one official who had been involved in the early stages of the case, the debate about "identifying a class" was still going on in September 1975.

While the debate continued, during the summer of 1975, a new investigation was launched under the direction of Barry Anderson, who then served as operations chief of the headquarters office of the Higher Education Division of OCR. The actual investigation was performed by two young and relatively inexperienced HEW employees and, interestingly, it did not go beyond the scope of the original two-department complaint. However, it did result in some startlingly different settlement recommendations. Under the old settlement, for example, the woman zoologist who had worked on a 12 month basis while on a 10 month contract was to receive a back pay settlement of $24,000. Under the new settlement, she was to receive $9,000. Most of the other back pay settlements were reduced somewhat, according to an official who worked on the original settlement, although the official pointed out that since an additional two years had gone by, one would have supposed the back pay figures should have grown.

The final settlement of the 1971 complaint, negotiated by Anderson, was completed in December 1975, almost two years after the earlier settlement had been approved by all the affected parties. By 1975 the women involved had been worn down by the struggle. They agreed to the settlement even though they did not believe it was equitable. To buffer the worst part of the settlement, complainants pooled some of their own back pay awards and shared them with the woman zoologist most severely affected by the cuts.

Anderson's explanation of his role in the Rutgers settlement is lengthy, contradictory, and hardly enlightening. It is, however, informative if one is seeking to understand the thinking of government antidiscrimination officials, particularly at OCR. His involvement, says Anderson, began in March 1975, after Mary Lepper was removed from her post as director of OCR's Higher Education Division. Roy McKinney was moved into that position and Anderson became chief of operations. OCR Director Peter Holmes and Lepper had become personally involved in the complaint, says Anderson, and when he entered the picture it was in the process of being recommended for enforcement. He fails to explain why enforcement was necessary when Rutgers had already agreed to and signed the settlement proposed by OCR.

"It was my assignment to review the adequacy of the case before it went to hearing," Anderson explains.

> Albeit reluctantly, I had to agree that we could probably go to enforcement but was unwilling to do so because we had a series of mishandlings of the case from the minute it was undertaken. Originally the women in the zoology and psychology departments tried to file a complaint which was a class complaint according to their view but a

mini-class, namely within their own group. They covered the water-front issues—salary, hiring, blah, blah, blah, blah, blah, and we had a lot of other complaints. The individual who was originally assigned the case approached it as if it were eight individual cases. In addition, at that time there was very little understanding on the part of our regional staff, as you can attest, as to how to prove discrimination. So the way they went about proving this case was strange. Lots of different people became involved in it on various occasions with the cumulative effect that nobody was getting anything done and we were getting hell from Senator Case and everybody else. So that's the environment that I moved into in March [1975] a couple of years ago. I looked at it and quite frankly I was appalled at how badly it was done.

Anderson says that what he first was asked to examine was "a recommendation for enforcement." In spite of his earlier statement that he "reluctantly" had to agree that the agency could "go to enforcement" he continued: "We just didn't have it. And moreover the issue in the case was salary. What happened to the other six—promotion, termination, whatever? People who had worked on the case didn't distinguish between equal pay for equal work, promotion or whatever. All they knew is that there were problems and that they should be solved."

Anderson claims: "The individual who settled part of the case was unable to secure monetary relief. I came along and was able to prevail upon Rutgers and we've secured the monetary relief. We got them unusual, dollar for dollar, what they lost, those eight woman." But hadn't Rutgers been willing to grant monetary relief to the eight complainants several years earlier, he was asked. "Yes," he replied, "oh, absolutely, all along, that's true."

Why was the final settlement smaller than the one to which Rutgers had initially agreed? "Well," says Anderson, "it was smaller because the individuals who had originally figured out how much was due people hadn't done their homework." The figure, he insists, "was computed wrong." What about the woman whose laboratory work required that she work 12 months on a 10 month contract? "Well, that wasn't the case," says Anderson, "that wasn't the case." What was the case was she went from 10 month to 12 month. They [early HEW investigators] had her doing that a year early. They also had another woman working six months when she only worked half a year. That's what happened." Isn't six months half a year, Anderson was asked. "Well, she was supposed to work a year and she only worked half a year, okay? And they [early investigators] had her carried as a year, working, and she didn't do that."

Why would OCR want to settle for less than Rutgers had agreed upon, Anderson was asked.

'Cause the Department of Labor requires that we can only get what was lost. We cannot get—that's one of our biggest bitches with the Department of Labor. They say that the only thing, when they've [complainants] lost back wages, the only thing you can get them is back wages. We [OCR] read the executive order as saying 'appropriate remedy,' whatever we can get: equitable relief, whether it be punitive damages, we don't care, and we don't care whether or not we call it back wages or not.

But later in the interview Anderson remarked:

You asked a question that really points out an extreme amount of naivete. Our relationship with the contractors and with institutions we regulate is a legal one. And we cannot ask for nor would I *ever* contemplate asking more than what an individual is entitled to. The courts do not recognize punitive damages in discrimination cases at this time and I do not—unless and until such time as I am instructed to do otherwise I will not. All I want is to make the person whole and that's all that courts have supported.

Why was the payment originally agreed to by Rutgers and OCR reduced? Is it not likely that the concept of making the victim of discrimination "whole" could include pay for periods when men were paid but when a woman performing similar or greater duties was left off the payroll? Anderson does not think so: "It [back pay] was reduced because that's not what the women were entitled to. And that's what I told them. I said, 'Look, I'm not a feminist. That's not my job. I may be a feminist in my private life but that doesn't influence my job. I'm a professional in civil rights. All you're entitled to is what you lost. And that's all you lost.' And that's basically where we came out."

Even though Anderson complained of the narrow scope of the earlier investigation and settlement and insisted that the limitation of the investigation to the "mini-class" had been a primary reason for delaying the settlement, in the end no attempt was made by Anderson or OCR to broaden the investigation to other issues or to other departments on the campus. The final settlement in 1975 was limited to back pay for the eight women in the orignal two-department complaint.

An examination of printouts from OCR's computerized case following system dated November 8, 1977, reveals that after 1975 there was no activity on any of the many other complaints that had been filed against Rutgers. The printouts also reveal OCR's official explanation for the headquarters hold on the original Rutgers settlement. Entries on January 16, 1974, tell us that conciliation conferences were held between Rutgers and OCR. The next two entries, dated November 19, 1974, tell us that the "conciliation effort failed" and that the case was referred to Washington headquarters for enforcement.

Chapter Four

THE AGENCIES EXAMINED: THE OFFICE OF FEDERAL CONTRACT COMPLIANCE PROGRAMS

"I've tried to rebuild the stature and integrity of the program. It's not easy when you've had so many deficiencies in the past."
Weldon Rougeau, Director, OFCCP, 1978

The overall impression one gains from the agency handling of the cases presented in Chapter 3 can only be one of disappointment. Nevertheless, if anything, the cases outlined display the brighter side of the enforcement coin. Of the five, findings of discrimination were made at some point in three cases. And one case out of the five resulted in some kind of restitution to complainants, inadequate though that restitution may have been. Agency records are replete with complaints filed years ago—some as early as 1968 or 1969—that have gone completely unexamined. Others have been examined spasmodically and filed away. Still others have been dismissed for no apparent reason other than the administrative convenience of the agency involved: their appearance on the books after years of neglect was undoubtedly an embarrassment.

But have we evidence of bureaucratic ineptitude outside of that presented by disappointed complainants? And what have the agencies to say in their own defense? In this chapter and the next we attempt to answer these questions in regard to the two major agencies, the Office of Federal Contract Compliance and the Equal Employment Opportunity Commission.

In 1978 the Office of Management and Budget (OMB), under the guidance of the new Carter administration, prepared a series of special analyses of the U.S. budget in areas of public concern, including civil rights. Perhaps one of the most interesting exhibits in the civil rights analysis is a graph entitled "Federal Contract Compliance Activities." It reveals that the compliance program has grown from an expenditure of 25 million in 1974 to a projected $45 million in fiscal 1979 and tells us that approximately half a million "hires and promotions" have been garnered during each year since 1974 "from affirmative action plans in non-construction contracts." In 1979, we learn, approximately 700,000 new hires and promotions will result from "the compliance reviews carried out by the agencies as they examine the activities of 25,000 non-construction contractors" (OMB 1978, p. 281).

The figures are impressive. Private business has a choice when it comes to executive order compliance. If business owners do not wish to be encumbered with the requirements of the order, they can choose not to contract with the federal government. If they choose to become federal contractors, they are obliged to follow the requirements of the order. The figures would seem to indicate that contract compliance works: that business executives, having chosen to negotiate with the government and become government contractors, have indeed learned to abide by the requirements of the executive order. However, the graph fails to tell us just who is being hired and promoted. It does not specify whether these hires and promotions went to white males or to women and minorities. Nor does it tell us how, or even why, the figures—collected, we are told, from the affirmative action plans of non-construction contractors—can or should be accepted as real rather than wishfully hoped for jobs and promotions.

Perhaps we can gain some clue about these "hires and promotions" from the Office of Federal Contract Compliance Programs itself. In a September 1977 self–appraisal, the OFCCP concluded that "there can be little doubt that OFCCP's affirmative action program concepts, principles, and procedures have accounted for significant, visible improvement in the recruitment, hiring, placement, and promotion of minorities and women into career areas and specific jobs from which they were largely excluded in the years prior to 1971" (OFCCP 1977, p 74).

Unfortunately, the report does not go on to provide some rational source for "visible improvement." To the contrary, just one paragraph after its self-laudatory assessment, the report admits to a problem: "One of the most critical defects in the administration of the affirmative action program requirements is the absence of a system which enables OFCCP to measure the success of these program requirements" (p. 75). No one, it seems, has been keeping track and the over 3 million "hires and promotions" presented in the Office of Management and Budget graph are nothing more than the happy fiction of some bureaucratic imagination. In reality, by its own admission, the OFCCP hasn't even got a system for measuring its accomplishments.

In its 1975 assessment of OFCCP, the U.S. Commission on Civil Rights found nothing to brighten the picture. In both its policy development role and its role as monitor for the enforcement agencies, the

Commission judged OFCCP ineffective and inadequate. In policy, the Commission found "OFCC's Sex Discrimination Guidelines are inferior to those issued by the EEOC and are seriously deficient." In supervision, the Commission found that the agency had never "removed that compliance authority . . . despite strong indications that compliance agencies, such as the Department of Health, Education and Welfare, the Department of the Treasury, and the General Services Administration, routinely commit violations" (U.S. Commission on Civil Rights 1975b, pp. 633,636).

The Government Accounting Office (GAO), the congressional investigative agency, was equally uncomplimentary of the OFCCP's efforts when it was asked to examine the agency in 1975. "The almost nonexistence of enforcement actions could imply to contractors that the compliance agencies do not intend to enforce the program," wrote GAO investigators. Ten years after receiving authority to supervise the executive order, the GAO found that the OFCCP "does not yet have a fully operational system for assessing progress of Federal non-construction contractors in increasing employment of minorities and women" (GAO 1975a, pp. 37, ii).

The House Subcommittee on Equal Opportunities of the Committee on Education and Labor agreed. In a 1976 report, following hearings conducted by the committee, it concluded, "the failure of the Department of Labor and the compliance agencies to effectively administer and enforce the Executive Order has led to the program being called a 'comic foam-rubber club' rather than the 'stiffest civil rights stick'" (U.S. House 1976a, p. 61).

In 1977 the OFCCP won praise from the Commission on Civil Rights for its new leadership. However, the commission still remained highly critical of the agency's inability to resolve some of its problems. "OFCCP," reported the Commission, "has not revised its guidelines on sex discrimination and thus they continue to be weaker than those issued by EEOC" (U.S. Commission on Civil Rights 1977a, p. 78). Most ironic of all, the Commission found that in 1977 the OFCCP was still unable to identify all federal contractors within its jurisdiction and had been forced to purchase a list of contractors from Dun and Bradstreet. What is more, the agreement between OFCCP and Dun and Bradstreet prohibited OFCCP from sharing the listing with the compliance agencies. Needless to say, Dun and Bradstreet developed the list using federal grant funds (p. 115).

Officials at the OFCCP have long maintained that the basic difficulty they have had in enforcing the executive order stems from the peculiar administrative structure that places rule making and supervisory authority in their agency while assigning enforcement authority to other government agencies.

The structure had a genesis that seemed sensible. Government officials most closely involved with contracting for goods and services were in the best position to know whether or not the companies they dealt with maintained discriminatory employment practices and were in the best position to contract only with nondiscriminating companies. It seemed to make sense to place the responsibility for defense contracts with the Department of Defense, education contractors with the Department of Health, Education and Welfare, and so forth.

Unfortunately several factors worked to contradict the seeming logic of the system. First, the immense scope of government contracting forced most agencies to form separate civil rights units to monitor compliance. Communication between those units and the units responsible for contracting with outside companies was not always adequate. Second, the heads of these civil rights units were appointed and often owed political loyalty to their own department heads and not to the Department of Labor OFCCP. Their goals were not always in keeping with the responsibility of OFCCP to enforce the executive order. Third, compliance agency heads were sometimes placed higher in civil service ranking and closer to cabinet department secretaries than the head of OFCCP. In a rank conscious bureaucracy, they did not often admit any obligation to conform to OFCCP wishes. And fourth, placing the responsibility for withholding federal funds within the government agencies responsible for giving them out created an obvious conflict of interest. Even in the best of circumstances and with a high level of administrative support for enforcement, the contract compliance system did little to counter pressure against enforcement brought by businesses and institutions with federal contracts. And during the Nixon and Ford years circumstances were far from ideal.

Howard Glickstein, who took over a new task force on civil rights reorganization set up by President Carter in 1977, pinpointed this major problem: "By and large, said Glickstein, "the companies found that they had very little difficulty with agencies they actually contracted with. They usually could work something out." With such a system, even if OFCCP officials had strong motivation to see that the law was implemented, it is unlikely they could have done much. But the system also gave agency officials the perfect excuse. Whenever confronted by criticism of their inability to enforce the executive order, they could turn to the administrative system and claim, with some justification, that it worked to undermine their authority.

OFCCP was in the peculiar position of releasing rules and regulations that could be publicly criticized by officials at far higher levels in other government agencies that were responsible for enforcing those same rules and regulations. Thus Caspar Weinberger, in his parting shot as secretary of HEW, told *Science* in 1975 that Department of Labor regulations on affirmative action were designed for such situations as stores, factories, and breweries.

> But colleges are not just dealing with clerks, and the regulations do not always fit the problems of a developing faculty. . . . The thing we want universities to do is broaden their base of recruiting, to make it national, so that numbers of persons have an opportunity to compete for a position. But once they've done that, they should appoint whom they think best, even if it is a white man. You have to avoid reverse discrimination, too (Culliton 1975, p. 618).

Clearly statements such as Weinberger's did little to help the executive order program maintain a tough image.

A year after Weinberger's statement, Laurence Lorber was appointed as OFCCP's new director. He was immediately described by *Business Week* as an "activist Director" under whom "the OFCC has moved into previously by-passed industries" (May 1976, p. 98). Lorber was well aware of the poor image of the agency. His first act upon taking over in March 1976, said Lorber, was to tell all compliance agencies they should begin enforcing the executive order. Apparently, he says, this was a "revolutionary statement."

Lorber admits that his statement had little impact and, like his predecessors, he blamed the weakness of his agency on its peculiar position in the bureaucracy. At HEW's Office for Civil Rights, he noted,

> they work for the secretary of HEW, not the secreatry of Labor, which means your control is not great. We have a lot of responsibility. I don't know how much of the authority we really do have on a day to day basis. I would be very candid and say we can't point with pride to our efforts recently in a whole lot of areas. The executive order program has taken a long time to get off the ground.

Leonard Beirman, who served as assistant director under Lorber and as acting director following Lorber's resignation, also assigned much of the blame for OFCCP ineffectiveness on the administrative structure. In addition Beirman adopted some of the criticism of his agency that had become popular with HEW officials. He, too, began talking about unrealistic OFCCP regulations: "When you write a regulation that has to apply equally to an insurance company and a steel mill you're in a lot of trouble to start with. You have to have a regulation with some built in flexibility because the country's so diverse."

Following the changeover to the Carter administration in 1977, OFCCP established a task force to examine ways to revitalize the

contract compliance program. The task force report, while it did finally
come up with suggestions for strengthening the agency, gave an inordi-
nate amount of attention to justifying the past inaction of the OFCCP.
Much of the justification followed the same line of reasoning used by past
directors to explain agency shortcomings: if the agency had not performed well it was not for lack of will to enforce the law but simply the
result of an unwieldy administrative structure.

To completely understand the reluctance of the task force to assign
any blame for the past lack of vigorous enforcement to the agency, it is
important to keep in mind that at the time their report was written in
1977, President Carter had formed his own task force on the reorganization of the entire employment civil rights enforcement structure. It
seemed clear at the time that the presidential group was working toward
a recommendation that one agency, most likely the Equal Employment
Opportunity Commission, be charged with all enforcement. Few entities,
either public or private, seek to self–destruct. Therefore it is not surprising that the OFCCP task force report strongly recommended the consolidation of all compliance agencies within the OFCCP and the continuation
of that agency as a separate entity.

Nonetheless, much of the reasoning used to explain past agency
failures and to support the continuation of a greatly enlarged OFCCP is
somewhat farfetched. At one point the report argues that the reason so
few actions had been initiated against large government contractors in the
past was that such "contractors tend to arrive at compliance settlements
rather than face loss of Government business" (OFCCP 1977, p. 24). Since
large companies stand to suffer considerably larger monetary losses than
small companies, the report argues, they tend to come into compliance
more rapidly. The report supports its contention with a circular bit of
interpretation. Since OFCCP has imposed few sanctions on large companies, large companies must be in compliance with the law:

> With the exception of the Timken Roller Bearing Company . . . the 16
> contractors which have been debarred from Government contracts
> have been employers who, for the most part, did not have a substantial
> dollar volume of contracts. Thus, *irrespective of the degree of reform,
> the imposition of sanctions will be largely confined to those employers
> for whom the cost of complying with the requirements of the Order
> exceeds the benefits to be derived from Government business* (pp.
> 23–24, emphasis in original).

The task force fails to note that a more plausible explanation might
be that sanctions have not been imposed on large companies (or small
companies, either, for that matter, since a record of 16 debarments over
an eight- to ten-year period is hardly impressive) because the government

has not brought action against them. Moreover, the assumption that small companies are more recalcitrant because they have less interest in keeping their relatively small contracts than do large companies in keeping their large contracts seems to have little basis in either fact or logic.

In another peculiar piece of reasoning, the OFCCP task force argued against the consolidation of all employment civil rights enforcement into one agency since neither the EEOC nor the OFCCP was completely effective: "Regardless of the location of OFCCP and EEOC, both have basic deficiencies which prevent them from maximizing efficiency in the total EEO effort and avoiding potential conflict, competition, duplication, and inconsistency. To consolidate or merge the Executive Order and Title VII programs in their current state would aggravate the fundamental problems which confront them" (p. viii). The "conflict, competition, duplication, and inconsistency" would presumably be made worse by consolidation into one agency. And, the report seems to assume, two poorly run agencies are better than one.

In spite of its curious reasoning and its tendency to justify the shortcomings of OFCCP's past performance, the task force did reach a sensible conclusion:

> "It is the recommendation of the Task Force that as a precondition to considerations of merger each agency [OFCCP and EEOC] should apply specific administrative and/or legislative reforms to correct its individual problems, and allow sufficient time to demonstrate the efficacy of such reforms. In instituting their respective reform measures, EEOC and OFCCP should coordinate their efforts to ensure that they arrive at a division of responsibility which will serve to compliment, support, and reinforce each other's efforts rather than to supplement, conflict, or compete with them. Thus, if there is an eventual merger, the consolidation would not require any fundamental rebuilding. Rather the consolidated programs would be "off and running" with immediate results (pp. 34–35, emphasis in original).

The recommendation was adopted by Carter's task force on civil rights reorganization and the job of consolidating contract compliance into a single agency fell to Weldon Rougeau, President Carter's first appointee as director of the OFCCP. Rougeau, who took office in April 1977, found himself in the unenviable position of supervising the consolidation of OFCCP, with 200 employees and a reputation for inaction, with 1,900 employees from the 11 compliance agencies that existed in 1978, most of them carrying a reputation for total ineffectiveness.

The merger took place on October 1, 1978. In planning for it Rougeau remained quite candid about the problems he expected. Under civil service regulations, he explained, only people who actually spent 50 percent or more of their time on executive order compliance could be transferred. OFCCP had the obligation to make offers to such people and the individuals could accept or reject the offers. From 50 to 60 percent of the positions transferred would probably be filled by compliance agency personnel, said Rougeau. The remainder of the positions would be filled through outside recruitment. Some of the smaller compliance agencies, such as the Maritime Commission Office for Civil Rights, were to be transferred in toto while larger agencies that had other statutory authority besides the executive order were to lose only part of their personnel and functions.

Not all personnel from the compliance agencies were expected to transfer with the executive order authority. However, well before the transfer, Rougeau was aware that some agencies would unload as much of their deadwood as possible. Indeed, one agency official gloated that 91 of the "worst" people in his agency would be "dumped" on OFCCP. (The same agency official was himself later transferred to OFCCP.) "It happens in every reorganization," Rougeau commented. "Agencies try to get rid of their deadwood. . . . We will have to weed them out in some kind of way. . . . This is an absolute must in a consolidated organization. We simply cannot have everybody the way they were before they came to the Labor Department."

A vigorous training program plus careful monitoring of all investigative work would be used, said Rougeau, to help in the weeding process.

> Performance standards will be set and people's work will be reviewed at critical junctures. If they fail to measure up to the standards that have been set, life is going to become very difficult for them. In my judgment it was not difficult at first with some of the agencies. There were no standards imposed and certainly there was never an accent on commitment to the goals of the overall program. I have let it be known . . . that I will emphasize the two Cs—commitment and competence. Commitment you are supposed to bring with you to the job. You can't teach that, you can't ingrain it. Competence we can play a hand in if the person has the basic skills to learn and perform well we can provide the wherewithal to enhance that and develop it and training is going to be a big part of our program. . . . There is just not going to be anybody sitting in these offices and not doing anything or playing footsy with contractors. We're not going to have that.

In spite of the obvious difficulties Rougeau faces, he entered into his task with a major advantage: he had not been a part of the OFCCP operation in the past. And much to his credit he did not feel obliged to adopt the pattern of the past: he did not attribute OFCCP's failures to its peculiar administrative structure. Instead of justifying the past, Rougeau talked of establishing credibility in the future: "I recognize that there is a lot of cynicism out there. I think we have to speak with actions first."

Among his first actions Rougeau stepped up the number of debarment proceedings taken against contractors who are not in compliance with the executive order. Without these proceedings, contractors who continue to discriminate or who fail to maintain adequate affirmative action plans can nonetheless continue to gain federal grants.

Rougeau believes that word of OFCCP's new compliance stance is spreading. More contractors are beginning to take show cause letters seriously. In the past, he explained, these letters—which supposedly put contractors on notice that they must, within one month's time, either comply with the law or come forth with good reasons for failing to comply—were widely ignored since the compliance agencies rarely followed through with enforcement action. OFCCP, said Rougeau, has begun holding regional seminars to familiarize employers with the requirements of the executive order. All the seminars have been oversubscribed. "I think it is probably an indication that more companies than ever before are concerned about complying and I think are concerned about knowing how we do our work and what they should expect when there are reviews at their facilities."

Universities, which in the past had some success at convincing agency officials that they must be treated as special cases will not be left out, Rougeau insisted.

> Sure, I value academic freedom quite a bit as an intellectual postulate but universities that get government contracts are in the same class as contractors who manufacture ball bearings and I'm not going to treat them any differently. I don't care how many arguments they raise. If they are getting the money from the government they are going to have to adhere to the rules and regulations that we set up. What we've said to the universities by our rejection of the agreements that HEW had negotiated with them is that there is a new day at hand—you're no longer going to be able to plan to make your affirmative action plan. As a government contractor you're supposed to have your plan in place for inspection and if we have to have a review then we look at that within 30 days. It's no longer going to be the way it was in the past.

Rougeau's emphasis on what the agency intends to accomplish is a refreshing change from the emphasis of the past when agency officials talked of what could not be done under the rules or regulations or under the peculiar administrative structure that existed. Whether the new emphasis will translate into action, however, remains in doubt.

—— *Chapter Five* ——

THE AGENCIES EXAMINED: THE EQUAL EMPLOYMENT OPPORTUNITY COMMISSION

"One of the great and interesting things about this work is that Title VII is very strong but the mechanism—the EEOC—was primitive compared to the strength of the law. I mean the process was primitive, the law is pretty strong."

Eleanor Holmes Norton, Chair, EEOC, 1978

Of all the federal antidiscrimination agencies, none produces more ambivalence in the minds of observers than the Equal Employment Opportunity Commission. Columnist James Kilpatrick, generally considered an opponent of strong government enforcement, recently called the agency "plainly the worst—the most maddening, the most arrogant, the most inefficient and the least effective" of all antidiscrimination agencies (1979). Proponents of enforcement found the comment amusing, but not because it was totally wrong. Kilpatrick, they insist, would find EEOC the most maddening because it has in fact been more sincerely engaged in the effort of enforcing the law. Other agencies have been less maddening, from the standpoint of the employer, because they have interfered less. Proponents would also—sadly—disagree that the agency has been the most inefficient and the least effective. For inefficient and ineffective as EEOC has been, it has nonetheless been miles ahead of the other antidiscrimination agencies.

The criticism that has been leveled at EEOC by proponents of civil rights enforcement has always differed sharply from that leveled at other agencies. One gains a picture of an agency firmly establishing policy and sticking to it and at the same time plagued with management problems, communication failures, inefficiency, and confusion that have made the enforcement of that policy all but impossible.

The 1975 report of the Commission on Civil Rights, for example, points out that EEOC, from its inception in 1965, has been "plagued by personnel problems which hamper its efforts to fulfill its mission" (1975b, p. 499). In 1972, the report explains, EEOC gained the power to file suit against private firms found to be discriminating when those firms refused to negotiate settlements on a voluntary basis. Yet, one year later, the agency's Office of General Counsel had 105 vacancies out of its allotted 270 slots. "Thus, the Office charged with administering the agency's most powerful compliance tool was operating at less than two-thirds of its capacity" (p. 500).

The Commission also found that during one nine month period in 1974 EEOC had conducted 586 reviews of voluntary compliance agreements that had previously been reached between employers and EEOC. Almost all of the reviews "resulted in findings of noncompliance," yet not one produced a referral to the Office of General Counsel for legal action (p. 528).

The litigation process itself came in for some strong criticism from the Civil Rights Commission, which held that EEOC attorneys have been too selective in taking cases to court. Agency figures showed an incredibly low caseload for EEOC attorneys: "As of March 1974," wrote the Civil Rights Commission, "an average of one case was assigned to each attorney, although the fiscal year budget projected five cases per lawyer" (p. 541). The low case load could not be explained by the magnitude of the cases involved: "As of August 1974 more than 40 percent of EEOC's lawsuits were against respondents having workforces of between 25 and 300 persons. Approximately 20 percent of the respondents have between 300 and 1,000 employees, 30 percent between 1,000 and 10,000 employees, and four percent over 10,000" (p. 541).

In its report, the staff of the House Subcommittee on Equal Employment (U.S. House 1976a) in large part concurred with the analysis of the Civil Rights Commission:

> While the EEOC has been the most aggressive of the three major federal equal employment opportunity agencies in enforcing the law and protecting the rights of groups and individuals subject to employment discrimination, it has failed to provide an adequate remedy to those suffering the effects of discriminatory employment practices. The agency's failure is attributable to a lack of continuity in leadership, mismanagement and an engulfing inventory of charges which threatens to keep the EEOC from becoming a law enforcement agency and remain a processing agency. The goals and procedures of the EEOC increasingly are designed to resolve as many charges as possible rather than to provide more effective enforcement of the law or to protect the rights of the charging party (p. 25).

In its second look at EEOC in 1977, the Commission on Civil Rights expressed considerable optimism at the chances for resolving some of the agency's problems. The Commission cautioned, "drastic measures are clearly needed if EEOC is ever to become an agency which effectively combats employment discrimination" but it also speculated that "the program which EEOC's new leadership is implementing has potential for revitalizing the agency" (U.S. Commission on Civil Rights 1977a, p. 177).

The report noted that EEOC continued to have severe personnel problems and maintained no effective system for measuring personnel performance. It had been anticipated that EEOC's conciliation efforts would prove more successful following the 1972 amendments that enabled the agency to take employers to court. Yet the Civil Rights Commission found in 1977 that the success rate for conciliations had risen only marginally, from 25 percent of the conciliation attempts in 1973 to 31.5 percent in the first eight months of fiscal 1977 (p. 197). What is more, the Commission found continuing severe inadequacies in case preparation and in the litigation system. Discrimination cases recommended for legal action by district offices were rejected 86 percent of the time in fiscal 1976. "Given the fact that there are over 300 attorney positions in the General Counsel's office alone, the agency's systemic litigation record in terms of numbers of lawsuits filed and amount of relief obtained remains inadequate" (p. 203).

Eleanor Holmes Norton, Carter's first appointee as EEOC chair, agrees with much of the criticism and claims that when she took over there was "nothing in the agency" that did not need drastic overhauling. Nonetheless, Norton is among those who have praised the early efforts of EEOC in helping to shape the broadest possible interpretation of Title VII law. For much of its first decade of existence, EEOC did not have the right to litigate Title VII cases. Its strongest weapon was simply voluntary conciliation of cases where it had found an employer in violation of the law. Court action was left in the hands of private complainants and the Justice Department. In spite of this major handicap, says Norton,

> EEOC improvised ways to influence the development of the statute to serve the broad purposes of dismantling discrimination. Left to its own devices, the Commission used *amicus* briefs, guidelines, and bold interpretations to set the pace for a liberal interpretation of the statute. The courts, accustomed to giving deference to the interpretations of administrative agencies, were not much interested in whether EEOC was a true regulatory agency or had enforcement power. Lacking precedents in the American experience for civil rights of enforcement, the courts accepted the expertise of the Commission and its view of the law. Never in the history of administrative law has an agency done so much with so little" (Norton 1977b).

In spite of its limited means, EEOC was able to lay out basic employment guidelines that developed the idea of disparate impact discrimination. The EEOC guidelines were later used by the Supreme Court as a basis for its precedent setting 1971 ruling in *Griggs v. Duke Power Company*. In the same manner, through guidelines on various aspects of discrimination and through using innovative commission rulings, the agency created the basis for the narrowest possible exemptions from the law under the bona fide occupational qualification clause of Title VII. The agency was also able to generate policy that eliminated state protective legislation, affirmed the right of individuals to go to court on Title VII issues following adverse rulings in binding arbitration, upheld the use of statistical evidence to establish prima facie showings of discrimination, and developed the theory that vague and subjective criteria for employment decisions, especially when used by supervisors who are male or white while workers are female or black, are a ready mechanism for discrimination.

To this date, says Norton, the pursuit of important legal precedents is one of EEOC's strong points. While much of the law has already been clearly established, she believes "there are some frontier issues still: reverse discrimination, comparable worth, some rarified testing issues, some issues around the use of statistics." Perhaps the most difficult remaining issue, says Norton, is the idea of comparable worth or equal pay for equal value: "That may be the hardest yet unconquered field." The idea of comparable worth comes from the fact that many jobs that are still largely segregated by sex command salaries that seem to have more to do with the sex of the job occupants than with their skill level, complexity, or value to employers. Thus secretaries who are mostly female may find they earn far less on the average than delivery truck drivers who are mostly male, even when they work for the same company. Norton points out that there have been at least half a dozen cases on the issue in the courts to date and that all have lost. Because it is an important area, however, she says that EEOC has contracted with the National Science Foundation to develop standards for measuring the value of various jobs "that are so impeccable that courts will come to respect the notion." Development of the standards will be followed by an effort to bring valid comparable worth cases in the courts.

The process for setting court precedents in EEOC law is always a long one, Norton says. However, EEOC's major problem has not been caused by any weakness in the law. It is, instead, that while the law has become strong, the means available to the agency for enforcement of it have been weak. For example, Norton points out that even after the agency gained litigation authority in 1972, it did not use its authority properly.

In extending litigation rights to the EEOC, Congress had anticipated that private suits would become rare and that EEOC or the Department of Justice would handle most court complaints. That hope was not fulfilled. Neither EEOC nor Justice ever managed to take on much of a case load and Justice, even in the few cases it did take, seemed consistently to steer clear of sex discrimination. Between 1966 and 1977, Justice filed only eight cases based on sex discrimination compared to 82 based on race discrimination. EEOC filed far more cases than Justice—a total of over 700 in all—but nonetheless the record was disappointing. The EEOC cases, however, did roughly parallel complaints filed with the agency as to the basis of the illegal discrimination (U.S. Commission on Civil Rights 1977a, pp. 200, 274).

The disappointing litigation record of both the Department of Justice and the EEOC was largely due to the quality of the investigative work performed by EEOC, according to Norton. Because the agency began its history with no power to litigate, it developed a "probable cause" standard for findings of discrimination. The standard, says Nortion, simply meant "could you conciliate the case?"—was there enough evidence of discrimination to sit down with an employer and attempt to work out some kind of voluntary agreement for change. But once the EEOC gained enforcement authority through the right to litigate the "probable cause" standard was no longer relevant. A finding of "cause" should have meant that the agency was prepared to defend the case at a court hearing. But no change in the "cause" standard was made following the change in the law, Norton points out.

When she took over the agency in 1977, one of Norton's initial moves was to require that agency findings be made on a "litigation worthy" standard rather than the old "probable cause" standard. Says Norton:

> Basically what we have tried to do is to put the agency on the only standard that any court or for that matter any employer would take seriously. EEOC was able to conciliate almost no cases because the respondents understood that district offices were operating on a non-existent standard—a standard that only EEOC recognized and that their own lawyers would not litigate. They knew that if we found cause and sent that to a litigation center, that the chances were 95, 96, 97 percent that the case could not be accepted. So what the litigation standard is, is simply that there is enough here, not that we could win, but that we could withstand a hearing without looking silly. I'm saying that the conciliation standard was so low that you would look silly.

Perhaps the most persistent criticism of EEOC in the past has been directed at the agency's inability to overcome its case backlog. The backlog grew from over 15,000 cases in 1969 to close to 130,000 cases in

1977, when Norton took over the agency. Every effort to bring the backlog under control had ended in failure: An early 1970s effort to institute "pre-decision settlement" as a means of reducing the backlog produced some ludicrous statistics. In 1972 the agency reported that in 2,442 cases it had reached "unsuccessful Pre-Decision Settlement": a euphemism, one assumes, for no settlement at all. A less publicized effort to reduce the backlog by setting case completion quotas for investigators failed in the mid-1970s.

Norton's own solution has, on paper at least, produced better results. Upon taking over the agency, Norton established three model offices to test her new system and then moved the system to all district offices. At the same time she restructured the agency, increasing the number of district offices, eliminating litigation centers, and moving attorneys from these centers to district offices where they would work alongside investigators during the early stages of case analysis. The middle level of bureaucracy that had existed in regional offices was also eliminated. Now district offices, where the new charge processing systems are supposedly in operation, report directly to Washington.

Basically, Norton split complaints of discrimination into two categories: backlogged cases and incoming cases. Some investigative units in each district office were assigned exclusively to handle cases already on the books. Others were trained in new case intake procedures that were keyed toward resolving complaints as they came through the door and thus eliminating the backlog at its source.

In order to reduce the backlog, old cases were to be handled by limiting the scope of investigation "to matters affecting the individual in most instances so the breadth of charges will not obstruct the resolution of these cases" (EEOC 1977). Moreover, the cases would be grouped by the employers they were filed against and the first investigated would be "those with the largest number of charges . . . and . . . those that can be resolved most quickly and efficiently." New cases were to be handled under a new "rapid charge processing" system which would place "stress on early resolution through negotiated no fault settlements . . ." (EEOC 1977).

In mid-year 1978, EEOC released a ten month report on the success of the dual track case system in the model offices. The report revealed a dramatic rise in negotiated prefinding settlements for cases handled under the rapid charge processing system from 13 percent for fiscal 1977 to 46 percent for the ten months between September 1977 and July 1978. In each model office the percentage of charges accepted under the rapid charge system dropped dramatically from the earlier system where the agency had apparently accepted all charges. The average drop in charges filed in the three model offices was 28 percent. A look at charges filed in the model offices during the month of April 1978 revealed that four months later 79 percent had been "resolved," 16 percent were "pending," and only 5 percent had been referred for more extensive investigation.

Meanwhile, the model office backlog processing units had managed to reduce their backlogs substantially compared to charge intake: the average by which case closures exceeded charge receipts in the model offices was 142 percent and the agency noted that "the great majority of closures are backlogged charges" (EEOC 1978c).

At the same time, the dollar benefits per individual complainant went up from an average of $1,582 for fiscal 1977 to $1,651 during the 1978 period covered. The figures may seem small but Norton believes that the new charge processing systems have produced more in the way of remedies for complainants than they could expect before. The stress on speed, she says, has been essential. "Without speed there can be no findings," Norton believes. The theory at EEOC used to be that speed would prevent findings of discrimination but Norton feels she has demonstrated that the opposite is true: "that because these cases are proved by circumstantial evidence, basically, the kinds of evidence that tends to be least lasting, that if you don't attempt a remedy early, for thousands of people—all but the strong cases—you will get no remedy at all." The effect of rapid charge processing, says Norton, has been "to triple and quadruple the remedy rate."

The new intake procedures have been made so thorough that charges actually taken are more likely to represent legitimate discrimination complaints, says Norton. Before,

> what EEOC did was to take their name, give them a number and send them home. Even they lost some of the information. . . . The problem is [in the past] they had a system which was very undisciplined in which to work and in order to keep from turning away an appropriate charge they came out with the magic idea of taking every charge, which means that the legitimate Title VII charges were competing with people badly in need of help but not under Title VII.

Norton explains that often people would come in to file charges who needed simply to be referred to an unemployment office or an apprenticeship training program. Under the old system, clerical help rather than trained investigators would record their "complaint" and place it at the end of the line in the backlog. The system not only prevented the individuals from gaining the help they really needed but it also padded EEOC's case backlog. Intake is now divided into two parts. First the complainant is given "pre-charge counseling" during which an effort is made to discover what the real problem is and whether or not it is a Title

VII problem. During this stage, Norton says, investigators are trained to put complainants in touch with agencies that might more appropriately handle their problems. If an investigator ascertains that the problem presents a legitimate Title VII issue, an extensive intake interview is performed on the spot, says Norton. The interview is aimed at gaining sufficiently detailed information to enable EEOC to attempt early settlement with employers. It is because of this detailed intake procedure that EEOC has been able to dramatically increase the rate of early settlements, Norton believes. Employers, she says, would rather find some remedy at an early stage when the cost of settlement is relatively low.

The new system is not without its drawbacks. First, rapid charge processing places a greater burden on potential complainants to articulate their discrimination charges. Unsophisticated complainants who have difficulty framing their charges would seem to be in greater danger of being turned away under the new system. But Norton insists that there are sufficient checks built into the system. Supervisors check over all intake work and Washington specialists do further checks of intake quality. (One mid-level EEOC official, however, expressed a great deal of concern over the failure of district office personnel to take in legitimate charges of discrimination under the new system. "They used to take everything as a discrimination complaint," she said, "but now they turn away almost everything." District personnel, she claims, still have a hard time understanding the meaning of discrimination.)

Second, the procedure seems to be one that functions most appropriately in a limited geographical area. While it may have been possible in New York City, where Norton developed the system, for potential complainants to spend long periods of time in face-to-face talks with agency investigators at the time of intake, it is not possible for the same pattern to hold nationally. A number of states remain without district EEOC offices, among them Alaska, Hawaii, Wyoming, Montana, Utah, Nevada, North Dakota, South Dakota, Nebraska, Kansas, and Iowa. While these areas may not generate the heaviest complaint volume, it seems clear that any complaints that do come from them are destined to be placed in the backlog because of the difficulty of conducting the kind of intake interview required by the rapid charge system. Indeed, there have been complaints from some charging parties in outlying areas: many have filed charges by mail and though months have gone by have, at best, received only a brief acknowledgement of their letters. The rapid charge system would seem to work best only in those states, perhaps even those cities, where EEOC district offices are located.

In fairness it must be said that to a certain extent the same difficulty existed in the old system. Complaints from outlying areas, if they were investigated at all, were often held up until sufficient numbers of cases were filed from those areas to warrant the expense of sending an investigator. By that time investigators often found themselves overloaded and able to give only scant attention to numbers of cases that had long lost strength due to their age.

Third, the new system increases the likelihood that complainants will be urged into settlements that place them back into discriminatory work situations. This problem has no real solution, Norton believes. Most people, she says, want only simple remedies. Either they want more money or a promotion. It is often possible to get these remedies at an early stage: "If you wait for cases to reach the cause-no cause stage you will come up with a fair number of no causes because many, many people who come to an antidiscrimination office have fairly weak cases. Many of these people can get remedies while the employer doesn't know quite what all the evidence is."

In fact, says Norton, even in what might have been good cases, the wait preceding complete investigation often destroys the case. "Many cases so fall apart before you get to them that they can't get the probable cause finding that you could have gotten for them in six months rather than 18 months." Moreover, the more difficult the remedy being sought, the less likely it can be achieved, especially in old, backlogged cases. "If someone wants a whole job back and you get to him two years later, you think they're about to put him back when they know you don't have any witnesses? When they know everybody's memory is dim? The harder the remedy, the more important it is to get to it early," Norton insists.

According to Peter Robertson, EEOC, who in 1978 served as a director of Program Planning and Review, the new standard for settlement of these cases is that both parties are in agreement. While he admits that this might leave a number of complainants in discriminatory situations, Robertson says the system is the only possible way to dispose of the backlog and get to the more important task of initiating major Commission charges of systemwide discrimination.

> We are probably pressuring charging parties a little to settle where if we had no backlog we wouldn't but you can't cry over that. You've got a choice, right now. . . . What do you do with 120,000 cases? You can sit around and call all sorts of nasty names about how we got there but that's not useful today. You walk in and there's a pile on the desk and the mere existence of that pile is such an inhibiting factor against doing this [systemic work] that you have got to deal with it and you've got to deal with it fast and you cut some corners. And you set up the best guarantee . . . the both parties agree guarantee. The only standard that goes here is what does the individual want to settle. And if the individual says, "I want the system changed," our answer is, "Today *we* decide when and where we change systems. It takes more resources to

change systems and we will decide where we're going to do that. Now, if you want to go to court, go on to court. We'll help you get a lawyer—we'll set up lawyer referral programs. If we can shake some money free we may even eventually start funding some lawyer referral programs. But in terms of which one of America's quarter of a million employers we go in and look at you are not going to make that decision by filing an individual charge." We cannot allocate limited resources by letting [individuals] decide.

Norton agrees. In fact, she says, the whole idea behind the rapid charge processing and backlog processing systems was to clear the decks for Commission launched systemic work. Had the Commission begun a major drive to attack systemwide discrimination against large employment systems before clearing up the backlog, it would have been severely criticized, Norton claims. "We are dealing with people who, if their charge had been gotten to in a reasonable time, could have gotten a remedy and today will not get a remedy for one reason only and that is because the Commission got to it two years late."

Norton is, of course, correct: there are thousands of people who have filed charges of discrimination over the years who will get no remedy or who, at best, will gain a few thousand dollars or perhaps a belated promotion for their trouble. There is no guarantee in the system that, once they have settled, they will not immediately experience retaliation. There is no guarantee, and little likelihood, that having filed a complaint, settlement will place them in a nondiscriminatory situation. Some could probably turn around following settlement and instantly file a second, equally legitimate complaint of discrimination.

The new leadership of the Equal Employment Opportunity Commission freely admits that this is so. The work of the Commission has been so badly botched in the past that hard decisions had to be made. The hardest of all, perhaps, was to decide that more benefit would come in the long run from major, Commission selected systemic work. The sacrifice, necessary though it may have been, was individual complainants who believed that the law was intended to protect them from employment discrimination now and not at some future date selected by the Commission.

—— *Chapter Six* ——

HOW TO LIE WITH STATISTICS, PACIFY THE GOVERNMENT, AND RETAIN THE STATUS QUO

"The problem [at Berkeley] was that what was an acceptable plan was largely covered by Labor Department regulations that seemed to me to be totally unrealistic in connection with universities and more suited for a brewery."

Caspar Weinberger, former Secretary, HEW, 1976

If it is true, as some of the recently appointed antidiscrimination officials believe, that the agencies will become meaningful enforcers under the Carter administration, we should find some evidence in the approach of the agencies to the use of statistics. In this chapter we explore several examples of how the statistical game was played by one agency both before the Carter administration and after the transition. Even though it lost its contract compliance authority in October 1978, as a result of civil rights consolidation, the Office for Civil Rights of HEW seems to be a logical candidate for examination since approximately 48 percent of all women employed in professions are involved in education (U.S. Department of Commerce 1976, p. 35) and since OCR still claims to retain authority to examine issues of sex discrimination in education employment through Title IX of the Education Amendments of 1972.

The criticism of OCR by the Commission on Civil Rights, the Government Accounting Office, and the House Subcommittee on Equal Opportunities has been similar to that accorded other agencies charged with antidiscrimination responsibilities (see, especially, GAO 1975b). The response to that criticism has also been fairly standard. Early OCR leaders blamed the agency failures on the unfriendly political climate for civil rights during the Nixon administration. Later leaders claim the fault lies with the contract compliance regulations they were required to enforce—the regulations, they claim, were not suited to the task in higher education. David Tatel, President Carter's first appointee as OCR director, believes OCR never stopped producing good work but higher-level political appointees stepped in to prevent enforcement. "Although OCR was pressed," he claims, "that wasn't because it didn't do its work." The true texture of OCR's enforcement efforts, however, can best be experienced through some examples of the agency's handling of its tasks.

In May 1970 a group of women at University of California at Berkeley released a report on the status of academic women on the campus. The report found that women were underrepresented in virtually all departments and ranks across the campus and that their access to the perquisites of academic life both as students and professional employees was more limited than that of their male colleagues. The report was followed by the filing of several complaints of discrimination with HEW and, when HEW failed to begin investigation, by the filing of a complaint in federal district court.

After four years of mid-level delay and waffling that made legally required deadlines for enforcement of the executive order on campus meaningless, and of high-level political interference to prevent the imposition of required legal sanctions on the Berkeley campus, an HEW approved affirmative action plan was finally produced in February 1976. On accepting the plan, then OCR Director Peter Holmes praised Berkeley for its "commitment . . . to the underlying objectives of equal employment opportunity. . . ." But the plan itself leaves the reader with the uneasy feeling that it fails to address the problems of increasing the participation of women in higher education employment. Overall, it promises an effort to increase the female faculty from 6.5 percent in 1974 to a modest 13 percent sometime in the 21st century. In reality, under OCR approved follow-up reports, the university seems, instead, to have reduced the percentage of women on the campus by several tenths of a percent.

Although statistics take up the bulk of the plan, their importance is downplayed by OCR officials and campus administrators alike. According to Holmes, "affirmative action is a nit picky, burdensome, paperwork requirement." Adds Martin Gerry, who served as Holmes's deputy during the Berkeley negotiations and later as director of OCR, the record keeping and statistical requirements of the regulations "are unintelligible and counterproductive."

On the campus, Vice-Chancellor Ira Heyman, who took charge of the Berkeley side of the negotiations, sees little sense in "the minutia of numbers" collected and analyzed. "The heart of the affirmative action program is hiring," Heyman insists. Provost George Maslach agrees: "I look upon those submissions as a legal requirement of boilerplate material that we had to do in order to maintain our legitimacy. Affirmative action is not, and never will be and never should be, a statistical approach. Affirmative action, when you get right down to it is a case by case development, and that's all there is to it."

Nevertheless, the statistical "boilerplate" offered by Berkeley and accepted by HEW's Office for Civil Rights is revealing. In the 1974 version of its affirmative action plan, Berkeley officials applied a standard probability test to the faculty workforce, which had been broken down at OCR request into small, individual departments, and came up with an analysis that indicated virtually no "statistically significant" underutilization of women and minority group members on the faculty. OCR saw nothing wrong with the figures until Elizabeth Scott, the one woman in the Berkeley statistics department, pointed out that given the size of most departments, Berkeley officials had used an inappropriate test—a test, said Scott, that made it possible for some departments to "*never* be caught discriminating no matter how badly they perform even up to never ever hiring a woman."

Once the implications of the analysis were made plain, OCR required the use of a numerical rather than statistical definition of underutilization. But the incident calls into question the sincerity of Berkeley's desire to increase the number of women and minority individuals on the faculty: Berkeley, after all, had some of the top statistical experts in the country from its own top–ranked statistics department to call upon in selecting its method of analysis. What is more, the incident calls into question OCR's desire to enforce the law: OCR was willing to rush into accepting the conclusion that Berkeley, with 6.5 percent women on its faculty, had no underutilization of females. What is more, the agency was willing to review Berkeley's heavyweight statistical analysis with its own regional office flyweight analysts who were untrained in statistics.

The part of the Berkeley plan that raised most eyebrows involved the timetable set by the administration for the achievement of "parity" or the percentage of women and minorities one would expect to find based on numbers of trained, qualified women and minorities in the workforce. In an early version of the plan, Berkeley set goals for hiring women and minorities that allowed as much as 15 years for the achievement of parity. In an 11 page critique of that early plan, sent to Berkeley Chancellor Albert Bowker in November 1973, Holmes points out that the higher education guidelines require "that goals should be set so as to overcome identified deficiencies 'within a reasonable time'" and objects, mildly, to the unexplained lengthy time frame. UCB responded, in the submission later accepted by the government, by *increasing* the timetable in many instances to 30 years, a figure most onlookers considered a joke. But OCR, in apparent seriousness, accepted the timetable without objection.

Vice-Chancellor Heyman argues that the long projections are neces-

sary since the university cannot fire tenured white males to create jobs nor
employ less rigorous standards for hiring women and minorities. But a
careful look at Berkeley's first follow-up submission to OCR reveals that
the size of the faculty overall had grown modestly over a two year period
while the relative size of the female faculty appears to have diminished.
These figures are hard to come by, for in another questionable activity the
record keeping method in Berkeley's follow-up reports differs markedly
from that used in the 1974–75 presentations. Thus it is all but impossible to
compare them and come up with a reasonable assessment of progress.
Physical education supervisors and agronomists, for example, were
included in the early submission as ladder rank faculty but excluded from
the April 1976 follow-up report to the government.

Lynn Bailiff, who at the time was responsible for analyzing campus
statistics, agreed that such changes can obscure whatever trend may exist
from one report to the next. He insisted nonetheless that UCB was going
to make even further changes in its method of reporting. It was a price the
university was willing to pay, said Bailiff, in order to "clean up its
classifications." And, indeed, Louise Taylor, who followed Bailiff in
taking charge of affirmative action statistics for the campus, has revealed
that such changes have continued.

The first follow-up report in 1976 not only changed the base of
people who were counted as faculty, but it also revealed that timetables
for hiring women had been changed. The modest goal of 13 percent
women in 30 years did not drop to 28 years, as one might expect since two
years had passed. Instead, it *increased* in the case of some departments to
"30 plus" years. The 30 plus figure was defined by Berkeley as a
"minimum of 30 years to achieve parity." In other words, it is a commitment *not* to hire to parity within at least the next 30 years. That Berkeley
administrators would even submit such so-called hiring goals and that
OCR would accept them was a clear indication of the state of enforcement in 1976.

Berkeley's second follow-up report was submitted in the spring of
1977, following the appointment of new leadership at OCR by the Carter
administration. It covers employment changes during the 1976–77 academic year and fulfills the promise of the university that it would once
again alter its data base and reporting methods. Thus it becomes even
more difficult to ascertain whether or not the university has made progress
under its government approved affirmative action program. The few
clues available in the report do leave considerable room for doubt as to
the progress of the university and as to the sincerety of its affirmative
action effort. They also leave room for doubt as to the sincerity, or at least
the competence, of the newly appointed OCR leadership in performing
their enforcement task.

In 1976–77, the Berkeley report tells us, there was a remarkable increase in female faculty to 112 compared to 1,354 males. This compares with 83 women and 1,303 men listed as ladder rank faculty the year before. The percentage of women on the faculty has grown from 5.99 percent to 7.63 percent in only one year. But elsewhere we are told that since the 1975–76 academic year only 12 women were hired while two were terminated. It doesn't even help if we assume that all the agronomists were really added back into the faculty in 1976–77, for there were only eight of them.

Elsewhere in the report we are told that there are 125 women on the faculty compared to 1,452 men. These figures appear in the university's department-by-department utilization analysis. Women have done even better in this analysis, if it is to be believed, for they represent 7.9 percent of the faculty here. We are warned, however, that a number of people have been included twice in the utilization analysis for 1976–77, whereas they were only included once the previous year. In the new report, all persons on split appointments are counted in both departments if they are at least half time in each. We are also warned that physical education supervisors, who were included in 1974 and supposedly excluded in the 1975–76 headcount, were really "erroneously included." About all we can figure out from all of this is that there appear to be a higher percentage of women on split appointment than men—a circumstance that is not always advantageous when it comes to promotion. We can also conclude that somewhere, more women were added to the total headcount than women hired.

After dealing with these figures for a time, one begins to wonder whether the constant shifting of the statistical base is really an effort intended to "clean up" the university's classifications or whether it is, instead, a technique for obfuscating the progress—or lack of progress—of faculty women on the campus.

Certainly the statistical obfuscation, if that is what it is, does not end with shifting the base each year. The 1976–77 submission, as we already saw, counts split appointment faculty twice in its summary tables on male and female headcount. But at the same time we learn that any fractional underutilization of women is rounded out. Thus, where nine-tenths of a woman may be needed to bring a department into line with female availability, the department is viewed as being in compliance and needing *no* female hires. Through this technique the university has reduced its already modest goal for women on the faculty considerably. Berkeley has managed to have it both ways: fractional women count as one whole person or even as two persons toward measuring overutilization or parity, but fractional underutilization of women disappears completely from the hiring goals.

In yet another questionable statistical ploy, the time until "parity" or a faculty 14 percent female, lengthened considerably in the 1977 sub-mission. While only five departments had goals of "30 plus" years for achieving parity in 1975–76, 14 additional departments had slipped backward to the "30 plus" goal by 1976–77. The university submission offers a very peculiar reason for this phenomenon: "the higher availability pools are largely responsible for the longer expected times to parity."

Where earlier reports had complained that achieving parity would take time because of the shortage of qualified females and members of minority groups, we are now expected to believe that the increase in their availability is "responsible" for the delay. The more women and minori-ties there are, the longer it will take to hire them!

When one examines the department-by-department utilization analy-sis, the reasons for slippage become clear. The Oriental languages department, for example, hired two men and grew from 13 to 15 members, only one of them female. The "expected" female headcount, if the department was at parity, therefore grew from 3.3 to 3.9 and the years to parity lengthened from 25 to 30 plus. In dramatic arts, the department grew from nine to ten men. The expected female headcount grew proportionally from 1.6 to 1.8 and the time to parity increased from 14 years to 30 plus. The department of rhetoric, on the other hand, hired a woman and lost a man. The expected female headcount remained about the same at 2.2. Having hired a woman, however, the department years to parity lengthened from 22 to 30 plus. Political science grew from 35 men and one woman to 39 men and two women and the hires to parity shrank from 4.5 to 2.5 women. Time to parity lengthened from 23 years to 30 plus years. Classics, on the other hand, shrank from 17 men and one woman to 15 men and one woman. The expected female headcount also shrank from 4.1 to 3.7 but the years to parity lengthened from 29 to 30 plus. In physics a slight increase in the availability of women and no change in the all male faculty of 57 produced a lengthening of time to parity from 27 to 30 plus years.

Once again the university manages to have it both ways. If more women become available, time to parity lengthens. If men are hired but no women, time to parity lengthens. If a woman is hired but no men, time to parity lengthens. If fewer women are needed, time to parity lengthens. If more women are needed, time to parity lengthens. If a man is terminated, time to parity lengthens. If a woman is terminated, time to parity lengthens. The Office for Civil Rights, needless to say, found the Berkeley submission acceptable. (It should be noted that enforcement proceedings were later begun against Berkeley, but the proceedings were not brought about by Berkeley's spurious statistics. Instead, the issue was the right of the government to copy files and remove them from the campus.)

The kind of statistical game playing exhibited by Berkeley in its

affirmative action plan and in subsequent updates of that plan is unfortunately not unique. Neither is the readiness with which OCR, both before
and after the change in administration, accepted the submissions. At the
University of Hawaii a similar complaint to the one filed by Berkeley
women was submitted to HEW in December 1972. In October 1973 the
university submitted an affirmative action plan to OCR. The plan insisted
that women were gaining promotion and tenure more rapidly than were
men in proportion to the number of women and men who were eligible.
The definition of "eligible," as it turned out, meant those who were
allowed by the university to be considered for promotion and tenure.
Within this group women did better than men. The problem was, of
course, that men were allowed tenure and promotion consideration in far
larger proportions than were women. Large numbers of women were
simply cut out of consideration at an early stage and thus did not even
appear in the statistics. Indeed, when one examined complete statistics
that included all eligible women, the rate of tenure consideration for men
was 30 percent higher than the rate for women. Discrimination in
promotion was even more pronounced: men were promoted at twice the
rate for women.

In August 1974, after several on campus investigations conducted
during 1973, OCR released an "interim report" on University of Hawaii
compliance that found much of the complaint submitted by ·campus
women to be valid. Among the OCR conclusions: "Women continue to be
underutilized in academic positions. Of 1,542 faculty positions considered
in this study, women comprise only 372 or 24.1 %."; "Women are underutilized in tenured faculty ranks. Women represent 24.1% of the total faculty
on the Monoa Campus, but only 16.4% of the 804 tenured faculty are
women." "There is an underrepresentation of women in academic
administrative positions." "The university has not made good faith efforts
to eliminate these problems and . . . no significant gains toward Equal
Employment Opportunity have been made."

The OCR finding was issued after the appearance of the university
affirmative action plan and was critical of that plan. In addition it pointed
out that specific actions needed to be taken with regard to each of the
charges in the 1972 class complaint. In fact, in his cover letter to the
university chancellor, the regional OCR director noted that "these charges
must be treated as 'affected class' situations as specified in 41 CFR Section
60—2.1 with appropriate corrective action programs to remedy deficiencies with timetables for completion."

The 1972 complaint to OCR had been lengthy and specific. It
complained of discrimination against female faculty and potential faculty
in hiring, promotion, tenure, retention, and salary and fringe benefits and
offered some specific statistics and detailed individual situations to back

up a number of the complaints. Thus, when OCR released its "interim report of the findings" in 1974, it informed the university it was able to "isolate each charge of the class complaint and discuss the findings on each issue." OCR's language, however, did not stop the agency from dismissing the complaint two years later, in April 1976, in part due to "non-specificity of the allegations of sex discrimination." The second reason offered for the dismissal was "insufficient data base on the part of the university."

The university had apparently bolstered its own case by failing to provide data. Yet the data OCR seemed unable to obtain was available as part of the public court record in a private Title VII complaint of sex discrimination against the university. And it indicated that the situation for female faculty had consistently deteriorated since the 1972 complaint had been filed. In 1967, one year before the university had an obligation under federal regulations to eliminate sex discrimination, the faculty was 27.5 percent female. (The year also marked the early stages of a State of Hawaii effort to "upgrade" the university.) In 1972, when the class complaint was filed, the figure had dropped to 24.3 percent female. In its 1974 interim report, OCR noted that the figure had dropped to 24.1 percent female. During the 1975–76 academic year, when OCR dismissed the class complaint, the figure had dropped again, to 23.5 percent.

Similar drops could be found in the tenure status of women. In 1967, 20.5 percent of the tenured faculty was female. In its interim report OCR said 16.4 percent of the tenured faculty was female. In the College of Arts and Sciences, which included 70 percent of the faculty but excluded female dominated fields such as home economics, library, and nursing, the percentage of females with tenure was even lower: it dropped from 15.6 percent in 1967 to 12.1 percent in 1975.

The figures apparently made no impression on OCR, which continued to find the University of Hawaii in compliance with the executive order and which assured the women who had submitted the complaint that any further problems "in the utilization analysis of the Affirmative Action Compliance Program of the university will be dealt with the context of that program."

Following the changeover to the Carter administration, OCR remained sufficiently impressed with the university's affirmative action progress that in September 1978 it released another letter of finding in which only minor reporting flaws were pinpointed. On the utilization of academic women, the OCR letter reported "steady improvement over the last three years." The "improvement" seems puzzling in view of the steady decline in the number of faculty women reported over the years. It seems even more puzzling in light of a report released within weeks of the OCR letter of finding by a university committee on the status of women.

That report found that the percentage of women continued to drop and stood at 20.1 percent during the 1977–78 academic year. How could OCR report "improvement" while the percentage of women dropped so radically from the 24.1 percent it had found (and considered low) in 1974?

The answer can be found in OCR's letter of finding: "The analysis for December 1975 showed 51 departments and 80 job titles underutilized in women; the updated analysis for December 1976 showed 42 departments and 58 job titles underutilized in women; and the analysis for December 1977 showed 34 departments and 49 job titles underutilized in women." Between 1975 and 1977 the university had decided to shift from one set of rational statistics on the availability of qualified female faculty to a far more conservative set of statistics without correcting its earlier figures. Thus the number of departments "underutilized" in 1977 dropped dramatically without any substantive change in hiring patterns. In 1978, with the new administration leaders in place at HEW, the figures satisfied OCR.

But perhaps we should not be surprised since OCR itself has considerable experience in similar statistical game playing in its presentations to Congress and in its own systems for collecting and analyzing complaint investigation data.

Among the charts presented by OCR to the House appropriations committee in 1976, for example, was one titled "Summary of Complaints Submitted Under the Various Authorities for Individual Years" (U.S. House 1976b, p. 787). From its title and contents one would assume that it purports to present year-to-year totals on exactly how many complaints of illegal discrimination have been filed with OCR under each of its legal authorities. This, in itself, is enough to make me suspicious—I have been told by past executives within OCR that there have never been accurate records kept of complaints filed and that figures were often manufactured for the benefit of Congress. However, one does not need to go outside the charts presented during this one year to find flaws. The total for the years 1969 through 1975 in OCR's "Summary" chart is 1,866 complaints in all under its various legal authorities. But in other charts presented during the same congressional hearing, we learn that complaints received by just two of OCR's four divisions alone exceed the total complaints the agency claims in its "Summary" (pp. 787, 788). What is more, the total number of Title VI complaints received by one division, the elementary and secondary division, in one three year period, exceeds by 869 the total number of Title VI complaints OCR claims the entire agency received over a seven year period!

The only possible conclusion we can draw is that OCR has presented Congress with charts that have no relationship with one another and no correspondence with reality. Surprisingly, however, not one member of the congressional committee thought to question agency officials about the glaring inconsistencies in their figures. The lack of questioning is even more disturbing when one inspects the chart presented to Congress titled "Higher Education Division Complaints as of December 31, 1975 (U.S. House 1976b, p. 788). We learn from the chart that of a total of 1,699 complaints between 1969 and 1975, 203 have been referred to other agencies, 556 have had "investigations started," 493 have been "resolved," and the remainder are in the backlog. The record, if it is to be accepted at face value, is hardly a good one: only 29 percent of the cases received by the division have been "resolved" while 58 percent remain unresolved. But what of the 29 percent? What does it mean when the agency claims to have "resolved" a complaint? The agency answer appears at the bottom of the chart: "*Resolved*—Complaints resolved (by any means other than referral—i.e. lack of jurisdiction, withdrawal, closed-to-cause, voluntary or mandated remediation) during the calendar year." Resolved, then, does not necessarily mean that the agency has investigated a complaint, made a finding of discrimination or no discrimination, and imposed a settlement.

None of the congressmen on the House appropriations committee were disturbed by the OCR statistical display. To the contrary, during the hearings, Martin Gerry, who by then had become OCR's acting director, engaged in the following exchange with New Jersey Congressman Edward J. Patten:

> Mr. Patten. You know, I attended a dinner up at Rutgers Saturday night. We honored one of the professors but he was only an excuse for the dinner. The reason for the dinner was to raise money for the scholarship fund. There were about 1,000 people there. I can tell you that was a different group than you would have seen 10 years ago. There was a pretty good mix there. So we have come a long way, despite what everyone else says. I mean, looking at that audience and those who were participating, the hopes of getting down to the job have been realized. Do you have any satisfaction that the money we are spending here is bringing results?
>
> Mr. Gerry. Yes, Mr. Patten, I do. I think in many areas there has been a great deal of progress, as you indicate. I think higher education institutions are certainly good examples. I think in terms of the overall value to the country of eliminating barriers to equal opportunity that have existed the return of the taxpayers' money is certainly a good one.
>
> I think it is money well spent given the overall impact and the strengthening of the country which has taken place as a result of improved civil rights enforcement (U.S. House 1976, pp. 797-98).

Exactly what was the "overall impact" from which Gerry derived so much satisfaction?

By 1977 OCR had developed a computerized case following system that had the potential of helping the agency to begin keeping accurate statistics on complaint resolution. As of October 1977 the system indicated that a total of 2,082 cases had been filed with the Higher Education Division alone over the years. Of these, 880, or 42 percent, had been closed without any finding whatsoever, because of "lack of jurisdiction," referral to another agency, incomplete information, withdrawal by the complainant, or for some other reason. Another 34 percent of the cases remained in administrative limbo, awaiting some action. In 334 cases, or 17 percent, OCR had concluded the cases lacked merit and had closed them. In only 144 cases, or somewhat under 6 percent, according to the agency's own figures, did OCR discover that a complaint had sufficient merit to warrant, and obtain, "corrective action."

The Higher Education Division has existed within OCR since 1972, thus the printouts cover roughly five years of work. The division employed approximately 100 people, most of them in professional positions. At best, then, it had taken three and one-half person years to gain each "corrective action."

Have these corrective actions been worth the price? In instances where it is possible to trace the exact corrective action, it does not appear that they have been. The University of Hawaii complaint, for example, is logged into the case following system as a case involving only salary inequity. In spite of the fact that the complainants in that case were informed that the complaint had been dropped, the case is logged into the computer system as one that ended with "corrective action secured." The only possible event that could be tied with that "corrective action" was that 14 female faculty members had been given pay raises to bring them into line with male peers. The pay study, however, had been launched by the Wage and Hour Division of the Department of Labor independently from the complaint filed with OCR. Moreover, a faculty committee, working with the advice of the Wage and Hour Division, had determined that a *minimum* of 75 women were entitled to such raises. Other issues that had been included in the complaint to OCR were neither handled nor resolved, although OCR chose to consider them closed with the submission of an acceptable university affirmative action program.

In an earlier individual complaint at the same university, the printout also revealed that corrective action was secured. The university had informed OCR that it would return a woman to her job after OCR found she had been terminated due to discrimination. The woman was never returned to her job but the "corrective action" remained on OCR's records. Several of the individual back pay awards made at Rutgers and discussed in Chapter 3 also appear among the corrective actions OCR claims to have secured. No mention is made of the failure of the agency to resolve other issues or the fact that Rutgers had agreed to larger settlements than those OCR eventually permitted.

Where it is possible to check specific cases, they reveal that the case-following system has sometimes been misused in other ways by agency personnel. Numerous investigative activities that should have been logged into the system are missing. The Berkeley complaint, for example, has only three entries: In May 1970 we find "complaint received," and in April 1974 we find two entries, "case closed—incomplete," and "complaint closed." In some instances, where several similar complaints have been lodged against the same university, some cases will inexplicably be marked "case closed—no jurisdiction" while others remain open. Some five-year-old cases indicate considerable investigative activity followed by findings of executive order violations but no corrective action. In a number of instances one finds the agency has indicated a violation of the law has been found but the cases are closed years later with an entry that reads "case closed—lacked merit." Large numbers of cases show only two entries: "complaint received" and, often several years later, "complaint closed."

Computer buffs have long recognized that computerized statistical systems are only as good as the programs fed into them. They say it succinctly: garbage in, garbage out. At OCR, even though the terms to be logged into the computer were clearly and specifically defined, there appears to have been no small amount of manipulation through the use of inappropriate entries and through the failure to enter all actions taken on complaints. In specific cases where agency actions could be traced from another source, the manipulation sometimes appears to have been used to cover agency bungling of case handling. There is more evidence, in the case of OCR's case following system, that it was the users, not the system, who were at fault.

But, strangely enough, the new Carter administration agency heads decided in 1978 to junk the computer system rather than the people who had misused it. Cindy Brown, who heads OCR's operations, admits the system was beginning to work: "we got the accuracy of it up quite high," she says, "but we still were never able to make the computer spit out all these analyses. It was very expensive. So we have gone to a manual reporting system which we've developed from scratch . . . I mean we developed it the sensible way instead of the way the case following system had been done."

In the future, says Brown, the agency may put all closed cases into a data processing system for analytical purposes: "cases that are history, that never change." But the computer experts I have questioned all agreed that systems for retrieving and analyzing constantly changing information are a far more efficient use of computers than systems for retrieving and analyzing static information. Indeed, they point out that the smallest bank with a computerized check entry and statement procedure must have a far more sophisticated program that handles far more entries each year than the OCR case following system.

But Brown came to an opposite conclusion: "People who have a lot of experience with management information systems tell us that you cannot rely totally on a computerized system, that you must have a manual system backup. That you can't get information fast enough or do with it what you want. I mean it's really interesting to talk to people who really work in the field, which I've done now, and they say, you know . . . computerized systems do not work that well."

One wonders how the Federal Reserve System, which must depend upon computers to accurately tabulate millions of daily transactions where inaccuracy could take its toll in the loss of millions of dollars, would react. But Brown, when her notion that hand counting case following statistics was more accurate and efficient than using computers was challenged, responded by insisting: "Well, we've had all sorts of experts looking at what we were doing. We brought in people with a great degree of experience."

The new hand tabulated statistics produced by the Office for Civil Rights are about what one would expect. Terms have been changed so that there is no way to compare them with the older statistical summaries produced by the computer. "Results achieved" from complaint investigation are now tabulated in terms of "closed with change" and "closed with no change" instead of "merit," "corrective action taken," and "lacked merit." And we are warned that the terms are not exactly comparable. Closed complaints are split by "investigated" and "uninvestigated" and it is not possible to tell how many complaints "closed with no change" were investigated and how many were closed without any effort at investigation.

About the only things possible to ascertain from the new reporting method is that letters of finding with "no violation" still run twice as high as letters of finding with "violation," and that the rate of closures of uninvestigated complaints has accelerated rapidly. Indeed, by September 1978 the agency was 482 "uninvestigated closures" ahead of its own projection. As for the quality of the complaint work being done, Brown assures us that "we don't have any indications that the quality has gone down at all . . . I think it's been maintained."

There is considerable evidence that the failure of OCR to pick up on the kinds of gross statistical scams in plans such as those produced at Berkeley and at the University of Hawaii is far from accidental. OCR's own manipulations of its case statistics lend credence to the notion. Certainly enthusiasm for enforcing the executive order on the campus was at a low ebb during the mid-1970s. But the continuation of this pattern into the Carter administration is perhaps even more outrageous in view of administration rhetoric about turning the tide in antidiscrimination enforcement and in view of the continuing Orwellian use of the term "affirmative action."

Following the debacle at Berkeley, a number of OCR officials admitted that their efforts were aimed more at forcing the Department of Labor to lift or revise the requirements of the executive order as they applied to universities than at accomplishing affirmative action on the campus. Said one: We followed those DOL regulations item by item by item by item. . . . That's the only way we could convince Labor it wouldn't work."

Berkeley officials expressed outrage at the suggestion. If they did that, said Provost Maslach, "they ought to be sued for immoral and unethical activities. This whole process cost us millions of dollars." Nonetheless, Maslach himself characterized the statistical demands of affirmative action as "boilerplate." And the interchange between Berkeley officials and OCR, as with University of Hawaii officials and OCR, leaves little room for university outrage. It is hard to imagine that any of the officials involved on either side were so naive that they believed they were engaged in serious statistical analysis in order to overcome a discriminatory situation.

It would seem that statistical game playing continues to be a favored means of gulling the government, or, as many observers view it, of pleasing the government and gulling the public. Indeed, if there is outrage, it belongs properly only with women who have had the door to campus employment closed so rudely in their faces.

—— *Chapter Seven* ——

THE REAL STATISTICS

"All of those people who have denied that there is discrimination . . . seek and grope for all kinds of explanations, but, of course, never admit there could be an explanation of discrimination."
Irene Bowman, Complainant, 1976

Considering the ease with which government officials accept and use meaningless or even fraudulent statistics, one must ask whether there exists any meaningful statistical evidence about the employment situation for women in the professions. At Berkeley and elsewhere OCR has been willing to believe that there is little underutilization of women since there are few trained women available; therefore there is little discrimination and little that can be done to increase female participation in the professional workforce beyond increasing the number of women students seeking training. Is OCR correct?

A great many people seem to think so. What is more, they believe that government actions to increase female participation in the workforce have produced "reverse discrimination"—a term used to describe discrimination against white males. The term gained considerable favor with academics who confronted affirmative action on the campus in the early 1970s and concluded with embarrassingly unscholarly haste that it was nothing more or less than preferential treatment for women and minorities at the expense of better qualified white males and thus at the expense of the merit system. Somehow the term captured the imagination of the American press. One could hardly open a magazine during the mid-1970s without reading anew about the horrors "reverse discrimination" had visited upon the world of professional employment.

"For a democratic society to systematically discriminate against 'the majority' seems quite without precedent. To do so in the name of nondiscrimination seems mind-boggling," said one writer in 1973 (Seligman, pp. 160–68).

"in the effort to stop discrimination against women and minority-group members, . . . the Federal government is imposing rigid employment policies on colleges—and may be threatening the quality of U.S. education," warned another writer in 1974 (*Newsweek*, July 15, 1974, p. 45).

"White people cannot be legally punished any more as a group than black people as a group, yet isn't that precisely the sort of injustice that occurs when a university announces it prefers to hire women or black people and will not seriously consider men or white people?" asked a university president in a 1975 speech (Hager, Los Angeles *Times*, February 15, 1975).

"Goals have become quotas. Women and minorities are given preference for both jobs and enrollment. Equal opportunity has been replaced by equal representation," insisted another writer in 1976 (*U.S. News and World Report*, March 29, 1976).

"It might be time to reaffirm, as was affirmed with the Civil Rights Act, that there will never be racial peace until the idea of racial discrimination is buried: that an end to reverse discrimination would help to reunite the United States," wrote another in 1977 (Bethell).

The term "reverse discrimination" was so frequently used that the very existence of such discrimination rapidly became a nonissue. The only question to be debated was whether and how to bring reverse discrimination to an end. The assumption behind the existence of reverse discrimination was never hidden by the writers, nor was it ever challenged by them. Yet it is so basically elitist that one would think it should have raised an editorial eyebrow or two:

> In the first place, if groups are now to be represented in the work force according to their percentage of the entire population . . . there must inevitably be a retreat from the criterion of merit. It is as though we are saying that all horses must now end at the finish post together, not merely start together, and if one horse lags then that is proof that it was somehow handicapped, not that it is simply slower (Bethell 1977).

Merit, then, is assumed to be the existing working principle for hiring and advancement in the job market as long as the federal government does not interfere with its strange notions about affirmative action. And merit is the justification for any unequal representation that may have existed before government interference. Thus government imposed "reverse discrimination" has tangibly damaged the merit system.

The formula is tidy, but it overlooks a few simple facts. If merit were, indeed, the basis for hiring, there would be no need for any antibias programs whatever because there would be no discrimination. The claim of women and blacks that they are left out of the workforce in disproportionate numbers is exactly the claim that merit is *not* the existing principle but preference *is*—preference for white males. The assumption that unequal results are not necessarily the consequence of unequal opportunity but merely the result of better "race horses" finishing first is basically elitist and racist: it is the unstated assumption that the better "race horses" are disproportionately white and male. The assumption that government antibias programs have drastically changed employment patterns and produced discrimination against white males is questionable, at best.

The proponents of the theory that reverse discrimination exists are always able to cite isolated instances, generally horror stories about well trained male academics forced to support their families by working as fry cooks or service station attendants. They tend to avoid statistics that, they claim, cannot tell the real story. And, indeed, the statistics cannot tell us about the horrors of "reverse discrimination" because they tell us, instead, that there is no pattern of discrimination against white males. They tell us that the age-old pattern of discrimination against women and minorities continues, despite the law, the government antidiscrimination agencies, and the courts. Let us examine some of those statistics.

Perhaps the least controversial part of antidiscrimination law has been the concept of equal pay for equal work. Few men will admit to opposing the concept. Indeed, many men who oppose almost every other phase of equity law begin their position statements by declaring, "I'm all for equal pay for equal work but. . . ." One would expect that given the wide acceptance of this notion some progress would have been made over the 15 year history of the Equal Pay Act toward narrowing the gap between male and female income. One finds, however, that the gap has widened. The Bureau of the Census reports that in 1960, before the enactment of the Equal Pay Act, the median income of female, full-time, year round civilian workers was 61 percent of the income of men in the same category. By 1970, seven years after the enactment of the law, the gap had grown: women earned 59 percent of the income of men. By 1974, two years after professional and administrative workers were added to the Equal Pay Act's coverage, the gap had grown still further: women earned only 57 percent of the earnings of men (U.S. Department of Commerce 1976, p. 47).

When examined in terms of educational attainment, the mark, we are often told, of earning ability, the gap is even more striking. In 1972, according to one government study, the median income for men with less than eight years of elementary school was higher than the median income for women with one to three years of college. Men who had dropped out of high school after one to three years earned $726 more than did women who had completed college (U.S. Department of Labor 1977a, p. 3). A study of 1976 earnings revealed the gap was even wider if only white men are considered. White men who dropped out of high school earned an average of $2,200 more during the year than women with college degrees (Vetter et al. 1978).

A number of writers insist that the gap is due to the fact that women have largely remained in traditional female fields—fields that do not pay as well as male fields. Thus a recent new thrust of the women's movement has been toward achieving equal pay for equal value and working to overcome the notion that, for example, a secretary is less valuable to a company than its truck drivers. It is certainly true that the barriers that remain in the way of women moving into traditional male occupations have remained intact, and it is worthwhile to examine the low value our society places upon certain types of work that have traditionally been performed by women. Indeed, other figures released by the government indicate that women are rapidly becoming a higher percentage of persons living in poverty, whether or not they are employed. In 1975, 58 percent of the persons living in poverty in the United States were female. By 1976, according to preliminary figures, the figure had risen to 66.6 percent: two out of three poor persons in the United States were female (U.S. Department of Labor 1977b).

The failure to assign sufficient value to tasks that have traditionally been performed by females in our society demands attention. At the same time, it should not obscure the fact that women have not even attained the far less controversial goal of achieving equal pay for equal work. While the failure to integrate the work force may be in part responsible for the relatively low income of women, the failure to achieve equal pay (and equal promotion opportunities) in that part of the work force that *is* integrated must also be blamed. Government figures for 1976 show that women earned less than men in every industrial grouping, from a high of 88 percent of the earnings of men in farm employment to a low of 45 percent of the earnings of men in sales (U.S. Department of Labor 1977, p. 36).

A legitimate question could be raised about the large occupational groupings used. Since women entered certain professions in large numbers only recently, is it not possible that the figures are merely the result of women having less seniority or being less experienced in certain broad occupational groupings? While every profession cannot be examined here, an examination of more detailed statistics in a few professional fields might help answer the question.

Two areas have been selected for closer scrutiny, each with a very

specific reason: the first is academic employment because the current
mythology of reverse discrimination has its origins in the academic
community and because white men in that community have been most
vocal in their insistence that women are gaining positions at the expense
of more qualified men. The second is science and engineering because
current mythology holds that *because* women have always been rare in
these fields, those women who earn science and engineering degrees have
an easier time than do men in finding jobs and are being offered higher
salaries.

Looking first at academics we find that the percentage of women
obtaining doctoral degrees has risen sharply over the past several decades. For the sake of simplicity, let us leave aside the argument that
academic men do not always have doctoral degrees and that therefore the
pool of qualified women for academic employment should not be limited
to Ph.D. holders, although it is true, of course, that universities have
always hired and tenured non-Ph.D. males. Only 45.1 percent of men
teaching in colleges and universities during 1971-72, for example, had
Ph.D.s or some other doctoral-level degree (Grant and Lind 1976, p. 96).
Nevertheless, universities continue to argue that in the name of excellence, they cannot be expected to search for qualified women among non-
Ph.D.s. But even using women Ph.D.s as a base, we find that the pool of
potential female faculty has grown considerably. During the 1949–50
academic year, only 11 percent of all Ph.D.s were awarded to women.
During the 1959–60 academic year, 12 percent of the Ph.D.s were
awarded to women. By 1970–71 the figure had reached 14.3 percent. It
rose to 15.8 percent in 1971–72, 17.9 percent in 1972–73, 19.1 percent in
1973–74, and 21.3 percent in 1974–75 (Ott 1976, 9.3).

Employment statistics for university faculty positions do not indicate
any similar increase in the percentage of women. In its annual survey of
faculty status and compensation for 1973–74, the American Association of
University Professors (AAUP) found that only 22.5 percent of faculty
members in colleges and universities were female (Dorfman 1975, p. 135).
One year later the survey revealed that only 21.7 percent were female
(Dorfman and Cell 1976, p. 221). By 1976–77 the figure had gone up again,
but only slightly: 22.4 percent of college and university faculty members
were women (Dorfman 1977, p. 167). And in 1977–78 it dropped again:
22.1 percent were women (Eymonerie 1978, p. 205).

The figures cannot be attributed to a stagnant employment situation
in universities. While university hires may be well below the heyday of
expansion during the 1950s and 1960s, there is some hiring going on and
women have even made some gains at the lower levels. In 1974-75 only
27.9 percent of all assistant professors were female (Dorfman 1975, p.
135). By 1976-77 the figure rose to 29.7 percent (Dorfman 1977, p. 167),

and by 1977–78 it rose to 30.1 percent (Eymonerie 1978, p. 205). Not a major change by any means, but a sufficient increase so that one would expect some increase in the total employment figures. A further look at the spread of women faculty members among the university and college ranks explains the discrepancy. While women made slight gains at the lower ranks, they lost ground in the upper ranks. In 1974-75, 10.1 percent of full professors were female according to the AAUP. By 1978 the figure, which had dropped slightly each year, reached a low of 8.2 percent. In 1974–75, 17.3 percent of associate professors were female. Though the drop was less severe in this rank, it was nonetheless reflective of a downward pattern for women in the permanent faculties of colleges and universities. By 1978 females constituted only 16.6 percent of associate professors.

The tenure statistics tell the story: in 1974-75 only 46 percent of women faculty members in American colleges and universities had permanent academic tenure, while 64 percent of the men were tenured (Dorfman 1975, p. 139). By 1976-77 women had lost ground: only 44 percent were tenured. The figure for men remained 64 percent (Dorfman 1977, p. 171). By the 1977-78 year, women managed to regain one percentage point: 45 percent were tenured. But during the same period men managed to widen the gap even further: 66 percent of all faculty men had tenure (Eymonerie 1978, p. 209).

The salary gap fleshes out the picture: in 1974-75, AAUP found that women at every rank earned less, on the average, than men at the same rank. Women professors earned 90.8 percent of the earnings of men professors. Women associate and assistant professors earned 96.2 percent of the earnings of men at those ranks, and women instructors earned 95.6 percent of the earnings of men. By 1977-78 the gap had narrowed only .03 percent for professors: women earned 91.2 percent of the earnings of men. In all other ranks the gap had widened: women associate professors earned 95 percent of the earnings of men, women assistant professors earned 95.3 percent the earnings of men, and women instructors earned only 86.5 percent of the earnings of men.

The in-rank gap tells only part of the story, however, for the same annual survey tells us that those women who are employed by universities and colleges tend to be predominantly at the lower ranks while men tend to be at the upper ranks. In 1974-75, 60.6 percent of all males working as faculty members were either professors or associate professors. But 66.9 percent of females were either assistant professors or instructors. Thus the salary gap for all academic ranks really paints a more accurate picture of the status of women on the American campus than does the in-rank salary gap. In 1974-75 the gap was significant: women faculty members earned an average of 82.6 percent of the earnings of men. By 1977-78 the gap had widened: women were earning an average of 80.1 percent the earnings of men. The gap had grown by more than .50 percent each year.

A close look at the lower two ranks is particularly informative. In 1974–75, according to AAUP, 31.2 percent of all faculty men and 41.4 percent of faculty women were at assistant professor rank. By 1977–78 only 27.3 percent of faculty men were assistant professors but the figure for women remained high at 41.6 percent. The reports also indicate that men have never been used in significant numbers as instructors or lecturers: 8.2 percent were employed at those levels in 1974–75 and 8.4 percent in 1977–78. But over 25 percent of all women employed on college and university campuses during each year of the survey were at these two low ranks.

It is important to note that in 1977 the AAUP began using raw data collected by the National Center for Education Statistics of HEW rather than its own data collection system. The figures for 1977–78, therefore, might indicate change that is the result only of a changed and enlarged data base. However, there is a high level of consistency between the 1977–78 figures and the earlier ones. Certainly the consistency is sufficient to permit the conclusion that women have not been working their way up the academic ladder in significant numbers.

In 1975 the AAUP annual report broke down male and female salaries for the first time and noted that "the very fact that the differentials exist for all ranks and classes of institution with a single exception is strong presumptive evidence that women are in weaker bargaining positions than men in the academic marketplace, and are forced to accept inferior bargains" (Dorfman 1975, p. 123). The single exception was in the lowest paid category: female instructors at private universities (but not public ones) earned a weighted average compensation that was $220 per year more than male instructors in the same institutions. And in 1977 the report found, "(t)he most that can be said is that there is no indication of significant progress" (Dorfman 1977, p. 149).

Given the pattern in faculty employment, the pattern in academic administration should not be surprising. Perhaps the first comprehensive survey of academic administrators by race and sex was completed recently under a Ford Foundation grant by the American Council on Education and the College and University Personnel Association. The survey found that for the 1975–76 academic year, men far outnumbered women in almost every major category of academic administration (Van Alstyne et al. 1977). In schools of law and medicine 100 percent of the deans in surveyed institutions were white and male. In predominantly white, public institutions, 96 percent of the university presidents were white males, 3 percent were minority males, and only 1 percent were women. In men's colleges, 100 percent of the presidents were men and in women's colleges 69 percent of the presidents were men. Similar patterns prevailed in every administrative position: 99 percent of executive vice-presidents in public, coeducational institutions, 98 percent of chief planning officers, 98 percent of chief business officers, and 95 percent of chief academic officers were male.

Women administrators appeared in significant numbers only as directors of food service (26 percent), bookstore managers (36 percent), head librarians (29 percent), information office directors (27 percent), deans of nursing (90 percent), deans of home economics (85 percent), and affirmative action officers (49 percent). None of these positions could be called key decision-making administrative offices (especially the last).

In salary comparisons done during the survey it was found that differences in compensation were more consistently related to the sex than to the race of the administrator. Both minority women and white women were paid about 80 percent of the salaries of men with the same job title in the same type of institution. The disparity applied even to affirmative action officers, where men were paid consistently higher salaries than women.

A second study of college and university administrators was conducted for the 1976–77 year by the National Center for Education Statistics (Eiden 1977). Here, too, the discrepancies between male and female administrators were marked. A preliminary study released by the Center indicated that the mean annual salaries for male administrators were considerably higher than those for female administrators in the same job group. The average salary of male presidents and chancellors was $35,135. For females the figure was $32,107. The gap was larger for deans and directors: male graduate program deans averaged $31,281, women averaged $26,114; male business deans averaged $28,221, while women averaged $20,097; male deans of arts and sciences averaged $29,021, while females averaged $24,631. The gap was largest for chief business officers: men averaged $25,413, while women averaged $16,497.

A later analysis (Astin 1977) reported that the situation for women in academic administration remained unchanged. Even when compared to the number of women faculty at each type of institution, women did poorly though faculty normally constitute the pool from which most academic administrators are selected. Astin reported: "Differences in *absolute* percentages of women administrators compared with women faculty, however, are substantial for all types of institutions, particularly the universities and public colleges. Using the percentage of women on the faculty as a guide, women are underrepresented as chief academic officers in the public two-year colleges by a factor of 10 to 1 and in the public four-year colleges by a factor of more than 20 to 1" (p. 63). Astin found that most of the college presidents who were female were in

Catholic women's colleges. Another report, in 1978, backed that finding: it noted that of the total of 100 women college presidents in the United States, 87 were nuns (*Spokeswoman*, April 1978, p. 6).

When college size is taken into consideration, reported Astin, "19 of every 20 freshmen enter an institution in which all three key administrative posts (president, chief academic officer, and dean of arts and sciences) are held by men" (p. 65). He concluded:

> Clearly, women are grossly underrepresented in all top administrative posts in American colleges and universities. What appears to be a modest representation among college presidents and academic deans is, on closer examination, a relatively high representation of women among administrators in colleges for women. Private universities and public institutions of all types show the greatest lack of women administrators. A handful of women occupy top administrative posts in public two- and four-year colleges, while virtually no women occupy these posts in public and private universities. Among both top and middle level administrative positions, there is a strong negative correlation between the average salary and the proportion of women occupying the position (p. 65).

A second category of professional employment that bears close scrutiny is science and engineering. Here, if we are to believe those who purvey the myth of reverse discrimination, women are not only gaining jobs that might otherwise go to better qualified men, but they are also being paid more than comparable men. The reason, we are told, is that there has been such a shortage of women in these fields in the past that any woman who enters science or engineering will be eagerly fought over by competing employers desperate to please the government equal employment investigators. In this competitive job market women can virtually write their own employment ticket.

It is certainly true that women are not entering the fields of engineering and science in any great numbers. In fact, a 1976 report issued by the U.S. Department of Labor indicates that, with some exceptions, women are not entering any of the traditionally male fields with any speed. The field of law seemed to account for the largest gains. In 1965, four percent of the professional degrees in law were awarded to women and by 1974 the figure had risen to 12 percent. Pharmacy made gains as well: in 1965, 17 percent of the professional degrees in the field were awarded to women while 26 percent went to women in 1974. Engineering, which had granted only .04 percent of its first professional degrees to women in 1965 was awarding five percent of such degrees to women by 1974 (U.S. Department of Labor 1976).

A study by the National Center for Education Statistics (Ott 1977) of doctoral degrees awarded from 1970–71 through 1974–75 shows the same modest trend toward increased number of women in engineering and science. In 1970–71, 16.3 percent of the Ph.D.s in biological sciences were awarded to women. By 1974–75 the figure had risen to 22 percent. In computer and information sciences, 2.3 percent of the 1970–71 degrees went to women and in 1974–75 the figure rose to 6.6 percent. In engineering the figure went from .06 percent of the Ph.D. degrees in 1970–71 to 2.1 percent in 1974–75. In psychology it went from 24 percent to 30.9 percent. In the physical sciences it rose from 5.6 percent to 8.3 percent. And in the social sciences it went from 13.9 percent to 20.8 percent.

It could be argued, then, that while their numbers are growing, women are not yet entering the sciences or engineering in sufficiently large numbers to have become a glut on the market. If, indeed, there is a premium on recruiting women doctorates in the sciences and in engineering, it should be reflected in low unemployment rates and in high salaries for the newly minted Ph.D.s as well as for women who gained their degrees in years past when there might have been overt bias against hiring women in these fields.

A 1975 survey of doctoral scientists and engineers published by the National Academy of Sciences refutes such contentions. The survey found that in virtually all age groups the unemployment rates for women with Ph.D.s in engineering and the sciences was higher than the rate for men. Only on approaching retirement age does the figure begin to balance. In the younger age group, from 30 to 34, unemployment for women Ph.D.s was almost five times higher than for men. Overall, unemployment for women was three percent, while it was 0.8 percent for men (National Academy of Sciences 1976; see also National Science Foundation 1977).

The study found that salaries for men and women with Ph.D.s in science and engineering did not substantiate the myth that women in these fields can write their own ticket. At every age level the median annual salaries for men exceeded those for women. The discrepancy is almost $2,000 per year in the initial post Ph.D. years with people 30 years and under and grows to better than $6,000 for men and women in the 55 to 59 year age group.

One might argue that the median annual salary for men and women in science and engineering is an unfair conglomerate figure that includes the social sciences, where there are more women and where salaries are lower, and engineering and physics, where there are fewer women and salaries are higher. However, a breakdown by field disproves this contention. In every field—mathematics, physics, chemistry, earth sciences, engineering, biological sciences, psychology, and social sciences—the salaries of women lag behind those of men. The disparity ranges from $3,000 in psychology to over $5,000 in chemistry (National Academy of Sciences 1976, pp. 22–23).

Another objection might be raised on the supposition that women enter into careers later and therefore tend to be in the lower range of the experience continuum. However, the salaries of women in the under 30 age group are consistently lower than the salaries of men. Given the length of time required to obtain a Ph.D., it is unlikely that the age group reflects a greater degree of experience for males (except, perhaps, in work as graduate assistants since male students still seem to have an edge over females in gaining such posts).

In a study prepared for the National Science Foundation (NSF) (Maxfield 1976), the data from the 1975 survey of doctoral scientists and engineers was compared to data in a similar survey conducted in 1973. The study adds some interesting insights into the status of the woman Ph.D. in science and engineering since it concentrates on the small segment of doctoral degree holders who were either unemployed, employed in nonscience or nonengineering jobs because they could not gain employment in their fields, or employed part-time while seeking full-time work.

The study notes, first of all, that unemployment among these highly trained individuals was far lower than the national average. In fact, the demand for skilled scientists and engineers rose during 1975 and unemployment dipped for them while national unemployment figures rose. Thus in February through April 1973, the unemployment rate for scientists and engineers with Ph.D.s was 1.2 percent compared with a national unemployment rate of 4.9 percent. In February through April 1975 the national unemployment rate had risen to eight percent, but unemployment among doctorates in science and engineering had dropped to one percent. Nonetheless, during both survey years, unemployment for women doctorates in science and engineering was three times as high as for men: 3.9 percent of the women were unemployed in 1973, compared to 0.9 percent of the men; three percent were unemployed in 1975, compared to 0.8 percent of the men.

The study compared unemployment rates by groupings of men and women who had received their doctoral degrees at the same time. It concluded: "Unemployment rates for female Ph.D.s were substantially higher than the rates for male doctoral scientists and engineers for nearly all years of doctorate . . ." (p. 13).

The study also found that "the percentage of women employed part-time, but seeking full-time work consistently exceeded the rate for men" (p. 14). For 1971–72 graduates surveyed in 1973, 3.9 percent of the women but only one percent of the men were employed part-time and seeking full-time work. For 1973–74 graduates surveyed in 1975, 3.5 percent of the women but only 1.1 percent of the men were in a similar position.

Single discipline studies in the sciences underscore the points made in the NSF study. A particularly disparate field, for example, is microbiology, where a 1974 study found that women were more dependent for their jobs on research funds while men tended to gain secure positions in research or academic institutions (Kashket et al. 1974).

In other words, women were more likely to be hired on "soft money" as research assistants or associates once a large grant had been obtained by an institution and were thus more likely to be terminated along with the completion of the grant. Women therefore tended to move up the professional ranks more slowly than did men. Not surprisingly, the study also found that women microbiologists earned less than men both across the board and when compared by both the highest degree earned and by rank. Moreover, the gap grew rather spectacularly with the increase in degree level or rank: "The differences in salary were 10 percent more for men at the bachelor's level, 15 percent more at the master's level, and 32 percent more at the doctoral level. . . . When salaries for the sexes were compared by rank, however, women were seen to earn less than men at every level except the lowest, that of research assistant" (p. 490).

The report concluded: "The woman microbiologist, upon entering the professional job market, faces (i) slower advancement; (ii) restricted extramural recognition; and (iii) fewer positions of a supervisory or administrative nature, when compared to men. Most striking is the salary differential, which increases with increasing educational level, with increasing rank, and with increasing seniority" (p. 493).

Yet another report, released in late 1978, indicates that in 1977, except for beginning engineers and individuals entering industry jobs with bachelor's degrees in chemistry, women's salaries continued to be lower than those of men with comparable training, education, and experience at every degree level and age level in every field with every type of employer—private industry, government, and academic. Unemployment rates were found to be between two and five times higher for women in each field compared to men with comparable degrees. Men and women scientists employed in academic institutions moved up the academic ladder at widely different rates. Women, as usual, tended to be clustered at the bottom of the ladder when compared to men with the same degrees earned during the same time periods. Federally employed women professionals did no better than those employed in the private sector or in academe. The average grade level and salary for women in every profession was consistently lower than that of comparable men (Vetter et al. 1978).

Given the realities of the job market for highly trained women in the academic world and in the sciences and engineering, the allegation that reverse discrimination is running rampant over the hides of white males is pattently absurd. Myths, one would think, would not thrive long on facts. But the myth of reverse discrimination persists, nourished by appealing horror stories about victimized white males, clothed in a mantle of supposed merit, and housed in a windowless shelter where the real facts of female employment are not permitted.

—— *Chapter Eight* ——

A JURY OF ONE'S PEERS

"I don't care whether it's Jesus Christ Himself or Einstein. You can always find some way, if you put your mind to it, in which that individual—black, white, male, female—is a little less good than perfection."

Patricia St. Lawrence,
Berkeley Genetics Professor, 1976

On August 1, 1977, Judge William Knox announced his final ruling in the case of *Sharon Johnson v. the University of Pittsburgh School of Medicine.* Johnson had been denied tenure and had accused the university of sex discrimination in its decision. After 74 days of on again-off again hearings that stretched over many months, after testimony that occupied 12,085 pages of court transcripts, after hearing 73 witnesses and admitting over 1,000 exhibits, Judge Knox found against Johnson.

During the hearings much of the testimony had revolved around Johnson's qualifications for tenure. Indeed, Knox had said in open court that he would hear expert witnesses on the subject and make his decision on the basis of their testimony. Yet, after admitting that testimony, Knox titled one section of his rambling, 90 page final decision, "The Court is Not a Super Tenure Committee to Pass on the Qualifications for Grants of Tenure in Colleges and Universities" (*Johnson v. University of Pittsburgh*, 15 FEP 1516 [1977]). Said Knox:

> We start with the proposition that tenure is a privilege, an honor, a distinct honor, which is not to be accorded to all assistant professors. It is a very high recognition of merit. It is the ultimate reward for scientific and academic excellence. It is to be awarded in the course of search for fundamental merit. . . . Such decision by its very nature cannot be made by a court but must be made by the faculty.

Again and again Knox returned to his theme: the judicial system does not have the knowledge or the authority to interfere with the peer judgment system:

> . . . while the court might feel that the plaintiff's research is valuable in the field of medicine and is on the very forefront of the expansion of human knowledge for the extension of life, it is not for this court to make such a decision which can only be made by those who have acquired Ph.D.s and spent years in the field."; ". . . a well informed decision can only be made by the colleagues with whom the faculty member has worked. Thus, the peer review system has evolved as the most reliable method for assuring promotion of the candidates best qualified to serve the needs of the institution."; "The court has little doubt as to the plaintiff's scientific qualifications . . . her scientifically accepted output has been greater than that of the others . . . but on the other hand we cannot say that the decision that her research was not relevant to the mission of a department of biochemistry in a medical school was unreasonable. This is a matter for academic expertise in the field and not for the court.

In sum, reasoned Judge Knox,

> On the one hand we have the important problem as to whether sex discrimination is operating to the detriment of women in the halls of academia. If so, Congress has mandated that it must be eradicated. Colleges and universities must understand this and guide themselves accordingly. On the other hand we also have the important question as to whether the federal courts are to take over the matter of promotion and tenure for college professors when experts in the academic field agree that such should not occur. In determining qualifications in such circumstances the court is way beyond its field of expertise and in the absence of a clear carrying of the burden of proof by the plaintiff, we must leave such decisions to the Ph.D.s in academia.

The implication of Judge Knox's opinion is that *no* expert witnesses can be used by judges. Why, for example, should it be any easier for a judge to decide on the sanity of a murder suspect based on expert psychiatric testimony than on the qualifications of a woman for tenure, based on expert witnesses in her academic field? And indeed, Judge Knox did not stop at the university door. He referred to an earlier decision in his own court in which "this court pointed out that it did not have sufficient expertise to appraise the qualifications of those in the teaching profession whether university professors or elementary school teachers."

Since 48 percent of all women in professional employment are engaged in teaching, Knox's contention is worth examining (U.S. Department of Commerce 1976, p. 35). It implies that while Title VII was intentionally extended to education employment in 1972, the method of achieving equity in such employment was intended to be entirely different from that used for other types of employment: it is to be primarily the concern of the employment system rather than the courts and the burden of proof is to rest on the plaintiff, even after she has established a prima facie showing of discrimination, rather than on the defendant.

When Title VII was first voted into law in 1964, it contained certain key exemptions: it did not apply to local, state, or federal government workers and it did not apply to the faculties of educational institutions. By 1971 a number of amendments to Title VII were up for vote in both houses of Congress. They were intended both to strengthen the bargaining power of the Equal Employment Opportunity Commission, the chief enforcer of Title VII, and to extend coverage of Title VII to many of the workers who had been left out of the earlier legislation. When the Senate Committee on Labor and Public Welfare completed its work on the new amendments, its final report included the following discussion of extended coverage:

> As in other areas of employment, statistics for educational institutions indicate that minorities and women are precluded from the more prestigious and higher paying positions, and are relegated to the more menial and lower paying jobs. . . . Women are . . . generally underrepresented in institutions of higher learning, but those few that do obtain positions are generally paid less and advanced more slowly than their male counterparts. . . .
>
> The committee believes that it is essential that these employees be given the same opportunities to redress their grievances as are available to other employees in the other sectors of business . . . (Legislative History 1972, pp. 420-21).

When the proposed Title VII changes came to the floor of the Senate, an amendment was put forth that would have reintroduced the exemption for higher education institutions. In the debate on that ammendment, Senator G. Mennon Williams insisted that professional employees in higher education are

> no different from other employees in the nation and deserve to be accorded the same protections. To continue the existing exemption for these employees would not only continue to work an injustice against this vital segment of our Nation's workforce, but would also establish a class of employers who could pursue employment policies which are otherwise prohibited by law (Legislative History 1972, p. 1251).

Later in the debate Williams analyzed the bill with specific reference to the standards that would be required for educational institutions. They would, said Williams, "now be expected to conform to the standards of equal employment opportunity as established under Title VII, and employment practices such as hiring, promotion, transfer and termination will be subject to strict equal protection standards" (p. 1770). Similar discussions were held in the House of Representatives and similar conclusions were drawn. In fact, the amendment extending Title VII to faculty employees of educational institutions contained no special conditions or exemptions.

Nonetheless, a number of university administrators and male faculty members have expended enormous effort in recent years in trying to convince the government agencies and the courts that exemptions for education employees are both legal and essential. Time and again they have insisted on "the positive commitment of colleges and universities to equal employment opportunity and affirmative action . . ." (Heyns 1975, p. i). Time and again they have added qualifications in view of the alleged "unique" characteristics of higher education employment.

While the executive order, as presidential mandate, applies only to employers who have contracted with the federal government to provide goods and services, the requirements governing its enforcement should, in theory, be in line with legal precedents that have been set under Title VII. One would suppose, for example, that universities would refrain from arguing that the disparate impact definition of discrimination set by the Supreme Court in *Griggs v. Duke Power Co.* had no place on the American campus.

But this is exactly what university officials did attempt during hearings held by the Department of Labor during 1975 to determine whether universities should be exempted from existing regulations. The major emphasis of the testimony was that the merit system, with criteria laid out by universities and with candidates judged by their peers, cannot be allowed to bend to government regulation. Moreover, women and minorities could only be stigmatized by government imposed affirmative action since those who do gain jobs or tenure, even now, are thought to have "been appointed because of . . . the need of the college or university to achieve a certain numerical result" rather than because of their merit (Bowen 1975, p. 26).

"It would be to the advantage of those federal agencies responsible for carrying out the mandate of the Executive Order and of higher education," said Roger W. Heyns, President of the American Council on Education, "if the requirements for and monitoring of equal employment and affirmative action on campuses were modified to take into account the unique characteristics of higher education that are necessary for a sound and excellent educational system" (Bowen 1975, p. 3).

"I would like to begin by associating myself, and I believe, the overwhelming majority of other college and university presidents, with the positive commitment to equal opportunity which many of us feel so strongly," said William G. Bowen, president of Princeton University (Bowen 1975, p. 6). "But," he added later in his testimony, "it does seem to me that over time the best protection against discriminatory decisions is likely to come from a combination of sensible policies affecting recruitment, selection and advancement; better designed procedures allowing individuals who feel aggrieved to receive a full, fair and expeditious hearing from their peers; and an ever more widely shared commitment to fair play" (p. 35)

In his testimony, James V. Siena, legal counsel for Stanford University, further stressed the importance of leaving more of the task of affirmative action in the hands of the university. Said Siena, "it should be made clear that matters of internal governance, such as how decisions are reached or how the administration is structured, should properly be left for final decision by the universities themselves. Here again, the emphasis must be on results, not on the imposition of a uniform process" (Bowen 1975, p. 84).

It is doubtful that Siena would get much of an argument on this point from those who advocate the imposition of *Griggs* case law on universities, for they would point out that if the end result is a workforce with a fair representation of women and minorities at hire and in the promotion process, than few will object to the procedures through which that workforce is achieved. But Siena goes one step beyond. There are two aspects to the problem, he says: "*First*, who determines whether the goals are satisfactory? *Second*, what happens if the goals are not achieved?" (p. 89). The answer to the first question, says Siena, is,

> before a university's goals are found wanting, there should be clear and convincing evidence that they do not represent a good faith effort to estimate the probable results of implementing affirmative action procedures. . . . availability data are too imprecise and the means at hand too crude to make refined judgments on this matter, especially for faculty and other highly skilled employees where the selection factors are complex (p. 89).

The answer to the second question, says Siena, is,

> we feel equally strongly that failure to meet goals should not be taken as evidence of a lack of good faith compliance, but should simply serve as a signal to HEW that the situation might require a more detailed investigation into whether a good faith effort has been made to implement affirmative action procedures. Moreover, failure to meet goals should not "shift the burden of proof" (p. 90).

The university, then, should be left to its own means and its own goals and, if it fails to achieve its goals, the university is under no obligation to explain itself. Here Siena departs from the *Griggs* formula, for under *Griggs* it is exactly this lack of results, this continuation of disparate impact, that requires of the *employer* an explanation of its business practices.

The sum total of the testimony presented by university officials at the Department of Labor hearings and at subsequent government hearings on campus enforcement was an insistence upon the commitment of the university to a policy of equity and an equally vigorous insistence that universities are unique and are therefore the best, indeed the only, organizations qualified to act as police, judge, and jury of their own equity attempts. The first of these claims—that universities share in the nationally stated goal of achieving equity for women—grows more questionable with each year while university hiring and promotion efforts are measured against national statistics that show that the position of women on the campus has worsened. The second claim—that universities are unique and thus must be allowed to retain, unchallenged, the current peer review system—is also open to question.

Let us examine several examples of the peer review system in action to see if the faith placed by so many in its essential fairness, lack of prejudice, and concern with merit is warranted. We pick first an example that comes from an elite institution, the California Institute of Technology. There can be no question of the excellent reputation of the institution: we are not talking here of a mediocre school that might be accused of using claims of merit to avoid compliance with the law. Can anybody doubt that Caltech is, first and foremost, concerned with maintaining its own excellence, regardless of the gender in which that excellence is packaged? Let us see.

❖   ❖   ❖   ❖   ❖   ❖   ❖   ❖

Jenijoy LaBelle was the first women in the entire history of the California Institute of Technology to be hired at professorial level, although one other women, mathemetician Olga Todd, had finally become a tenured professor: the honor was awarded her only after she had spent years at Caltech as an untenured research associate.

LaBelle was hired by Caltech in 1969, as a 26-year-old Ph.D. in English literature who had, in her short academic career, already obtained two Woodrow Wilson fellowships. She also happened to be a very attractive young woman and Caltech immediately set about exploiting that fact. She was asked repeatedly by the university's publicity department to appear on television shows and to grant magazine interviews to tell the world what it was like to be the first and only women professor at the prestigious science school. The publicity might have engendered some resentment on the part of professors at Caltech and LaBelle now feels she was naive to allow herself to be exploited. However, the public relations work she did for the university did not prevent her from compiling an admirable academic record. By the time she was considered for tenure during the 1973–74 academic year, she had a number of publications in respected journals and had a coauthored book accepted for publication by a major publishing house.

It should be pointed out that Caltech does not have a graduate department in the humanities. Thus, the academic division that houses the humanities is primarily a service division intended to broaden out the background of Caltech students who will be, it is always hoped, among tomorrow's leading scientists. But Caltech is oriented toward research and publication and that orientation has spread to the humanities and social science division. There, as elsewhere at the Institute, professors are expected to produce a high volume of credible, high-level research and publication while teaching excellence is given little more than lip service.

Although there was no written statement concerning the number of publications required for tenure or the caliber of journals in which those publications appeared, it was clear from the publishing records of those tenured members of the humanities and social science division that LaBelle's record was a good one. The tenured English faculty, made up of about half a dozen scholars, agreed that this was so and voted unanimously in favor of tenure.

At that point the division chair selected seven outside experts and wrote asking them to comment on LaBelle's work. Later it was discovered that the chair had selected most of the experts from names he solicited from an untenured male assistant professor of English who one must assume was in competition with LaBelle for a tenured post: he was hired one year after LaBelle and thus would be up for tenure consideration a year after her. "It seemed very odd," comments LaBelle, "that the chairman would go to a junior member of the department and ask for names to judge my work rather than to tenured people. It turned out that almost everyone who was asked to judge my work has been a former associate of [his]. . . . Of course, my advice was not asked when it came to sending letters for him."

Nonetheless, the letters evaluating LaBelle's work were largely favorable, though they were not without some blatantly sexist remarks: "I've looked over the work . . . and find to my surprise that she's a good girl . . ." said one, ". . . what the hell, say I, there were distinguished female professors of English . . ." Another, from a professor at a university that had only recently turned coeducational, informed Caltech that the professor would have to vote a "reluctant no. . . . On the other hand," he added, "were [she] being considered at Vassar for example, where my wife teaches . . . I would strongly support [her]." Another evaluator closed his letter by sending "best regards" to the competing male assistant professor.

Despite the largely enthusiastic outside comments, the division chair decided against tenure for LaBelle, insisting that her teaching was undistinguished, that her scholarly productivity left "substantial doubt," her university committee service was lacking, and she fell short in "collegiality." According to a later finding made by the EEOC, "He had no documentation to support any of these opinions. In fact, existing evidence clearly contradicts his claims."

LaBelle and the members of the English faculty protested the decision to the Caltech provost and, largely because the positive evidence in her dossier seemed to belie the negative division decision, university administrators decided to call in another expert in English literature as an outside arbitrator. LaBelle agreed to abide by the arbitrator's decision and she assumed that the divisional chair had also agreed. But when the arbitrator decided that LaBelle deserved tenure at Caltech, the divisional chair insisted that he had never made any such agreement. Instead, he discounted the decision, according to the EEOC, "stating that perhaps the expert had at some time seen [LaBelle] and been influenced by her attractive appearance."

The division chair, still seeking to build a negative dossier, next sent letters to all of LaBelle's past students asking for honest and "brutal" appraisals of her teaching ability. The response did not help his case: most of the students found LaBelle an excellent teacher. The division chair then decided that teaching ability, too, was beside the point, and that, instead, the division should "change and raise the criteria for tenure." The division faculty then voted, according to EEOC, "to adopt what they called the 'Princetonian Standard,' requiring the acceptance of a book length manuscript for publication by a major university press." Meanwhile, LaBelle's English department rival, who had not published as extensively as had LaBelle, was granted an unusual early promotion to associate professor without tenure.

The divisional chair then gathered several more outside opinions of LaBelle's work. Since his own field was not English it would appear he once again consulted one of the English professors for names and, perhaps not coincidentally, two of the three experts from whom he solicited opinions were friends of LaBelle's rival. One of the outside, expert opinions came from the rival's former professor, who was himself interviewing for a prestigious position on the Caltech campus at that time and who happened to be staying at the home of his former student. In his hastily pencilled "expert opinion," he admitted that he had read only 40 pages of LaBelle's work. Nonetheless, he felt qualified to dismiss her as unsuitable for a post at Caltech. The letter was later typed by the divisional secretary at Caltech and added to LaBelle's files.

Early in 1975 the university administrative council, made up of divisional chairs, voted to deny LaBelle tenure. The humanities and social science chair then informed her that the reason for the denial was that she had failed to meet the newly created "Princetonian Standard." But a few months later LaBelle met the standard: she had a book length manuscript accepted unanimously by the editorial board of a major university press—none other, in fact, than the Princeton University Press. The book was later nominated for several awards. In addition, LaBelle had six more articles accepted for publication by that time.

In the fall of 1975 LaBelle asked the divisional chair for reconsideration. The answer was a flat no. She then appealed to the administrative council and that group decided that a reconsideration was in order. However, the mechanism for reconsideration, they decided, should be left in the hands of the reluctant divisional chair. The chair determined that he would call in a third group of experts, this time paid referees, and send them the entire dossier already assembled on LaBelle. He also decided he would send them the packet of the male tenure rival and ask them to choose between the two. The cards were by this time clearly stacked in favor of the rival. The lengthy correspondence in LaBelle's file made it clear there had already been a negative decision and that there was a heated tenure dispute in progress. The file also contained all the previously solicited negative letters. The rival male, on the other hand, entered the competition with early promotion to associate professor status, which could only indicate to outsiders that he had been rewarded by the institution for his merit. But even this stacked deck did not suit the chair. He attempted to send LaBelle's dossier with some of her written materials removed.

LaBelle never found out who the "experts" for this third round of outside opinion were. But it is clear once again that the chair, whose field was history, not English, had solicited some advice before making his choice: all the experts were from a school of literary criticism diametrically opposed to LaBelle's and in line with her competitor's.

"The comments of this third group of paid referees indicate that the prior letters did influence them, particularly those letters with negative evaluations of [LaBelle]," EEOC wrote in its findings. Not surprisingly, the chair found this procedure sufficient and the university told LaBelle that it would abide by the original, negative tenure decision. Meanwhile, said EEOC "(t)he competing male, who was recommended for tenure in accordance with Respondent's 'normal' procedures, was accorded tenure to become effective July 1, 1976—the effective date of [LaBelle's] termination."

❋   ❋   ❋   ❋   ❋   ❋   ❋   ❋

We look next at the evidence of peer review that so impressed Judge Knox in the Johnson case. The University of Pittsburgh has a well-respected medical school that has consistently won a large number of federal grants and that has remained in the forefront of medical research. Sharon Johnson came to the university medical school with a background that was unquestionably outstanding. She had graduated at the top of her class at the Massachusetts Institute of Technology, where she received her Ph.D. in chemistry in 1959. She served as a fellow at the Mellon Institute in Pittsburgh for six years and taught at Vassar College at the associate professor level before coming to the University of Pittsburgh. She also worked for a time as a senior chemist at Westinghouse Laboratories. By that time she had published seven articles and a monograph.

In 1967 Johnson was hired as an assistant professor—a cut in rank from her previous academic position—by the biochemistry department of the University of Pittsburgh Medical School. By 1971, when her tenure was considered, she had continued to add to her substantial professional reputation. She had published numerous scientific papers, obtained a number of large research grants from the National Institutes of Health and the National Science Foundation, and been elected to membership in the prestigious American Society of Biological Chemists.

The tenured professors of Johnson's department—all men—met in October 1971 at the request of the department chair to advise on tenure for Johnson. Johnson was not informed of the meeting nor was she given the opportunity to present any documentation concerning her accomplishments. No outside referees were consulted. Yet the professors, in their wisdom and apparently without any reference to documentation on her work, decided Johnson did not come up to their standards.

In what appears to be an after-the-fact effort to bolster the recommendation against tenure, the department chair next sought the opinion of two outside experts. But the effort was hardly a neutral and unbiased attempt to gain facts that might enlighten the chair and the university. The letters, written to "Dear Nate" and "Dear Bob," carefully explain that the department had already reached "the tentative conclusion that Sharon should not be promoted to the tenure level" and explain that she "comes up with very low marks particularly with regard to her teaching abilities, her general ability to organize material, her reliability for getting a job finished, as well as her scientific interaction with the rest of the department." Her work is characterized as lacking in "depth, excitement, and obvious significance." Having dropped these hints, the two colleagues were then asked their unbiased opinions about Johnson's work.

A more neutral tone might have inspired more open responses and the timing of the letters—after the decision was all but assured—was somewhat unusual. But in spite of this, the answers, while guarded, were hardly derogatory. Instead, one noted: "There is no question that the work is solid." The other stated: "There is no doubt that Dr. Johnson is an extremely competent person. Her work in all cases is carried out with the maximal technical competence and is frequently very important. . . . I would think she should be appointed to a tenured position." Not unexpectedly, the positive assessments made no change in the negative departmental decision. And by the time Judge Knox came to write his final opinion he was ready to conclude that "it was not inappropriate to provide background information to these experts. . . ."

Johnson's efforts to gain some review through the university system did not result in a serious examination of her academic credentials. It did, however, produce one major result. Her department chair began keeping a record of her "inappropriate" activities, documentation he seems to have assumed would be useful should she become too persistent in pursuing her tenure claims. In July 1972 the chair filed a memo that he characterized as "the initiation of a record of her attendance." The following October he wrote to the Medical School dean "to merely bring you up to date on Dr. Sharon Johnson's activities in the department over the past six months or so. As we have discussed previously, I have not been making an organized effort to monitor Dr. Johnson in any way—thus, there is little precise documentation of her activities but rather a series of observations which reflect the overall profile."

Included in the "profile": "There has been no direct verbal communication between Dr. Johnson and myself—occasionally she has written a letter to me." "She was bipassed [sic] by her peers . . . in their assignment of faculty examining committees for graduate student comprehensive examination. . . ." And, "(t)here are, of course, many other subjective aspects of Dr. Johnson's performance—inappropriate demands upon the secretarial staff, annoying and disruptive remarks at faculty meetings, attempts to undermine the morale of the department by soliciting support from students and postdoctoral fellows in the department and decoration of her office with male pinups." (Johnson had a poster of Olympic swimming champion Mark Spitz on her office wall.) The chair concluded that "all of these things are, of course, contributory to an increasingly difficult situation which I firmly believe is slowly but surely affecting the general atmosphere of the department in an unpleasant way."

In 1973 Sharon Johnson obtained a preliminary injunction from Judge Knox that prevented the University of Pittsburgh from firing her until a full-scale hearing on her charge of sex discrimination could be held. At that time the university's insistence on its right to unrestrained peer judgment did not impress the judge. In his finding on granting the preliminary injunction, Knox pointed out that there had been no criticism of Johnson's teaching prior to the semester during which the tenure decision had been made. In fact part of the evidence presented during the preliminary injunction hearings was the previous year's teaching evaluation in which Johnson came out third from the top out of eight department members. Knox considered the belated criticism of Johnson's teaching to be important evidence that the department was creating a pretext for the discriminatory denial of tenure. Indeed, he criticized the department for basing much of its decision on alleged inadequacies during one lecture she gave during the fall of 1971. But in his final decision, Knox quoted at length from the tenured faculty criticism of the same lecture and concluded ". . . it was not unreasonable for the tenured faculty to consider this in reaching a decision. . . ."

Two witnesses to the allegedly disastrous lecture were brought into court. One was Robert Glew, a protege of the department chair. During the hearings, the judge had expressed "great concern about the credibility of this witness." At one point Glew stated that he had helped mollify students upset with Johnson's lectures "by providing the tutorial sessions that for those that would—for those that might have been terribly disruptive, if they would be willing to hold their tongues, knowing that they would get support at least short-term support within a few days or so. . . ." Under examination by Johnson's attorney, Glew admitted that in fact he was not providing special tutorial sessions because of the Johnson lectures:

> I had already begun—had for the previous weeks—with a small number of students primarily minority students from the Medical School been carrying on review sessions . . . and it seemed to me a very easy matter without doing anything dramatic to simply expand that audience to include those students who were not necessarily in academic difficulty or students who were not necessarily lacking confidence but students who felt that they were missing something in Dr. Johnson's lectures.

The judge ignored this acknowledgement and his own doubts about the witness's credibility and in his final ruling credited Glew with giving extra sessions because of Johnson's failure: "The student dissatisfaction with Dr. Johnson's performance was so widespread that another junior faculty member, Dr. Glew, at the request of the students, initiated a series of evening lectures which covered the same material presented by plaintiff."

The second witness to the unsuccessful lectures was Frances Finn. After she testified, the vice-chancellor for the health professions wrote to the Pitt chancellor confirming that Finn had been granted a promotion and an increase in salary. It said, in part, "Dr. Finn's character and ability are well recognized, and I may add that in the hearing before Judge Knox, beginning with the preliminary injunction sought by Dr. Sharon Johnson, Dr. Finn was, in my opinion, the most effective witness for the University by a wide margin. For these reasons, I support the recommendation that Dr. Finn's salary be increased from $12,000 to $14,000 per annum. . . ." Evidence presented by Johnson indicated that Finn had actually received a triple promotion during the year, from research associate to assistant research professor to associate research professor. Her salary had increased, during the same one-year period from $6,000 to $14,000, according to testimony presented by statistician Gerald Gardner, who had examined and analyzed Pitt's employment statistics for Johnson. The figures stood out since Pitt was at the time in the midst of a salary freeze. Finn is married to the former chair of the biochemistry department. But Judge Knox, in his final ruling, stated that he "paid little or no attention to charges of influencing the testimony of Dr. Frances Finn." He referred to the mention of her testimony in the letter to the chancellor as a "crudity."

In his preliminary injunction ruling, Knox had found ample evidence of discrimination at the University of Pittsburgh Medical School and had faulted the university for failing to offer any defense for its statistical shortcomings:

> The defendants offered no contradictory statistical testimony and did not in any way cast doubt on [the] figures. The defendant instead attempted to show that sex discrimination did not enter the decision of tenured faculty to deny plaintiff tenure and promotion to an associate professorship, and also introduced evidence, most of it gathered after the making of the decision to discharge her, to indicate that she was a poor teacher.

In his preliminary finding, Knox had shown no reluctance whatever to take on the peer judgment system. He even went so far as to find "intentional wrongdoing" on the part of the university for failure to implement its affirmative action plan and "from the fact that the decision to refuse tenure was made without consideration of any criteria other than the evaluation of the teacher's teaching ability from reviewing four lectures. No substantial attention was paid to the plaintiff's work with graduate students or her standing as a research scientist. We also have the subsequent attempt to secure material which would bolster the decision of the tenured faculty when they saw that trouble was brewing." The judge then found "a prima facie case of intentional discrimination on the basis of sex" based on statistical evidence and evidence of disparate treatment.

What is more, during the full hearing, the university offered little statistical evidence to rebut Johnson's statistics, or at least little that impressed the judge, for in his final ruling he still concluded that the statistics indicated sex discrimination at the University of Pittsburgh School of Medicine. However, rather than faulting the university for these statistics, as he had in the preliminary injunction, he now said, "Since the factors involved in determining achievement of professional accomplishment are subtle and subjective, they would be difficult to study by statistical analysis." He also insisted: "The causal connection between these figures and the decision with respect *to this individual plaintiff* has not been shown."

Thus, even though he described the university affirmative action program as "negative action, not affirmative action," even though he had been presented with overwhelming testimony from outside witnesses as to Johnson's competence, and even though the hearing revealed that the peer review system at Pitt was, to say the least, not quite free from self-serving and face-saving, Judge Knox concluded "the peer review system has evolved as the most reliable method for assuring promotion of the candidates best qualified to serve the needs of the institution." Johnson's burden had not been met, according to the judge.

In *McDonnell Douglas v. Green* (411 U.S. 792 [1973]), a case much cited by Judge Knox in the preliminary injunction ruling in which he found substantial reason to believe Johnson would prevail in her case, the proof pattern is outlined with great care: Plaintiffs have the burden of proving a prima facie case of discrimination, defendants then have the opportunity to offer nondiscriminatory reasons for the employment practices and actions taken, and plaintiffs then can offer evidence that the "nondiscriminatory" reasons are actually pretextual and a cover for discrimination. But in his final ruling Knox insisted on a far more substantial—indeed, almost impossible—burden for Johnson when he declared "plaintiff has not shown by the weight of the evidence that such reasons are *so insubstantial and irrational* as to serve as a mask for what is forbidden by the law" (emphasis added). So bedazzled by peer review was Knox that he asserted, "It is also true that the court should not be involved in constantly reviewing the multitude of personnel decisions made daily by public agencies *even though the individual decision subject to review may be mistaken or actually bad*" (emphasis added).

❖   ❖   ❖   ❖   ❖   ❖   ❖   ❖

Howard Glickstein, who taught at Notre Dame, served as staff director to the U.S. Commission on Civil Rights and headed President Carter's task force on the reorganization of the antidiscrimination agencies in 1978, commented several years ago: "It is with a sense of deja vu that I listen to fellow faculty members tell me about the delicate,

complicated issues involved in making decisions about academic competence. This was the same rationalization used by officials of the plumbers
unions to explain to the U.S. Commission on Civil Rights why there were
so few black plumbers "(Glickstein and Todorovich 1975, p. 14).

Lowell Powell, former chair of the Equal Employment Opportunity
Commission, stated: "The concept that institutions of higher education
are 'above', or at least not in the same relationship to the rest of society, is
shared by a large segment of the population, and by most institutions of
higher learning as well. This view is frequently held, notwithstanding
glaring realities to the contrary" (Glickstein and Todorovich 1975, p. 14).

However, the very fact that higher education received a hearing
before the Department of Labor and a number of similar hearings both
formal and informal before the Civil Rights Commission, Congress and
even the president indicates that not everyone in government remained
unmoved. And it must be said that, while higher education officials were
unable to bring about major changes in the regulations concerning
campus enforcement, they have not been totally ineffective. Their efforts
have helped keep campus enforcement as an example of the worst
possible government antidiscrimination enforcement.

What is more, the pleas of university officials have met with a warm
reception in the federal courts. Judge Knox was not alone in his insistence
in the Johnson case that employment decisions for faculty must be left to
"the Ph.D.'s in academia" rather than the courts.

Before the 1972 extension of Title VII to cover education employees,
decisions favoring peer judgment were common. In a promotion case
brought by Lola Beth Green, a North Texas district court judge ruled in
1971 that he would not override the "rational and well-considered
judgment of those possessing expertise in the field" (*Green v. Board of
Regents of Texas Tech University* 335 F.Supp. 249; affirmed, 474 F. 2d 594
[5th Cir, 1973]). The full irony of the *Green* judgment cannot be
appreciated without realizing that Green's English department colleagues, "including the then chairman and the former chairman" had
voted in favor of her promotion. Only a university vice-president for
academic affairs stood in the way. The vice-president later admitted on
the witness stand that it was, indeed, true that the university did not pay
women as much as men and did not promote them as often. He insisted,
however, that these facts did not indicate sex discrimination. Because of
the decision, Green retired from Texas Tech at the rank of associate
professor, although she had served the institution for 27 years.

Surprisingly, such decisions continued to be common after the
amendment of Title VII to cover education employees. Thus, in the 1974
ruling in a sex discrimination case brought against New York University,
the Second Circuit court in New York included the following piece of
logic:

Of all fields, which the federal courts should hesitate to invade and take over, education and faculty appointments at the University level are probably the least suited for federal court supervision. Dr. Faro would remove any subjective judgments by her faculty colleagues in the decision-making process by having the courts examine "the university's recruitment, compensation, promotion and termination and by analyzing the way these procedures are applied to the claimant personally." (Applt's Br. p. 26). All this information she would obtain "through extensive discovery either by the EEOC or the litigant herself." (id.) This argument might well lend itself to a *reductio ad absurdum* rebuttal. Such a procedure, in effect, would require a faculty committee charged with recommending or withholding advancements or tenure appointments to subject itself to a court inquiry at the behest of unsuccessful and disgruntled candidates as to why the unsuccessful was not as well qualified as the successful. This decision would then be passed on by a Court of Appeals or even the Supreme Court. The process might be simplified by a legislative enactment that no faculty appointment or advancement could be made without the committee obtaining a declaratory judgment naming the successful candidate after notice to all contending candidates to present their credentials for court inspection and decision. This would give "due process" to all contenders, regardless of sex, to advance their "I'm as good as you are" arguments. But such a procedure would require discriminating analysis of the qualifications of each candidate for hiring or advancement, taking into consideration his or her educational experience, the specifications of the particular position open and, of great importance, the personality of the candidate (*Faro v. N.Y. University*, 8 FEP Cases 609).

In a race discrimination case brought in 1975, the Southern District Court in New York ruled:

The weight to be given scholarly writings and their publication in a tenure decision involves judgmental evaluation by those who live in the academic world and who are charged with responsibility of decision. Scholarship and research have been described as "the indispensable tools of the scholar's trade," and as such they should be left to the scholars. Absent a showing of discrimination or other violations of constitutional or statutory rights, the court is guided by the words of Judge Moore (in *Faro*): "Of all fields, which the federal courts should hesitate to invade and take over, education and faculty appointments at a University level are probably the least suited for federal court supervision." This surely is not a case for federal intervention (*Labat v. Board of Higher Education, City of N.Y.*, 10 E.P.D. Par. 10,563, p. 6335 [S.D. N.Y. 1975]).

In *Peters v. Middlebury College*, in 1976, the judge ruled: "Absent an impermissible discrimination, the federal courts will not intrude to supervise faculty appointments and tenure" (12 FEP Cases, 297–305 [1976]). And in *Cussler v. University of Maryland*, the judge made a similar ruling (430 F. Supp. 602 [1977]).

Most of the judges seemed to allow that deference to peer review operates only in the absence of discrimination, but it is clear from the cases that a great deal of evidence of discrimination was offered. This is evident, for example, in the text of the *Peters* decision itself where the judge wrote: "Until Dr. Madeline Gohlke was appointed to the faculty in 1968, there were no full time women faculty members in the English department at Middlebury College. There have been no full professors who were women at Middlebury at any time. There are four women at Middlebury who are tenured members of the faculty; none in the English department." Peters was able to introduce evidence of considerable antagonism among members of the English department faculty toward her feminist views and toward courses she introduced on women in literature. Although some doubt had been raised by an on-campus committee about "the effect that plaintiff's feminist activities and beliefs had on the decision not to reappoint," both the committee and the judge ultimately decided that the effect was insufficient and could therefore be ignored. And even though there was evidence that Peters' teaching was not adequately audited by faculty members and was well received by students, the judge demurred to the peer judgment that found her teaching inadequate for rehire.

Margaret Cussler's charge was that the University of Maryland had denied her a promotion to full professor and continued to underpay her because of sex discrimination in the sociology department. She, too, was able to bring in considerable evidence of discrimination, including a report by a committee within her own department that concluded the department had been recalcitrant in its hiring and promotion of women. In spite of her evidence, a courtroom exchange on the efficacy of the peer review system indicates that the judge remained unmoved. The defense attorneys in that case brought a female university president who testified that even if sex discrimination did exist on the campus, neither university administrators nor courts should override departmental decisions. Cussler's attorney, Sylvia Roberts, commented, "I believe the U.S. Congress gave us that right." Her comment promted Judge Edward Northrup to reply, "I don't say the U.S. Congress is always correct. If they're right 50 percent of the time, they're doing good" (Diamondback 1977).

The attitude of the judge in the *Cussler* case was hardly unusual: not only have judges been unwilling to consider sex discrimination a serious charge, but they have also gone out of their way, in a number of cases, to malign or belittle the victims of that discrimination. Thus, in *Faro*, the judge indicated his hostility to the plaintiff by insisting, "Dr. Faro, in effect, envisions herself as a modern Jeanne d'Arc fighting for the rights of embattled womanhood on an academic battlefield, facing a solid phalanx of males and male faculty prejudice."

And in *Johnson* the judge goes out of his way to refer to the *Faro* language: "We need not characterize the plaintiff as envisioning herself a modern Jeanne d'Arc as the plaintiff was termed by the Second Circuit in *Faro v. NYU* 502 F 2d 1229 (1d cir 1974) to recognize that the case is regarded by many as a test of the rights of female professors to gain tenure and promotion in academia under Title VII. This is regarded as one of the bastions of male chauvinism." Further, having already, on the record, expressed serious doubts as to the credibility of Robert Glew, one of the university's major witnesses against Johnson, Judge Knox concluded that the very same man was "one of the targets in the present case. . . ."

In contrast, in *Cramer v. Virginia Commonwealth University* 415 F. Supp. 673 [1976], a case brought successfully by a white male charging that affirmative action had lost him a potential job, the judge went out of his way to express sympathy for the plaintiff, insisting that the only persons to benefit from affirmative action plans were "the thousands of persons engaged in the civil rights business, bureaucrats, lawyers, lobbyists and politicians." The plaintiff and his fellows were, said the judge, "flattened by the civil rights steamroller." (*Cramer* will be heard by the Supreme Court, following a Circuit Court ruling upholding the lower court.)

✲   ✲   ✲   ✲   ✲   ✲   ✲   ✲

The good faith and nondiscriminatory intent universities so carefully insist is theirs while they battle the law in the agencies and in the courts may still convince university officials themselves. By 1976, however, it began to wear a little thin in some places. In an article in the *Journal of College and University Law*, for example, Professor Ray Aiken, who serves as legal counsel for Marquette University, reviewed the cases in which universities had successfully defended themselves against discrimination charges by drawing forth judicial deference to the peer review system and then went on to note that the level of deference was not yet sufficiently high: "To achieve for higher education a tolerable legal atmosphere will require that the attitude of legal deference signaled by these cases becomes solidly ingrained in the total substance of the law dealing with processes of academic evaluation, selection and rejection," said Aiken (1976, p. 105).

He continued:

> At the moment, that is by no means the situation in which we find ourselves. Higher education finds itself especially vulnerable to an

unrelenting and formidable attack by public and private agencies single-mindedly dedicated to the achievement of one social or political objective or another; and those agencies treat the broad standards of academic evaluation as largely irrelevant—even hostile—to their own purposes and responsibilities. Armed with a great array of investigative, regulatory, and prosecutorial weapons they have compiled a spotty record of occasional administrative and quasi-judicial victories over public and private colleges and universities which, even if rather regularly overturned in the courts, nevertheless sap both the energies and the resources of the institutions and their personnel" (p. 105-06).

This view, expressed in 1976, stands in sharp contrast to the statement of Senator Williams that "(t)o continue the existing exemption . . . would also establish a class of employers who could pursue employment policies which are otherwise prohibited by law."

Educational institutions still seek to remain such a class of employers. And with the help of federal judges it appears that they will be able to retain their exemption from the law of the land for some time to come. Only one recent legal decision offered temporary promise that the picture in the future might not be as grim as it has been in the past. In January 1978, First Circuit Court Judge Hugh H. Bownes found in favor of Christine M. Sweeney, who had brought a Title VII action against Keene State College for discrimination in promotion and salary level (*Sweeney v. Bd. of Trustees of Keene State College et al.*, 569 F 2d 169 [1978]). Judge Bownes met the issue of peer judgment squarely, recounted the decisions that preceded his, and admonished his fellow judges for their ready deferral to academics:

However, we voice misgivings over one theme recurrent in those opinions: the notion that courts should keep "hands off" the salary, promotion, and hiring decisions of colleges and universities. This reluctance no doubt arises from the courts' recognition that hiring, promotion and tenure decisions require subjective evaluation most appropriately made by persons thoroughly familiar with the academic setting. Nevertheless, we caution against permitting judicial deference to result in judicial abdication of a responsibility entrusted to the courts by Congress. That responsibility is simply to provide a forum for the litigation of complaints of sex discrimination in institutions of higher learning as readily as for other Title VII suits.

The Sweeney case was promising indeed. It reversed a trend that had consistently plagued academic women bringing Title VII suits and reminded judges of the intent of Congress in extending Title VII to education employees. The decision was the first at the circuit level in which a judge has been unwilling to leave the business of overcoming race and sex discrimination in higher education to the very system Congress concluded had brought about the problem in the first place. Thus Judge Bownes noted:

> Particularly in a college or university setting, where the level of sophistication is likely to be much higher than in other employment situations, direct evidence of sex discrimination will rarely be available. The Congress was no doubt aware of this fact when it extended Title VII to colleges and universities for the first time in 1972. The legislative history contains numerous indications of Congress' concern for the status of women in academia. Statistical evidence presented to the Congress at that time made glaringly clear that "(w)hen they have been hired into educational institutions, particularly in institutions of higher education, women have been relegated to positions of lesser standing than their male counterparts."

In its fall 1978 term, however, the U.S. Supreme Court rapidly moved to nip whatever hope might have sprung from the *Sweeney* case. Under *McDonnell Douglas*, the high court had said that an individual was expected to make a prima facie showing of discrimination in Title VII cases by establishing that she or he was a member of the protected class, that she or he was denied employment or some job advancement opportunity, that she or he was qualified for such opportunity, and that similar employment had gone to others following the denial. Once a prima facie case is established, the burden shifts to the employer/defendant. If the defendant succeeds in establishing a legitimate, nondiscriminatory reason for his actions, the plaintiff once more takes on the burden to establish whether or not the legitimate reason is merely a pretext for actual discrimination.

In the spring 1978 term, the Supreme Court, in *Furnco Construction Co. v. Waters* (46 L.W. 4966), reemphasized the *McDonnell* formula in terms that seemed to leave it unchanged. But the Court used the term "articulate" interchangeably with "prove" in speaking of the employer's burden to counter a prima facie showing of discrimination with proof of acceptable nondiscriminatory reasons for the employer's actions. In *Sweeney* the Court, while insisting that *Furnco* merely clarified the existing McDonnell decision, really bends both *McDonnell* and *Furnco*, by making a distinction between "articulating" and "proving" and thereby lifting from employers virtually all the burden they formerly bore:

> In Furnco Construction Co. v. Waters, 438 U.S.—(June 29, 1978), we stated that "(t)o dispel the adverse inference from a prima facie showing under McDonnell Douglas, the employer need only "articulate

some legitimate, nondiscriminatory reason for the employee's rejection" . . . We stated in McDonnel Douglas, supra, that the plaintiff "must . . . be afforded a fair opportunity to show that [the employer's] stated reason for [the plaintiff's] rejection was in fact pretext." 441 U.S., at 804. The Court of Appeals in the present case, however, referring to McDonnell Douglas, supra, stated that "in requiring the defendant to *prove absence of discriminatory motive*, the Supreme Court placed the burden squarely on the party with the greatest access to such evidence." . . .

While words such as "articulate," "show," and "prove," may have more or less similar meanings depending upon the context in which they are used, we think there is a significant distinction between merely "articulat[ing] some legitimate, nondiscriminatory reason" and "prov-[ing] absence of discriminatory motive." By reaffirming and emphasizing the McDonnell Douglas analysis in Furnco Construction Co. v. Waters, supra, we made it clear that the former will suffice to meet the employee's prima facie case of discrimination. Because the Court of Appeals appears to have imposed a heavier burden on the employer than Furnco warrants, its judgment is vacated and the case is remanded for reconsideration in the light of Furnco. . . . (47 L.W. 3330 [1978]).

The heavy burden placed on plaintiff Johnson to show "by the weight of the evidence" that an employer's alleged reasons for an employment action are "so insubstantial and irrational as to serve as a mask" for discrimination seems ludicrous in contrast to the employer's burden, spelled out in *Furnco* and *Sweeney*, merely to "articulate" any apparently legitimate reason for his actions. But this, at the moment, is the way the scales of justice are weighted for academic women attempting to challenge the peer review system.

There is no sign as yet that universities are giving up the militant effort to "require that the attitude of legal deference . . . becomes solidly ingrained in the total substance of the law dealing with the processes of academic evaluation, selection, and rejection" (Aiken 1976, p. 105). To the contrary, the courts have done their best to aid in the achievement of that goal. With *Sweeney*, which had appeared so hopeful a case at first, the Supreme Court seems to have joined in that effort.

—— *Chapter Nine* ——

THE SEARCH FOR
A SATISFIED CUSTOMER

"A good deal of luck was on my side. I'm not kidding myself: there are other women with just causes who don't get anything."
May Hollinshead, Complainant, 1978

On February 17, 1976, Judge W.D. Murray, senior judge for the District of Montana, ruled that Montana State University was in violation of Title VII of the Civil Rights Act and had engaged in discrimination against women as a class and against four of five named plaintiffs. The case, *Mecklenburg v. Montana State University* (13 FEP Cases 462) is one of the few victories for women under Title VII and the only successful class action court ruling against a university to date. (In March 1978 an out of court settlement was reached in the class action complaint of *Lamphere v. Brown University*. Terms of the settlement were somewhat similar to those of the federal court ruling in *Mecklenburg*.)

Because they are so rare, a detailed examination of the Mecklenburg case and of several other winning sex discrimination complaints is in order. Perhaps such an examination can reveal the secret of success. Certainly that secret has eluded a great many women who have gone to the agencies and the courts convinced that they had excellent and well documented cases of sex discrimination to present. We begin with *Mechlenburg*. Helen Cameron (the Mecklenburg of the suit) was first employed in the biology department at Montana State University (MSU) in 1968 at the rank of assistant professor. Because she had obtained her degree at Montana State, officials insisted that she give up an ongoing research grant in 1971 and spend the academic year elsewhere. When she returned in the fall of 1973, she discovered that men who had been hired when she was hired had been promoted to tenured positions as associate professors. She remained an untenured assistant professor. "At first I was told that I wasn't promoted because I had never been away," says Cameron, "then that I wasn't promoted because I was away, then that I wasn't promoted because I had been away. I wasn't promoted because I didn't have a grant but they wouldn't let me finish the grant I had, they insisted I leave and give it up."

Other women at MSU had also experienced discrimination. But most of them had remained isolated. During Cameron's absence in 1972, investigators from HEW's Office for Civil Rights paid a routine visit to the campus. As with most other universities it dealt with during this period, HEW soon became embroiled in a prolonged exchange over what types of data the university must collect and the format for presenting the data. But the visit did stimulate faculty women on the campus to meet and to begin comparing notes and collecting information about the status of women at MSU.

Of the 135 women faculty members on the campus, only five were full professors and three of the five had been hired at that rank: women simply were not being promoted on campus. Among the women faculty there were a number of 20-year assistant professors who were considered untenured by MSU despite their long service, since associate professor rank was required for tenure. Moreover, salaries often had an inverse relationship to length of time in rank, with the long time female assistant professors earning the lowest wages.

"We were simply judged on a different scale than the men," says Cameron.

> Each of us began to compare her salary with those of men of comparable training, experience and responsibilities, and our rate of promotion with those whom we knew were comparable. We began to discuss our poor chances of getting onto a committee of importance, much less into upper administration. We began to compare notes on the administrators' opinions, verbally expressed, of the "quality" of our research publications or the "independence" of our research or the "market value" of our field. Each of us was given different reasons, but each of us came out rather badly relative to the men with whom we compared ourselves.

The women then asked to meet with university officials to present their ideas for campus affirmative action. "Our request was duly acknowledged and duly ignored," Cameron notes. "The more outspoken we became, the more we learned about the mechanisms for maintaining discrimination."

During the 1973–74 school year, Cameron was again turned down for promotion. However, the rule requiring associate professor rank for tenure was changed that year and Cameron gained tenure at assistant professor rank. Her new found security allowed her to take a leading role in attempting to gain a hearing from the university for the grievances of faculty women.

The path followed by the women at Montana State was similar to that followed by women on many campuses. They took their information to the administration and to the faculty and, when they found they were rebuffed again and again, they began filing discrimination complaints with the federal agencies. When they found the agencies unwilling to act, they took their complaints to court. They filed a class action suit in federal district court in July 1974.

"It was the hope of the plaintiffs that the filing of a class action suit would serve to force the university administration to squarely face the problem of discrimination and sit down and negotiate to eliminate this problem," Cameron says. But university officials had already learned they could ignore both individual complaints filed with EEOC and the continuous flow of directives concerning the development of affirmative action that came from HEW. Even a petition in support of the court action signed by over 100 of the 135 faculty women at MSU did not convince administrators to take the new threat seriously. Further, Cameron points out, the risk at every stage of the battle was on the side of the five named plaintiffs. They had, for example, initially filed as "Jane Does." But when the university refused their attorney access to computer data they were forced to demand access in court. The judge ordered access but, in exchange, granted the university demand that the names of the five plaintiffs be released. What is more, the plaintiffs were forced to pay for computer time at the university. While the costs were eventually recovered when they won, the risk plus the out-of-pocket expenses were all absorbed by them. "The administrators themselves never have had to assume the risk of paying such costs out of their own pockets should they lose," Cameron points out.

In his ruling, Judge Murray found:

> The evidence shows discrimination against women as a class by the defendants at Montana State University in that females are underutilized as deans, vice presidents, department heads and as instructional faculty in many departments of the University. Women have also been discriminated against as a class in the areas of promotion, tenure, salary, and appointment to important university committees. . . . The promotional decisions at Montana State University reflect the defendant's implementation of a non-standardized merit system. . . . Thus those who play a role in the promotion process may apply a number of vague and subjective standards, and there are no safeguards in the procedure to avert sex discriminatory practices.

Murray had done what theorists at the EEOC insist should be done in academic cases. He had adopted the "belief of the Equal Employment Opportunity Commission that the legal principles which were developed under Title VII from 1964 to 1975, are capable of coherent application to employment systems in higher education and that the legal principles should in no fashion be modified or changed" (Robertson 1975, p. 27). He found that a prima facie case of discrimination was established by the statistics and he found the university's defense, both for its statistical pattern and for its actions in four of the five individual cases, to be a pretext for illegal discrimination.

Just as the *Mecklenburg* decision must have pleased EEOC, since it vindicated that agency's long held legal position regarding universities, so the decision infuriated those university officials around the country who were determined to maintain the peer review system against all encroachment. Wrote one leader in the legal fight to maintain the status quo, Murray's decision was "a fundamentally bad decision, and one which is virtually unprecedented in its unrestrained invasion of the universally-accepted academic selection process at all of the faculty and administrative levels of the institution" (Aiken 1976, p. 108). He also faulted the decision "because it happens to reflect rather accurately the legal posture that has been tenaciously assumed by the Equal Employment Opportunity Commission officers and investigators" (p. 109).

The writer assumed that the decision would be appealed by Montana State. He also assumed that the EEOC would continue to push "its dubious conception of what is a proper basis for asserting that institutional practices are unlawful." As long as EEOC "remained unreformed," he warned, "the exposure of colleges and universities and their personnel at least to intolerable harassment and expense, if not to final adverse judgment, will continue unabated" (p. 109).

Compliance with Murray's orders, he said, was impossible unless university officials

> abandon their established procedures for faculty and staff selection and promotion, or at least create a "standardized" merit system which avoids "variables" and does not depend on "vague and subjective standards" (unless, perhaps, they operate to favor females.) . . . And what is to be done with the male members of the present faculty and administrative staff? It would appear either that the total numbers employed must be substantially expanded in all ranks, or that males must be demoted or discharged simply *because* they are males. In other words, considerations of academic quality and proficiency must become secondary to those of sex, under penalty of contempt and liability for further damages (p. 110).

An appeal of the *Mecklenburg* ruling, he insisted, was an absolute necessity because "when the cost of settlement implicates the financial position of the institution's associated personnel, or the academic integrity of the institution it becomes unthinkable and intolerable to consider *detente* or compromise. The invasion must be resisted at any cost" (p. 110).

If anything is to be gained from an examination of "winning" cases, two questions must be answered: Why did they win? What did they win? Our militant critic of the *Mecklenburg* decision was wrong in assuming that Montana State would appeal and an examination of why it did not appeal throws light on the first of these questions.

According to Cameron, the chair of the Montana State University Board of Regents had favored an out-of-court settlement of the complaint all along. However, the campus president and other top level administrators who favored a court battle prevailed. Such deference to the authority of a technically lower level official is not unusual in the academic world, even when large sums of state tax funds must be expended to support the deference. Another state university recently filed in state court to overturn an arbitrator's ruling that a woman must be granted tenure and back pay. The action was taken at the insistence of a department chair, although higher level university officials supported the arbitrator's ruling and although, under the arbitrator's orders, the university must pay the full-time salary of the woman while the appeal is in progress. When personal expense is not involved, university officials are all too often willing to defer to the injured pride of their lower level colleagues.

In Montana, however, two series of events took place to prevent an appeal. The first involved the MSU faculty, which Cameron says had also opposed the suit and favored a negotiated settlement. At this point, however, due to several problems, including the suit, the faculty passed a vote of no confidence in the president and forced his resignation along with one of his vice-presidents. Two other vice-presidents left at the same time, although for reasons that were apparently unrelated to the president's resignation. The second set of events involved the plaintiffs themselves. "We were prepared to raise a political stink over spending any more state money," Cameron says. "This is a small state and it would not be that hard to raise a stink through the press over the university fighting any longer." One of the plaintiffs contacted the state commissioner of higher education and the chair of the MSU Board of Regents and, says Cameron, "apparently the commissioner and the chairman of the Board of Regents, or both, got it squashed—the attempt of the university to appeal."

One reason for the victory at the district court level, then, was simply that the case was not appealed by the university. A second reason can be found in the final ruling itself. The plaintiffs had wisely avoided the qualifications and peer review issue, pointing out only that the university was so arbitrary and capricious that it did not have any reasonable structure for employment decision making. The plaintiffs managed this, says Cameron, because the university was unable to offer any evidence as to the excellence of favored male professors. MSU simply did not do a good job of urging the efficacy of the peer review system. Instead, officials had defended their poor statistical picture with a series of long held myths about women.

In his final ruling, Judge Murray paid little mind to these defenses: "at any rate," he commented, "the explanations [e.g. climate, geographical isolation] given by witnesses testifying for the university and suggested in the Affirmative Action Plan . . . are totally speculative." And, said Murray, "(t)he defendant's explanations for the discrepancies in the promotions of men and women at Montana State University (e.g. assertions that women's careers are more limited by family obligations or that women are less ambitious than men) are wholly conjecture."

Cameron also says that the university did not attempt to explain or defend its own rather peculiar statistics, statistics that minimized the lack of progress of women faculty members by such devices as looking only at salary within rank, thus ignoring completely the fact that women are promoted more slowly than men. This failure, according to Cameron, was largely due to the fact that the university statistician had made blatantly sexist remarks: it was feared that if he were on the stand, plaintiffs' attorney could encourage him to reveal himself before the judge. The university's rather shaky statistics were therefore left to stand on their own.

In contrast to such cases as *Johnson v. University of Pittsburgh* and *Cussler v. University of Maryland*, both of which took months of courtroom time, the *Mecklenburg* hearing lasted only one week. Plaintiffs' attorney hammered home the statistics and did not get into the issue of the qualifications of women who had not been rewarded by the MSU system. Meanwhile, the defendants did little to rebut statistics or to assert the argument that universities have the ultimate right to judge their own employees by whatever standards they may choose.

While it would be pleasant to believe that the case was won because it was a meritorious case, this cannot be said with conviction. Without doubt, the case *did* have merit. But an unconvincing and unenthusiastic defense plus political manuevering that prevented an appeal seem to have had more to do with the victory than did the merits of the sex discrimination complaint.

The second question also bears investigation: What did they win? The writer who pleaded for an appeal of the decision bemoaned the "demotion or discharge" of males to make room for women. And he also decried the death of the vague and subjective standards he considered so essential to the entire peer review system. But here, again, he was wrong. No such dire results have occurred. Indeed, little has changed at Montana State University. Judge Murray's decision itself contained no settlement mechanism. He stated, instead, that plaintiffs were entitled to damages, as a class, and he enjoined the university "from further discrimination against the named plaintiffs as individuals and the class of women they represent." The manner of ending discriminatory practices at the university and the manner of assessing damages due to the plaintiffs were left to be worked out by an agreement between the university and the named plaintiffs, although the judge retained the right to approve any such agreement.

Under the "master plan" worked out as part of the settlement, a back pay survey was performed for all women who had worked on the MSU campus between 1973 and 1976. Ultimately 80 women received back pay in amounts ranging from a little over $100 to $13,000. The total back pay award approved by Judge Murray was $400,022.89. In addition, a promotion committee was set up to examine possible inequitable promotion denials. Five women gained retroactive promotion through the committee. The master plan also required that search committees for new faculty and administrators include some women and called for the establishment of a standardized and equitable merit system that would apply across the campus.

None of the facets of the settlement were completely satisfactory in the end, according to Cameron and co-plaintiff Bette Lowery. Back-pay awards, while they were the most satisfactory part of the settlement, were arrived at in a manner that left a number of women at inequitably low salaries. Librarians, for example, who are part of the faculty at MSU, were found to perform duties distinctly different from other faculty members. Their salaries were not compared to persons in male dominated professional fields but to the salaries of other university librarians in the Rocky Mountain region. By this measure, as one might easily have guessed, their low salaries were attributed to their profession rather than to sex discrimination. The campus equity committee concluded "there was no sex discrimination in the salaries of the M.S.U. female librarians." Other women were matched to male faculty members who were supposed to be closest in degree, area, and background. But, says Cameron, the system at MSU had been so arbitrary over the years that some men with Ph.D. degrees or with excellent research records were earning less than men in other fields with poor records and with master's degrees. Thus some women with excellent records were compared to lower paid men with good records rather than higher paid men with poor records. And where no match could be found in the primary field, some women with Ph.D.s were compared to male Ph.D.s outside their field rather than higher paid males in their field who held only master's degrees. Eleven of the twelve women in the College of Letters and Sciences were matched to the man with the lowest possible salary, says Cameron.

The promotion settlement proved even less satisfactory. The committee set up to examine promotions—a committee augmented by several administrators—began its work badly by funneling all promotion requests through department heads. According to Cameron, "the probability of being able to go through one's department head for help and support in such a situation, particularly for women in predominantly male departments, is not high." In spite of Judge Murray's finding that MSU had discriminated against women in promotions, the committee could find only five women eligible for retroactive promotion out of the total female faculty of 135. Cameron claims at least 30 women should have received promotions.

Search committees proved equally unsatisfactory. According to Lowery, one such committee set up to find a high-level administrator began its work by determining that the position called for a "crusty old man." When she objected and it became clear she intended to submit a minority report, the committee rushed its report to the president and the candidate was picked before her protest could be delivered. On another committee, says Lowery, a woman applicant was considered "overqualified" while a man who had been holding the position on a temporary basis was judged adequate and therefore recommended as "best qualified." Meanwhile, the promised written standards for determining merit in hire, tenure, salary, and promotion decisions have never materialized. The ratio of men to women on the campus has remained about the same and salaries for men are beginning once again to creep ahead.

"The comment I have heard several times now is, 'We're working on the inequities, but this time they are men's'" says Lowery. She believes many men on the campus feel they are being inequitably treated because of the salary gains made by women under the court ruling: "I really think there is a deep rooted feeling that the men should be ahead of the women in salary. The prevailing attitude on campus seems to be, 'Now you've done your thing, you should be happy because you got your money and let's go back to business.' And I'm all for that but I think business should include equity. But it doesn't seem to."

Says Cameron: "We are exactly back there now. Promotions are being turned down for women. If anything we are farther behind the firing goals and timetables than when they were written. . . . There are no committees advising the president which contain women and minorities. . . . There is nothing being standardized, though the university is supposed to write standard procedures."

The plaintiffs in *Mecklenburg* are considering going back to court.

But they realize, says Lowery, that they have entered into a gray zone. In almost every area the university could claim that it is working on the problems. The committee of women that helped support the plaintiffs in their work is no longer functioning and, Lowery points out, many timid women are happy with their back pay awards and "will remain happy and probably it won't be a crisis for them until they need another promotion or they wake up and realize that they've been increasing in pay just a little bit and the men have been jumping ahead and they look around and they're behind again." Lowery doubts that such women could be readily mobilized at this point should the plaintiffs decide to return to Judge Murray. "If we could get some of those women who are still being discriminated against to step forward and make the statement I think it would take us out of the gray area to a darker area, almost a black area. . . . These are some of the same people who were afraid of going in with us the first time who have good cases—we've been so carefully taught."

In sum, the "winners" in *Mecklenburg v. Montana State University* have received something short of equity. What about other "winners?" Have women who received EEOC determinations of discrimination or HEW findings or state court determinations in their favor or out of court settlements fared any better? Let us examine a few sample cases.

❈   ❈   ❈   ❈   ❈   ❈   ❈   ❈

One of May Hollinshead's earliest and most painful academic memories occurred when she was a graduate student in 1941. The chairman of the anatomy department, who later became Hollinshead's major professor, told her he would rather have a mediocre male graduate student than a brilliant female. "He told me, 'When you women start being reproductive you stop being productive.' And there was nothing I could do."

Hollinshead is now teaching in the anatomy department of the College of Medicine and Dentistry of New Jersey. She has worked there since 1956, when the college was known as Seton Hall College of Medicine and Dentistry. And she believes that many male professors still feel the same way, though they would not dare admit that they do. Because of such attitudes, Hollinshead's training in graduate school was twofold. She studied her field and learned, as well, that women often have to fight for a decent professional position. That training helped her later.

In 1971, when Hollinshead had served at the rank of associate professor for ten years, she requested promotion to full professor. At that time only 22 women served on the college faculty along with 173 men. No woman had ever been promoted to the rank of full professor. The school's only woman full professor had been hired from outside on the basis of credentials that were far superior to most of the male full professors at the school, according to Hollinshead.

Hollinshead's request for promotion was considered and turned down. Her on compus appeals for reconsideration were all rejected. During the same period, 13 men were considered by the medical school for hire or promotion. Hollinshead was the only woman under consideration for any personnel action. All 13 men were granted hire or promotion.

In June 1972 Hollinshead filed complaints with both the EEOC and the New Jersey Division on Civil Rights. Fourteen months later she was still an associate professor and a finding that discrimination was probably the cause of the promotion rejection was issued by the New Jersey Division of Civil Rights, which had taken charge of the investigation. The finding noted that Hollinshead's colleagues claimed she had been denied promotion "because her level of scholarly productivity seemed to have plateaued." But the division found that "three men who had plateaued were promoted. One had not published for two years before he was promoted, another had a three year gap in publication preceding promotion, and a third had a four year gap. The "entire scholarly output" of one of the male full professors, noted the New Jersey Division, "was one paper and two abstracts." By comparison, Hollinshead had a consistent publishing record during these years. The division concluded, "the complainant was subjected to a different, more severe, set of standards than her male colleagues and as a result she was denied her promotion." It also found that she had been paid less than five male associate professors and two male assistant professors in spite of the fact that by that time, with 12 years at rank, she was "the senior assoicate professor at the college."

After it issued the finding, the New Jersey Division on Civil Rights scheduled a conciliation meeting. However, the College of Medicine and Dentistry refused to promote Hollinshead. A full scale public hearing was the next step in the process but it was April 1974, almost two years after the complaint was filed, before the hearing began. It lasted a total of six days spread over six months.

In his report, the hearing examiner concluded that there was "no question as to the quality of Dr. Hollinshead's work being worthy of promotion to full professor." He found that the difference between the salary she earned as an associate professor and the salary she would have earned as a full professor from 1972 on was due to Hollinshead, and he concluded that "(t)he denial of her promotion to full professor is the result of sex discrimination." Nevertheless, he stopped short of ordering that promotion. In deference to the peer review system and to past judicial reluctance to interfere, and wishfully thinking that the promotion procedure "has been revamped to insure greater opportunity," he recommended that Hollinshead's papers once again be submitted to the faculty committee for "a fair and nondiscriminatory review."

The hearing officer's finding was submitted to the director of the New Jersey Division on Civil Rights. Nine months later the director issued his final determination and order. The ruling upheld previous findings within the division but ordered a promotion for Hollinshead, retroactive to July 1972: "Contrary to the objections of Respondent's counsel, the entire body of testimony, briefs, objections and recommendations in this matter compels me to find that the Complainant was denied a promotion to full professor solely because of her sex. The only reasonable remedy is to grant the complainant the promotion which she was illegally denied." He ordered back pay retroactive to 1972 to bring Hollinshead to the level she would have earned as a full professor and he also required the college to pay Hollinshead a $500 fee for "humiliation damages."

The matter did not end there. The trustees of the college—a public, tax supported institution—voted to appeal to the New Jersey State Courts. While the college was preparing its case, the Equal Employment Opportunity Commission released a finding in Hollinshead's favor. EEOC had determined that she had been discriminated against in the promotion denial and also found that the entire college discriminated against women in hiring and in promotion. By all the measures applied, the college was found lacking in its treatment of women "both before and after Title VII became applicable on the campus." But the addition of yet another finding of discrimination did not deter administrators at the College of Medicine and Dentistry from continuing the court battle.

Fortunately for Hollinshead, the ruling by the New Jersey Division on Civil Rights made it possible for the division, using the state attorney general as its legal counsel, to go to court on her behalf. Thus she was spared the expense, if not the physical and emotional pain, of a long and difficult state court battle. Unfortunately for the taxpayers of New Jersey, the college, too, could use the state attorney general's office since it, too, is a state agency.

Hearings were held before a three-judge panel of the New Jersey Appellate Court on December 8, 1975. On March 25, 1976, four years after she had filed her complaint and 14 years after she had become an associate professor, the court released its finding in favor of Hollinshead. Soon after she was promoted to full professor, retroactive to June 1972. Back pay and humiliation damages were awarded to her and the college was required to begin the development of a meaningful affirmative action plan.

While Hollinshead's complaint was involved in the administrative process, her department chair had begun changing her teaching assignments. From 1956 until the initial finding was made by the New Jersey Division in 1973, Hollinshead taught both medical and dental students, as did the rest of the faculty of the department. But during the 1973–74 academic year the chair cut her assignments to teach embryology to medical students. The following year she was cut out of the microscopic anatomy laboratory course for medical students and was "the only faculty member of my department assigned exclusively to the laboratory teaching of dental students—despite the fact that the department included three dentists." Dental school assignments, says Hollinshead, are the "Siberia" of teaching, not because the students are not bright but because they do not require the depth and detail of information that goes into medical classes. If assignments are limited to dental students, she points out, a teacher can quickly get rusty and increasingly less able to handle the more challenging medical assignments.

In 1975 it became apparent to Hollinshead that she would not receive an adequate explanation for the assignments and that she would once again be assigned exclusively to dental courses for the 1975–76 year. At that point she filed a complaint of reprisal with the New Jersey Division on Civil Rights. After another trying series of investigations and hearings, the division issued another finding against the college. But it took until June 1977 for the college to guarantee Hollinshead fair treatment, a share in embryology lectures to medical students, and primary assignments to teach medical students for a five year period.

The harassment did not end at that point. It merely found other victims. Hollinshead notes that she received no help from her few female colleagues. Several men did help her, however, and they suffered for doing so. Two colleagues who had testified for Hollinshead at the reprisal hearings soon found that their own teaching assignments were limited to dental students and one of the two discovered that his contract would not be renewed after the 1977–78 academic year. Another colleague, whose promotion to full professor had been recommended two days prior to the reprisal hearings, found several days after he had appeared with Hollinshead at the hearings that the promotion had been rescinded.

Hollinshead's salary had been lower than male colleagues from the beginning of her employment in 1956, thus the promotion to full professor brought her a salary that was still proportionately lower than her male colleagues. Nonetheless, if one discounts the years of pain and humiliation she experienced, it is possible to answer the question, what did she win, by stating that she *almost* gained equity. It is more difficult to find a clear answer to the question, why did she win. It would be possible, but foolish, says Hollinshead, to claim victory "because my heart was pure, my cause was just. . . . I know other situations where the same thing could be said." Women in those situations did not win, she points out.

Hollinshead attributes her victory to having an excellent attorney on her side at state expense. Had she been left to depend on the EEOC she could not have gained victory, she believes. The EEOC did try to interest the Justice Department in the case, but Justice showed no interest. The law in New Jersey permits the attorney general to represent two state divisions against each other and she was assigned an exceptional attorney. Both the law and the assignment, says Hollinshead, were rare pieces of luck. "Despite my success in two cases," she says, "the result of the Sharon Johnson case at the University of Pittsburgh Medical School clearly indicates that the courts still protect decisions made by males in male dominated institutions and that male judges plead the aura of academe as an excuse for not intervening in institutions where sex discrimination is well documented."

❖   ❖   ❖   ❖   ❖   ❖   ❖   ❖

Oglethorpe University is a small, liberal arts institution in Atlanta, Georgia. It has a full-time faculty of approximately 30 people and uses a large staff of part-time teachers. When Barbara Clark began teaching there in 1971, the school had only one tenured woman and about 13 tenured men. The full-time faculty as a whole had only five women, including Clark.

Clark earned her Ph.D. from the University of Georgia and taught at that school for three years. She headed the English department at Floyd Junior College in Rome, Georgia, for one year before coming to Oglethorpe. Among the honors she has accrued are election to Phi Beta Kappa and Phi Kappa Phi and selection as the first graduate of Georgia State to receive a Woodrow Wilson Fellowship. Her teaching career at Oglethorpe was successful. She quickly won the respect of students and ranked near the top of the faculty in teaching evaluations. In 1973 the university president nominated her as Outstanding Educator of America on the basis of her excellent teaching. The nomination was successful and the honor was granted Clark in 1974.

Although publication is considered in tenure decisions at Oglethorpe, it is not crucial, says Clark. Teaching and service to the campus community are considered of primary importance. And in 1973 Oglethorpe's president was so pleased with Clark's teaching and campus service that he informed her that he intended to award her early tenure with her 1974–75 contract. However, the early tenure recommendation was never made. Instead, a meeting of all Oglethorpe's tenured faculty members was held on February 8, 1974. No credentials were reviewed at the meeting, which lasted only 45 minutes, but the tenured faculty voted on tenure for five of their colleagues. In three cases tenure was recommended. Clark and one other faculty member received negative votes.

When Clark was notified that she would not be granted tenure she asked for the opportunity to present her case to the faculty. After initially rejecting the idea, the administration decided to allow Clark to make her presentation. She was met by a wall of stony silence: the administration, says Clark, apparently feared a potential lawsuit and warned the faculty not to talk. The recommendation against tenure remained unchanged. Clark filed a complaint with the Equal Employment Opportunity Commission.

In spite of the generally positive response to Clark on the Oglethorpe campus, the negative decision was not entirely a surprise. When she first began working at Oglethorpe there was only one other full-time teacher of English on the faculty—a man who already had tenure. Her senior colleague did not waste time letting Clark know that she was not welcome: he did not intend to allow her or anyone else to become a permanent member of the faculty in English. He considered the area his "kingdom," Clark reports, and assured her she could count on being employed at the institution for no more than three years. He planned to protect his domain by keeping "a temporary person to teach the freshman courses and others he didn't want to teach."

Over the years, Clark's colleague continued to antagonize her and a number of women students. In 1971, she reports, "he told me that women were made to serve men in bed, as his wife serves him breakfast in bed." On other occasions he referred to Clark, in her presence, as a "broad" and a "bitch." His term for older, returning women students was "little old ladies in tennis shoes." Eight women students complained of his behavior to Clark and, in some cases, complained to the university dean as well, insisting that "they would either transfer away from Oglethorpe or change from an English major before they would take another course" taught by this man. When Clark asked the professor to try to be more polite to the women students, he replied, "Why should I cast pearls before swine, when they only come out covered with shit?" When Clark complained to the dean, he ignored the issue of the women students and assured Clark that he controlled the vote at meetings of tenured faculty and therefore she need not worry about her colleague's threats to prevent her from gaining tenure. But the dean, himself, was later heard by a woman student to say, "Everybody knows that men are better teachers than women."

In 1973 Clark's senior colleague became chair of the Oglethorpe humanities department. It was during that same academic year that Clark was turned down for tenure. A subsequent investigation revealed that the dean had in fact done nothing to interfere when the man expressed his negative opinions of Clark at the tenure decision meeting.

EEOC issued a determination in the Clark case in August 1975, finding Oglethorpe in violation of Title VII. The ruling cites Oglethorpe's disproportionately high number of full-time male faculty members and tenured faculty members: "It is apparent from these statistics that females are disproportionately concentrated in lower level, non-tenured positions." It also cites the use of vague and subjective criteria in the tenure decision and points out that a visiting committee from the Southern Association of Colleges and Schools had concluded in 1974 that Oglethorpe needed to formulate its tenure criteria more precisely. "Thus in this case the major circumstance to consider is the fact that the entire process of determining who shall or shall not be granted tenure is apparently accomplished in a highly subjective, essentially non-reviewable manner, by males." The agency next turned to overt evidence of sexism on the part of Clark's English teaching colleague. The professor admitted to EEOC investigators that he had used sexist terms in addressing Clark but characterized his remark about women's place being in bed as a joke. The agency, however, did not take his remarks lightly and found that his criticism of Clark had been a major cause of the tenure denial.

Immediately after the EEOC determination was released, Clark's attorneys approached the university for a negotiated settlement. The fall 1975 semester was about to begin and a new university president had begun his duties at Oglethorpe. It rapidly became clear that he did not wish to begin his term in office with a legal battle. Clark also took the EEOC determination to two members of the Oglethorpe Board of Trustees: she informed the trustees that she did not want to sue, only to return to her teaching job. They, too, clearly wanted to avoid costly litigation and the possibility of damaging publicity for the university.

Within days, Clark, who had been clearing her office in anticipation of termination at the end of August, found herself back at work. The agreement, worked out by her attorneys, allowed her two years at Oglethorpe at the assistant professor rank she already held. At the end of each year she was to be given the opportunity for tenure consideration by the president, without benefit of a faculty committee, based on her teaching and service record at the university. In June 1976 Clark was granted tenure at Oglethorpe. One month later she was promoted. The promotion decision, which was handled through the faculty, had apparently been in process at the same time that Oglethorpe's new president was making the tenure decision.

Why did Clark succeed where others failed? One reason is that she had the good fortune to be on the receiving end of a rapid and well executed EEOC investigation. Clark explains that there had been a suit filed against the Atlanta EEOC litigation center at about the time she filed her complaint. Because of some legal complications, she says, the attorneys at the center were unable to litigate and were given investigative work. Her case was given to a woman attorney. When the legal problems cleared up, the attorney was officially removed from Clark's case. However, she had become sufficiently intrigued by that time to continue the investigation on her own. Thus Clark was able to gain a determination from the agency in a little over one year.

While the statistical picture at Oglethorpe showed a disproportionately small percentage of women, it is clear that statistics could not have held up on their own in court since the entire full-time faculty at the university is quite small. A pattern of disparate treatment bolstered the statistics. But the overt—and thus rare—evidence of a sexist attitude on the part of a male who was a key figure in the tenure denial clinched the decision.

Another obvious reason for Clark's win is that she teaches in a small, private college. The speed with which Oglethorpe settled was a result, says Clark, of the school's aversion to litigation and bad publicity. Prior to the EEOC finding, Clark's attorneys had drawn up a court complaint. They were prepared to initiate legal action when they went to the university to negotiate. Oglethorpe's new president did not want to begin his career with the embarrassment of a lawsuit left over from actions taken during his predecessor's reign. Large litigation contingencies are not part of the budget for small private colleges. Unlike state universities, they cannot depend upon the services of state attorneys general. Nor can they depend on keeping litigation costs hidden in large state budgets as can state attorneys and state universities. The school itself is not inexpensive for students and, like many small private colleges, must struggle to keep student numbers up. And for both students and institutional gifts, the school is largely dependent upon good publicity. There was an element of fear of the federal government as well as fear of publicity and the embarrassment it might bring, says Clark. Nonetheless, it is clear that the university had resources that far exceeded those Clark could tap for a legal battle. But the administration chose not to expend those resources in a public dispute that would generate unfavorable publicity. Under the circumstances, the positive EEOC determination was viewed as a very real threat.

In spite of the fact that Clark was able to continue her teaching at Oglethorpe uninterrupted, she was forced to settle for less than she would have had if there had been no discrimination. She had to face another difficult and anxiety filled year awaiting the tenure decision of the new president. Her career was at the mercy of the university that had treated her unfairly in the first place. She, like Hollinshead, experienced harassment in connection with her teaching assignments—her attorney was forced to include a clause in the final settlement agreement with Oglethorpe to protect her from further retaliation. And the grant of tenure

came one year later than it should have. Moreover, Clark suffered from
high blood pressure during her years of insecurity. Although the symp-
toms disappeared once her position was assured, there is no way the
school can repay her for the years of poor health. "My first year back,"
says Clark, "included 'punishment' as well as anxiety!"

❖   ❖   ❖   ❖   ❖   ❖   ❖   ❖

In 1970 Valentine Rossili Winsey was awarded a $1,200 salary
increase, told she was "extraordinarily competent and hard working," and
handed a terminal contract from her job as associate professor at Pace
College in New York City. "It took me two years to find out why," says
Winsey, "years of back-breaking research, phoning, typing charts, corresponding, working with NOW, with men and women in public office . . . in short, doing whatever would help expose the pervasive prejudice against women which had so recently victimized me."

In addition to her credentials as a psychologist, Winsey holds a
master's degree in speech communications and a Ph.D. in cultural
anthropology. At Pace she taught courses in four disciplines, helped
create an anthropology/sociology major, and chaired a committee (of
nine men and herself) to revise the core curriculum. So widely appreciated was her work that a year before her termination notice she
received an $1,800 raise and the dean's promise that in 1970 he would
support her petition for promotion to the rank of full professor. "Instead,"
she says, "with no warning, with no opportunity for appeal to a faculty
committee responsible for such important decisions, I was awarded the
$1,200 raise . . . AND a terminal contract."

Though Winsey had extensive past teaching experience to her credit,
Pace initially was reluctant to hire her in a full-time position. She began
her teaching at the college as an adjunct associate professor. She recalls
that at the time her attitude was "I'll show them that I'm so hard working
and terrific that they'll WANT to come across." For two years, Winsey
says, "I was fitting in wherever I could, teaching sometimes six days a
week, two nights a week. It was a checkerboard schedule to oblige the
college. However, I believed that by cooperating as fully as I could, my
contributions would finally redound to my advantage." Meanwhile, men
with lesser qualifications were being hired by Pace as full-time faculty
members. Realizing, at the end of two years, that her efforts to prove her
worth would gain her nothing, Winsey says, "I decided to quit." But a new
dean who seemed intent upon building a solid teaching faculty told
Winsey she was too good to lose and sent her first to the chair of the
speech department for a possible full-time position. The chair, who
described himself as an "old salt," protested that he did not like women
around since their presence prevented him from using four letter words.
Nor would he pay her what he paid men because, he added, to do so
would "demoralize" the department.

The dean next sent Winsey to the chair of the social science department, who did, indeed, hire her full time in the rank of associate professor, "at the magnificent sum of $12,000," says Winsey. "Later I was outraged to learn that a male had been hired at approximately the same time in the lower rank of assistant professor . . . but . . . his salary was $19,000. It's bad enough to be paid less than a man on the *same* level, but when you're paid less than a man on a lower level, it's demoralizing!"

When the time came for Winsey to apply for promotion to full professor rank, her broad background, which the dean had insisted earlier was too valuable for Pace to lose, suddenly emerged as a defect. Her chair declared that his department promotions committee felt she was "not specialized enough" and "too all-overish. . . . Most of the men, my chairman informed me, 'resent your coming in as an associate in the first place and if I were to promote you, it would demoralize the whole department.' "

At that point Winsey attempted an on-campus review of her promotion. It soon became clear, however, that her efforts had greatly upset both her department chair and the dean. So, says Winsey, "in the interest of harmony I informed my chairman that I would wait another year." During that time, she told him, she would work on whatever he felt was needed to improve her chances for promotion. However, her extraordinary forbearance did not stop her chair or the dean from characterizing her as "troublesome." And the characterization led Pace administrators to decide that the best thing to do was to fire her. Thus her department chair first apprised her of the $1,200 raise and "in the next breath" informed her that he would never again hire a "trouble maker." She was being terminated "for her own good," since, having failed to gain promotion, she "wouldn't be happy here."

"I was stunned," says Winsey, "it was too much to contain at once." Shortly thereafter, when Winsey was invited to sign the terminal contract offered her, she refused. Instead, deeply pained, she surrendered the option of a final year of work in favor of seeking legal redress from the New York Commission on Human Rights.

The next months required enormous effort on Winsey's part in collecting information and prodding the sluggish bureaucracy of the Commission to move. Her situation was further exacerbated by the termination of her husband's job as assistant public relations director at the John Jay College of Criminal Justice of the City University in New York (CUNY). There were no connections between her problems at Pace and her husband's termination at CUNY that could convince a judge, says Winsey. Nevertheless, word of her battle had reached people at CUNY, whose administrators made it evident that they were not happy with the issues she had raised. Her situation was made even worse when the New York Commission insisted that she retain a private attorney to represent her "despite their staff of lawyers whose job it was to assist plaintiffs appealing for help. Their expressed opinion was that I stood a better chance of achieving justice if I got my own lawyer."

After two years of persistent and grueling effort, the Commission issued a "Decision and Order," finding that Pace had discriminated against Winsey and against women as a class. It ordered the college to reinstate Winsey with a total financial settlement of about $25,000, including $1,500 damages for mental pain and humiliation. Pace was also ordered to institute an affirmative action plan revising some of its hiring and employment practices and to report back to the Commission periodically on the plan's progress.

"At this point I was faced with a very sobering choice," Winsey writes.

> "Both my private lawyer and the Commission lawyers advised me of my option to disassociate the decision in my favor from the Commission's precedent-setting 'Decision and Order' involving the affirmative action ruling. This meant that I would most likely be reinstated by Pace with back pay, and my future would then be secure. But, I was also advised that if I did so, the effect of the total decision rendered by the Commission on behalf of all women in higher education would obviously be weakened. . . . My husband and daughters agreed that I should stick it out to the end.

Not unexpectedly, Pace appealed the Commission ruling in the New York State court system. Over the next few years Winsey and the New York Commission, backed by the Corporation Counsel, suffered several setbacks. The lower court set aside the Commission ruling and the New York Appellate Court supported the lower court. But in October 1975 the New York State Court of Appeals, the highest state court, partially overturned these decisions. It found

> there was sufficient evidence which the Commission could credit that Dr. Winsey was being treated differently than a man would have been because of her necessarily agressive pursuit of promotion despite an acceptable teaching record at Pace. What became apparent is that she was a "troublesome" woman. What Dr. Winsey did to cause her termination would not have been considered "troublesome" if she had not been a woman. It often happens that those who are not supine and fight for their rights will be regarded as troublesome and those disturbed by the struggle would wish that the troublesome one "would just go away." To terminate Dr. Winsey's employment for this reason . . . is to have unlawfully discriminated against her.

But the court's ruling on classwide discrimination was disappointing:

"There is insufficient evidence to support a finding that Pace's appointment practices were discriminatory on an institution-wide basis." The court added: "This is not to say, however, that Pace or any other school of higher learning can never be shown on a sufficient record based on statistical data to have discriminated unlawfully on the ground of sex."

With regard to Winsey, the court expressed some interesting and familiar reservations: "Neither the Commission nor the courts should invade, and only rarely assume academic oversight, except with the greatest caution and restraint, in such sensitive areas as faculty appointment, promotion, and tenure, especially in institutions of higher learning. . . . In the professional or academic milieu subjective judgments necessarily have a proper and legitimate role. . . ." Rather than ordering Winsey's reinstatement, the Court ordered the entire case remanded to the Commission to "make new findings and appropriate determinations with respect to the complaint of Dr. Winsey as an individual that she was unlawfully discriminated against on the ground of sex." (The Commission extensively circulated a memorandum advising of the Winsey victory. When I wrote to the Commission for a copy of the full court finding, I was informed that "budgetary restrictions make it impossible to furnish copies." When my husband made an independent request for a copy several days later, he was promptly furnished with one.)

Winsey has her own theory about why she won: she is convinced that the victory is in large part due to the fact that Pace is a private institution. Even though the school has greater financial resources than many other private schools, it does not have the ability of state institutions to bury expenditures for fighting discrimination complaints in large state budgets. A second reason for her victory is contained in the decision of the Court of Appeals, which leans heavily on evidence of "explicitly discriminatory comments to her or with reference to her by the head of the speech department and other comments by the dean and head of the department of social science indicative of sex discrimination." What is more, following her resignation she received a highly laudatory letter about her professional credentials and capacities from the president of Pace. The school, itself, had established not only that she was extraordinarily competent, innovative, and dedicated, but also that its own administrative personnel were overtly sexist in their decision making.

What Winsey gained falls short of equity. Although she was reinstated with tenure in September 1976, the ruling left Pace to decide on Winsey's promotion. As of fall 1978 she was still an associate professor, although men in her department have averaged two years in each rank before promotion. Winsey has not yet received remuneration for the time she was unemployed, or for the pain she suffered. Instead, she has been forced to hire another attorney in a battle over the monetary award.

Throughout her battle, Winsey prided herself on maintaining physical and emotional health. But years of unconscious teeth grinding while the fight was in progress have led to painful problems requiring oral surgery "at astronomical costs. A good title for the *Winsey v. Pace* odyssey," says Winsey, "would be *The Ordeal of Winning*." And perhaps she is right. Certainly I have yet to find a "winner" who has obtained a fully satisfactory settlement or who obtained a settlement with ease. If anything, all of the case histories in this book may make the battle for equity seem too simple and smooth for we have had to leave out all but the most essential details in each case.

❖   ❖   ❖   ❖   ❖   ❖   ❖   ❖

The answers to our two questions are not promising. When we examine why these women won where others did not, we must admit that the reasons are mostly extraneous to the merits of their cases. They won because officials in the employment process were not clever enough to disguise their sexism and thus their institutions could not deny overt discrimination but could only attempt to pass it off as a meaningless joke. They won because they had political help from state officials or university trustees, or because their institutions feared bad publicity. Given dissimilar sets of outside circumstances, other women with equally meritorious cases have lost.

When we examine what they won we find that inevitably it was less than equity. Even Barbara Clark, who came closest to equity of those we interviewed, had to accept an added year of insecurity while placing complete trust in a new university president. She had no way whatever of knowing whether he would chose fair consideration or a whitewash of previous university actions. Clearly equity would have demanded that she be returned to Oglethorpe in a tenured position.

Winning, for most of the complainants, placed them in situations that may have been more advantageous than before the battle. Nonetheless, these situations were *still* discriminatory. The concept of making the victim of discrimination whole has not yet made it into the real world, even for those victims who have won.

—— *Chapter Ten* ——

WORKING FOR UNCLE SAM

"... *as a white women of moderate means, with a husband who is devoted to providing me with emotional and economical support, if I can arrive at a point of complete hopelessness and impotence in achieving my rights as a human being, what hope can there be for my sisters who do not possess the same degree of personal support? What faith can a black woman or a woman who is raising a family alone, for example, find in a system which is not adverse to techniques of intimidation and reprisal? Indeed, where there is fear for one's livelihood, either implied or actual, there can be no justice!"*

Diana Gutmann, Complainant, 1977

Diana Gutmann filed a complaint of sex discrimination against her supervisors in the Naval Air Systems Command in June 1975. She had worked as a civilian employee for the Department of the Navy for ten years and in 1975 served as a GS 7 administrative assistant for planning. For five years, according to her complaint, all her requests for training had been denied and her career had apparently reached a dead end. Her immediate supervisor had, however, assured her that he wanted to place her in a ladder training position if such a position could be established within his office. In 1975 just such a position became available. It was advertised as a GS 9, 11, or 12 level position and required no formal college level degree. Gutmann was selected as "highly qualified", along with four other applicants. But Gutmann did not get the job. Instead, without interviewing anyone but his preselected candidate, her supervisor told the division administrative assistant, "I'm going to hire a GS 12 male with a college degree for the position; women should go barefoot in the winter and pregnant in the summer."

Before Gutmann filed her formal complaint, she was required by government equal employment opportunity (EEO) investigation policy to go through an informal complaint resolution process. Her informal complaint had been investigated in May 1975 and the investigating officer had concluded that the "barefoot and pregnant" statement made by her supervisor was not sexist at all but merely "insensitive and imprudent." He also concluded that there had been no discrimination in the hiring process and "no deliberate, nor any discernible institutional, pro-male, or pro-college degree bias involved in the selection." In his judgment, the individual selected for the position was "head and shoulders the best." His only recommendation was that the selection "be reaffirmed and hiring be accomplished forthwith." He did not even see fit to reprimand Gutmann's supervisor for his "insensitive and imprudent" remarks.

When Gutmann filed her first formal complaint, she asked only for training opportunities that would allow her to advance her position within the Naval Air Systems Command, an apology from several supervising officers who had made clearly sexist remarks, and attendance at EEO seminars by those supervisors to help educate them to equal employment problems. The result of her formal complaint was an immediate campaign of reprisal and harassment against Gutmann and the individuals who supported her. Her supervisor began "keeping book" on her—noting her hours at her desk and complaining when she took time off to perform her duties as the unit's Women's Program chair, even though such duties were authorized by the secretary of the navy. His personally detailed log of her presence and absence in the office even covered times when he himself was out of the office on sick leave. At one point her supervisor issued a letter of caution to Gutmann in which he charged that she had taken too much time to perform duties in the Federal Women's Program (FWP) and in matters relating to her complaint. The letter concluded: "If it has developed that you are unable to participate in the FWP and continue to perform your assigned duties, then you may have to be relieved of your responsibilities in the FWP. . . . Henceforth, preparing of your EEO complaint will no longer be an acceptable excuse for not performing your assigned duties."

In other harassing tactics, key witnesses had their personnel files searched without prior consent. Some had their own jobs threatened and were intimidated before hearings in which they were to give testimony on behalf of Gutmann. Defamatory statements were made about witnesses and about Gutmann. On one occasion a higher ranking supervisor responded to a question about Gutmann by saying, "well she's in that, ah, Women's Program [the Federal Women's Program] too, but I can't really call her a creep, because Mrs. Jewell out there is one too."

Gutmann's performance ratings also began to slip following her formal charge. Her rating on resourcefulness and methods of working in the two performance ratings prior to her filing had read: "Mrs. Gutmann exceeds expected standards in this area," and "Tries to be innovative and exercises initiative in spotting and correcting errors." In motivation, quantity of work, and timeliness, the two earlier ratings read: "Mrs. Gutmann is most conscientious in meeting deadlines and accomplishes all assignments on the basis of assigned priorities and generally in accordance with her own best judgment," and "Most conscientious in meeting deadlines and accomplishing all assignments per assigned priorities; generally in accordance with her own best judgment." Following her formal complaint, the same supervisor began writing such comments as: "Some evidence of new ideas to accomplish tasks. Usually content with old ways." "Often waits unnecessarily for direction. Shows little interest in some tasks." "Meets deadlines on routine tasks. Difficult tasks marginal in quality if completed on time. Does not meet all workload requirements." Gutmann's overall performance prior to filing her complaint was consistently judged to exceed or meet expected standards. After her complaint was filed her work was judged to meet standards only "marginally."

Gutmann eventually amended her discrimination complaint, expanding it to a class complaint on behalf of all women in the Naval Air Systems Command and increasing the remedy to include retroactive promotion, back pay, and insured access to training that would enhance her future professional opportunities. Because of the performance ratings, and a number of other retaliatory actions, she was also forced to file charges of reprisal, harassment, and intimidation against several supervisors.

In December 1975, following the formal, in-house investigation of her complaint, the commander of the Naval Air System Command informed Gutmann that her allegations of sex discrimination could not be sustained by the record. Gutmann next requested a formal hearing before a Civil Service Commission complaints examiner. But the hearing produced a finding of no discrimination, no reprisal, and no retaliation.

Before the Civil Service Reform Act of 1978, procedures for discrimination appeals allowed governmental departments to accept or reject Civil Service Commission findings and the pattern normally was that departments rejected commission findings of discrimination and accepted findings that vindicated departmental managers. But apparently the finding of no discrimination in Gutmann's case was sufficiently outlandish to catch the eye of the secretary of the navy. He felt obliged to partially reject the finding and, instead, handed down his own finding that some discrimination had occurred. Only the lowest level supervisor was charged with discriminatory actions in the secretary's finding, however. All senior officials were vindicated by the secretary, who found that none had discriminated against Gutmann. Nor did the secretary find any truth

in Gutmann's reprisal claims. Only "with respect to the allegation of sex discrimination against Mr. Mason relative to the filling of the position," did the secretary "not accept the recommended decision of no discrimination." The secretary's office noted that Gutmann's supervisor, "in the eight years in his position as Branch Head, . . . has never promoted a woman to the GS-9 level or above." As to the supervisor's statement that he intended to hire a GS 12 male with a college degree and that women should be barefoot in winter and pregnant in summer, the secretary found that "(h)e may very well have used the latter expression in the context of a jest as he claims, and as the Examiner so finds." However, the secretary gave less credence to the supervisor's claim that he used the word "male" without meaning he intended to hire a man: "his claim that 'I used male as a noun, not as an adjective,' is not persuasive. Neither is his attempt to support his claim by equating his use of 'male' to the use of terms like 'manpower' or 'he' in publications, such as the Congressional Record."
    Concluded the secretary:

> We find that it was Mr. Mason's desire not only to fill the position with an experienced person at the highest possible grade, but it was also his intent to fill the position with a male with a college degree. In light of the foregoing, we conclude that sex was a factor in Mr. Mason's improperly restricting consideration for the position at the GS-12 level and denying you [Gutmann] full and fair consideration for that position. We therefore make a finding of discrimination in regard to Mr. Mason's disparate treatment of you.

The Secretary nonetheless denied retroactive promotion and back pay on the grounds that, even though sex was a factor, Gutmann would not have been selected since "another highly qualified GS-9 female was among the best qualified candidates."
    No disciplinary action was suggested against the discriminating supervisor. Nor was Gutmann granted any kind of relief. The position, however, had remained unfilled since the dispute had erupted. Now a board was to be set up to oversee filling the post. Thus Gutmann was told she would once again be evaluated along with the four other candidates. But the evaluator, although now watched by a board, was to be the same discriminating official. Gutmann was promised that the supervisor would be required to prepare "a proper supervisory appraisal" of her work and that the appraisal would be reviewed by higher level officials.
    At that point Gutmann had two possible means available for appealing the decision. She could go to the Civil Service Commission or to the federal courts. She chose the courts. And eventually she won an out-of-court settlement. In May 1977 the Department of the Navy agreed to

grant retroactive promotion to GS-9 level as of April 29, 1975, and an additional promotion to GS 11 two months from the date of the settlement. A promotion to GS 12 was also guaranteed under the terms of the settlement and was granted to Gutmann in December 1978. Gutmann was awarded $9,800 in back pay and several hundred in court costs. Attorney's fees were left for decision in a separate court hearing.

The cost of the dispute had been high for Gutmann: "I lost my faith in the system itself since I and all those who have spoken out in my behalf have been subjected to reprisal, intimidation, and harassment." Federal government managers are not concerned with getting at the truth, Gutmann insists, "but rather with an intensive and sophisticated strategy of cover-up a la Watergate!" The navy, she says, has adhered "to the old line management concept . . . that of never admitting error or accomodating, regardless of the circumstances. In the long run, it is the navy that loses. . . ."

In his August 1976 finding, Secretary of the Navy H. J. Broderick totally ignored the class issues Gutmann had raised in her complaint. The complaint might have served as an ideal opportunity, given an open attitude and the will to enforce the antidiscrimination laws, for the secretary to demand a comprehensive look at the employment situation for women in the navy. Instead, the secretary let matters ride and left it for a 1978 report of the Civil Service Commission to discover that the navy management—including its equal employment opportunity management—was in a state of shambles. According to the report, navy civilian jobs were "wildly overgraded," with many offices housing too many supervisors and not enough workers. Merit promotion programs were widely ignored, with the majority of installations studied for the report using improper rating and ranking procedures for awarding promotions. Meanwhile, according to the report, "Navy continues to run behind government minority and female employment averages in almost all areas, and it falls farther behind each year. . . ." Progress during the 1971–76 period was found to be roughly one-third the progress rate recorded by government overall. Only 6.3 percent of navy civilian professional jobs were held by women compared to 20 percent for government as a whole. At GS 12 and above, the navy percentage of women and minorities was only one-half the governmentwide average. And more than a quarter of the installations studied had not set up required upward mobility programs while another quarter of the installations had "minimal" programs (Cramer 1978).

✿   ✿   ✿   ✿   ✿   ✿   ✿   ✿

The navy may indeed lag behind the rest of the federal government in the employment and promotion of women. However, other agencies are not far behind the navy in their reputation for ignoring equal employment opportunity. June Chewning filed a class action complaint in federal court against the Department of Energy in 1976, after years of frustration in trying to advance her claims through the Energy Research and Development Administration (ERDA). Like Gutmann, Chewning first filed her complaint when she was denied promotion. She had first worked for the Atomic Energy Commission (AEC)—one of the agencies that later made up the Department of Energy—in 1966, transferring to the agency from the Department of Defense. She rapidly developed expertise in manpower analysis and future manpower needs in the atomic energy field. Several years after transferring to the AEC, Chewning's division was abolished and the function she performed was transferred to another division with Chewning serving as acting branch chief. Since her former branch chief had left the job, Chewning seemed to be the natural successor to the post. She had been performing the tasks as acting head of the branch since the transfer and no one in the new division was sufficiently familiar with the work to qualify as branch chief. Nonetheless, she was passed over for the position and a man from the new division was promoted to head the branch, even though he knew nothing of its functions.

From that time on, Chewning experienced harassment. The new chief, she says, had no qualifications and "felt insecure." In contrast, Chewning had developed an international reputation in nuclear manpower assessment. The new chief simply could not accept Chewning's expertise, she says. He resented the fact that people called to ask her questions and ordered her to route all phone calls to him. Says Chewning, he accused me of "running my own little shop" and he tried to separate her from her outside professional contacts. "There developed almost a conspiracy," she recalls. She was given bad supervisory evaluations of her work, loaded down with "nit-picky tasks" that consummed her days and forced her to take her work home with her most nights, denied a within grade promotion that would normally have been automatic, and prevented, until almost the last moment, from accepting an invitation to present a paper to an international conference. Only her self-initiated transfer to another division enabled her to present the paper and only a battle within the personnel structure of the agency eventually won her the within grade promotion on a retroactive basis.

Chewning's experience in the complaint processing system closely parallels Gutmann's. The first investigation of her 1974 complaint was so poorly conducted that it had to be repeated. The second was equally bad. The investigator, says Chewning, belittled her claim that she had been denied training opportunities that had been given to men by listing her training in his report and ignoring the more generous training given men. He consistently overlooked letters of commendation in her file while harping on recommendations received by the man who was promoted to head her branch. He made positive mention of a 2.2 college grade point average received by the male and ignored any mention of her grades or the fact that she had achieved Phi Theta Kappa and other honor society memberships. He even insinuated that she many not have graduated from college at all.

Although the government complaint processing system is supposed to take a maximum of 180 days, Chewning waited over 400 days while the process plodded ahead slowly and unsympathetically. When she did decide to file a class action complaint in federal court, however, her training in manpower analysis was put to good use. The memorandum in support of her motion for summary judgment contains one of the most impressive statistical showings of discriminatory treatment by a federal agency compiled to date. The figures, based on ERDA's own data, cover training practices, hiring, promotion, and grade level.

By virtually every possible measure, ERDA statistics displayed a discriminatory training pattern. Men were more often selected for training programs. they received more hours of training than did women, and men received most of their training during preferred on-duty time while women were more often required to spend their own time if they wished to receive training. During every fiscal year studied, the cost of training for men far exceeded the cost for women. In fiscal 1974, for example, the direct cost for training per male was $176.17 and the indirect cost was $174.81. For females, the average direct cost was $67.33 and the indirect cost was $24.87. During the same year, men received training benefits that outdistanced the benefits for women in almost every possible field. Executive management training given men averaged $10.25 per training hour, more than double the per hour figure of $5.04 spent for women. Legal and scientific training costs per hour for males was $17.39 compared to $6.09 for females. In the trade and craft area males benefited at the rate of $20.38 per training hour while females received no training whatever. And even in clerical training the average cost per training hour for men outdistanced the cost for women by $3.48 compared to $2.36.

In the ERDA Executive Development Program Chewning found even more serious discrepancies. About 30 percent of eligible males were appointed to the program in 1974 compared to 16.20 percent of the eligible females. Furthermore, ERDA maintains a long-term training program for professional employees that often involves sending them to first-class educational institutions. For the 1977 fiscal year, 97.80 percent of those assigned to such programs from headquarters were male. Only 2.20 percent of those assigned were female. Nationally, the corresponding figures were 97 percent men and 3 percent women.

Chewning also discovered that women were denied their requests for training at 3.3 times the rate for men. She pointed out, "(t)he amount of training that one receives also will necessarily bear heavily on what grade the individual may be placed into, and his or her chances of promotion, and other or similar employment based considerations." Her court memorandum on ERDA training statistics concluded:

> Finally, the very reason for training is to upgrade skills. If ERDA should assert that women do not possess the necessary skills to qualify for high level positions, then ERDA has an *affirmative* obligation to provide them with training at a higher ratio than their workforce participation rather than at the lower levels of training they have been providing. Therefore, if ERDA asserts women are underqualified to fill their technical positions, then the training statistics presented are more indicative of discrimination than they would at first appear.

Turning to ERDA's professional workforce, Chewning discovered that "there is a severe overall under representation of females in professional categories, that the women in the workforce are predominantly in the lower grades, and that the women are severely underrepresented in various of the technical and professional positions." In 1972, for example, less than 10 percent of the professional workforce at ERDA was female. Of the women who were employed, only 13 percent were in grades 14 through 18 or in executive positions that comparatively could be considered grades 19 through 23.

Chewning also compared the female workforce to availability figures that had been prepared by ERDA itself. She found that women fell below availability in *all* categories. To name but a few: women made up 1.84 percent of engineers but only 0.5 percent of the engineers at ERDA; they composed 38.08 percent of mathematicians but only 14.30 percent of ERDA mathematicians; 5.73 percent of physicists were female but ERDA had no female physicists; 10.66 percent of physicians were female but ERDA had no female physicians. By 1976, although the percentage of female professional employees had risen slightly to 11.90 percent, and the percentage of women at grade 14 or above had risen to 24 percent of female professional workers, the absolute disparity remained incredibly large: 75.97 percent of female professional employees still remained at GS 13 or below compared to only 23.16 percent of the men.

Chewning next looked at average months since last promotion and here, once again, she found enormous male-female discrepancies. For men and women in the GS 12 and below professional population at ERDA in 1975, there was an eight month longer average time since last promotion for women. Men remained in grade 15.65 months before promotion, on average, while women remained in grade 23.57 months. The cumulative effect of such delays for women could obviously be severe in terms of a lifetime career and lifetime earnings.

Grade at time of hire proved to be another factor adversely affecting women. Chewining points out that, theoretically, professionals hired into the lower grades generally straight out of school should enter government service with approximately equal qualifications and should thus be hired at the same mean grade. In 1972, however, the mean grade at hire for men was 12.85 while it was 11.64 for women. By 1973 the gap had grown to 13.10 for men and 10.91 for women. In 1975, the last year presented in Chewning's statistics, the gap remained large: males entered government service at ERDA at a mean grade of 13.52 while women entered at 11.43.

Chewning's statistics were so well developed that the government finally had to acknowledge that there was clear evidence of sex discrimination in the new Department of Energy. In July 1978 the Department of Justice signed a consent decree stating that they had no other explaination for the disparities between men and women in ERDA's workforce. They agreed that back pay awards and promotions for many of the 255 women working in professional positions in the new Department of Energy Washington office were in order. The case had by then been bifurcated and evidence of classwide discrimination had been reserved for one hearing while remedy discussions were to be held in a second hearing. But the body of evidence collected by Chewning was apparently so overwhelming that the Department of Justice, which is responsible for defending government agencies in such suits, saw no point in attempting to contradict it in court.

According to newspaper reports of the settlement, the government's own experts had agreed that there was a salary disparity of at least $8 million between men and women professionals doing the same kind of work at the Department of Energy. Apparently there was also considerable evidence of sexual harassment of women employees and of assignment of highly trained women scientists to menial tasks. "They just didn't like women over there," commented one attorney. Other attorneys claimed that the problem had its roots in the fact that the Department of Energy and its predecessor agencies, AEC and ERDA, were originally staffed by ex-military types who were insensitive to women coworkers. "It amounted to a buddy system and the agency was known as a good agency to transfer to in order to get a promotion if you knew the right people," one attorney commented (Washington *Post*, July 15, 1978).

According to press reports, the settlement could amount to as much as $12 million and thus become the largest settlement to date for a government agency. But the settlement is not without its troubling aspects. The Justice Department acknowledged that discrimination clearly exists at the Department of Energy but did not admit to how much discrimination there might be or exactly who might be affected. Thus, in order to gain a share of the settlement, individual women may have to file claims with a court appointed master. Each woman would then be in a position where she would be claiming back pay and other benefits without any court record to back her specific claims. Chewning and her attorneys are asking the court to accept a computer assisted determination of the amount of back pay and the "rightful place" for each woman, using the regression analysis formula used to establish the government's liability.

While the settlement certainly will help a number of women at the Department of Energy, which ranks eighth among the 12 cabinet-level departments in its use of women, it is unlikely that it will produce departmentwide equity or even full equity for all of the women who must bring their claims before the court-appointed master.

Chewning admits that the battle has been a rough one and that the rewards may be less than adequate. Nevertheless, she would do it again. "If you approach it with the right attitude, it just makes you grow," she comments. The opportunity for growth is certainly there. And women throughout the federal government have, so to speak, taken advantage of it. Generally, they have been somewhat more protected from losing their jobs than have women in other areas of employment. But they have not been free of the harassment, intimidation, and reprisal that seems to be a common response to those who file discrimination complaints.

❖   ❖   ❖   ❖   ❖   ❖   ❖   ❖

Even the antidiscrimination agencies have not been free from complaints of discrimination and the supervisors within those agencies have not always reacted in a manner free from intimidation or harassment attempts. Complaints of discrimination have been filed against all the major antidiscrimination enforcement agencies by their own employees and they differ not at all in the kind of discrimination complained of, or in the reaction to it from agency managers.

The Equal Employment Opportunity Commission was recently found to have discriminated against an employee because of her Hispanic background. A federal district court judge in Washington, D.C., ruled that the Commission had discriminated against Iada Berio in promotion denial and ruled that Berio's supervisor had been guilty of retaliation against her once she filed her complaint. The Commission reacted in much the same manner as other federal agencies that have no direct antidiscrimination enforcement responsibility. An agency spokeswoman said no decision had yet been reached on whether EEOC would appeal the ruling. However, she insisted, the EEOC was definitely not guilty of discrimination. In court the agency had defended itself against Berio's charges by insisting that she was denied promotion because she simply was not qualified for her job. The lack of Hispanics in the agency headquarters (there were only 26 in August 1977, compared to 534 blacks) was blamed by the agency on the lack of qualified Hispanics available. EEOC fought the case, despite the fact that Berio won a rare ruling from the Civil Service Commission that found she had experienced discrimination and retaliation (*Wall Street Journal*, October 9, 1978). Berio's supervisor, meanwhile, received a promotion within the agency (Los Angeles *Times*, January 6, 1979).

It is, of course, true that antidiscrimination agencies may be more vulnerable than most employers to frivolous suits by disgruntled employees since they are more vulnerable to receiving bad publicity about such suits. But it is also true that none of these agencies have particularly spectacular records on the employment and promotion of women. There is simply no reason to believe that the same kind of discrimination that takes place against women in other federal agencies would not take place in the antidiscrimination agencies. A proportion of the complaints, at any rate, must be given credence—probably a far higher proportion than agency officials would like to admit.

One such complaint was filed in 1975 by a woman we shall call Barbara Jackson, an equal opportunity specialist who worked in the national office of one of the major antidiscrimination agencies. Jackson had taken the business of equal employment investigation quite seriously when she was first employed in one of the agency's district offices. Indeed, she had handled complaint investigations so well that she was able, in several instances, to reach agreements between employers and complainants that included substantial awards of back pay. Her work soon came to the attention of the agency director and she was transferred to the Washington headquarters office to help in the conciliation process in several difficult cases in the far west where assistance from the national office had been requested. When she completed that work, she was assigned to head a task force to revamp the agency's operating manual.

But step by step, the work she had done was being undone by a white male supervisor. One of the back pay agreements she had completed after months of delicate negotiation was stopped after it had been approved by all the employees involved, by the employer, and by the district office. Her careful conciliation efforts as part of a national team sent to aid the western region were unraveled by the supervisor and employer representatives who had been sent to Washington to talk to "higher ups" while the agreement was being fashioned on the west coast. Finally, her 18 month effort as head of a task force to refashion the agency operation manual was taken from her. The same white male supervisor did some hasty cut and paste work, combined the manual she had shepherded with work done elsewhere in the agency, and took credit for the finished product. Visiting reporters, including this author, were given copies of the draft manual that resulted and left with the unmistakable impression that what they were given was the work of the male supervisor.

The basic charge in Jackson's complaint was that she had been denied promotion because her work product had been taken from her and credited to the male supervisor. Her record for several years of employment indicated that she had been unable to complete any of the tasks assigned her. As an element of her complaint, she also charged that the women who had lost back pay in the settlement she had successfully negotiated and the national office had rescinded had also been discriminated against as a side effect of the discrimination she had suffered.

The work product charge was hardly frivolous. When it came time to consider Jackson for promotion, she was given credit for only one job—a job she had completed years earlier as a trainee. Jackson also charged harassment and reprisal that continued even after she left her job. Phone calls were not referred to her new office and anonymous callers have contacted her new supervisor to inform him that she is a troublemaker.

Jackson left her agency for a job in another antidiscrimination enforcement agency several years ago and progressed rapidly enough in her new position to leave little doubt that she had the ability to perform well as an employment discrimination specialist. Indeed, her new agency had perhaps the best record in the federal antidiscrimination enforcement effort before the 1978 consolidation wiped it out as a separate entity. The percentage of women and minority employees in the industries the agency monitored actually increased over the years. Officials at her former agency angrily refused to comment on Jackson's charge. They claim that it is improper for them to comment since the charge is still in the investigative and hearing process—it has been there for almost four years. And they add that she was really an inept employee after all and that her complaint had to be nothing more than sour grapes since others had to step in to bail her out when her tasks were inadequately completed.

Jackson's complaint has been bounced back and forth between the Civil Service Commission and her former department for over three years. At one point, following the inauguration of President Carter, new officials in charge of her former agency admitted that there had been a clear case of discrimination against her. But nothing was done about it, either to compensate her for the damage done to her career or to discipline discriminating supervisors. In fact, some of her former supervisors have gone through several promotions and several increases in job responsibility within their equal employment agency. Her immediate supervisor—the man Jackson claims played the major role in taking away her work product—also managed to survive the reorganization in 1978 and ended up on his feet once again, in a highly responsible job within the consolidated enforcement agency. It is a reality that produces chills in some quarters. These are, after all, the people who will continue to make policy in the antidiscrimination effort.

Jackson has reached the point where she must decide whether to stick with the government's investigative and hearing system or file a private claim of discrimination in federal court. Remaining with the government's investigative system has been complicated by the new civil service regulations. Her case could involve issues of merit as well as sex discrimination. Thus her complaint would not automatically be sent to EEOC under their new authority to investigate claims of sex discrimination in federal employment. On the other hand, filing in court is expensive and may be as time consuming as staying within the government system.

Jackson's case cannot be spelled out in any more detail as yet, nor can her real name or agency be revealed. Although it should have been resolved long ago, her complaint remains in the government hearing process and is not yet a matter of public record. But even in rough outline, her case is important to relate—all the more important because it has not yet been resolved, despite the change in administration.

The antidiscrimination agencies, of all government agencies, should know beyond doubt all the devices used by employers to counter charges of discrimination. Whether or not those charges are accurate is entirely beside the point. The enforcement agencies, one would think, should recognize the tactics and reject their use on the part of employers seeking to divert attention from the real issues. They should, instead, concentrate on fact finding that would establish the truth about allegations of employment discrimination. Instead, it would seem that they have learned to use those very tactics to fend off charges against their own employment patterns.

—— *Chapter Eleven* ——

DO AS WE SAY . . .

"I feel that the fight that we fought at the Justice Department . . . those first cases . . . made the department aware that their record was very bad when their record should be the best. They . . . are supposed to be fighting these cases on behalf of [complainants] and they practice discrimination."

Lella Candia, Complainant, 1978

Government service, like academe, is a world where merit has become the central myth of employment. As with a great many myths, merit serves a useful purpose. It permits those who have prospered within the system to respect and value their own worth: after all, the system has rewarded them, it is a merit system, ergo, they are meritorious. And it provides a ready rationale to impose on those who fail: the system has not rewarded them, it is a merit system, ergo, they have no one to blame but themselves.

The difference between the two systems is one of form rather than substance. The academic merit system depends upon the rhetoric of soft philosophy where collegiality, peer judgment, and necessarily vague and subjective standards play a key role. The civil service merit system depends upon the rhetoric of hard science where objective evaluation, testing devices, and comparison of exact numerical scores are considered vital.

The system set up to ensure merit in government service came into existence in 1883, 90 years after the beginning of federal government employment. But from the beginning, the merit system excluded certain groups. "The harsh reality has been that certain minority groups and women have not had the door of the Federal Civil Service system open to them," the U.S. Commission on Civil Rights reported in 1975. "Indeed, although a merit system would ostensibly preclude treatment on the basis of race, ethnicity, or sex, nevertheless, overt discrimination against minorities persisted for more than 50 years after the Civil Service Act and against women until the last decade" (U.S. Commision on Civil Rights 1975b, p. 7).

Even after the hiring of women and blacks was permitted, members of both groups were subjected to various forms of continuing discrimination. Blacks were subjected to segregation within a number of federal departments until "well into the administration of President Franklin D. Roosevelt" (U.S. Commission on Civil Rights 1975, p. 8). And "(o)vert discrimination against women was permitted under the merit system until well into the 1960's, by virtue of a rule which permitted appointing officers to refuse to consider female candidates certified as qualified by the [Civil Service] Commission" (p. 9).

Federal workers, like education employees, were excluded from coverage when the Civil Rights Act was passed in 1964. The act merely contained the statement that U.S. government policy was to ensure nondiscrimination in federal employment. Federal workers, like education employees, had to wait until the 1972 amendments to Title VII were passed to gain legal rights to fair treatment in employment. Even at that late date, the treatment of women in federal employment was dramatically discriminatory. Women made up one-third of the federal work force. Yet 75 percent of all workers in the lowest four grade levels, but only two percent of the employees above the GS 15 level, were women (Legislative History 1972, p. 1,757).

Under the 1972 amendments to Title VII, all government agencies were required to develop affirmative action plans and the Civil Service Commission was ordered to approve plans, monitor agency equal employment programs, and review its own merit system standards and complaint procedures to bring them into line with the requirements of Title VII. Federal employees also gained the right to go to court to seek relief against the government. But in spite of the changes in the law, the Civil Rights Commission in its 1975 review found little change in fact. "In both 1970 and 1973," the Commission reported, "women constituted 75% of the employees" in the four lowest grade levels. During the same period, "women employed above the Grade 15 level increased from 2 to 2.3 percent, which constituted a rate of change so slow that, if continued, would result in only 5 percent of these jobs being held by women at the beginning of the 21st century" (U.S. Commission on Civil Rights 1975b, pp. 15–16). In 17 agencies and one federal department—Interior—the employment record was so bad there were no women above the GS 15-level (p. 16). Federal affirmative action, said the Civil Rights Commission, required only that agencies have a program and see that it was enacted, with no regard for whether or not the program actually eliminated the underutilization of women and minorities. It was, said the Commission, "as if a doctor were prescribing aspirin to a cancer patient and periodically evaluating the progress of the patient simply by determining to what extent aspirin doses were being administered" (p. 96).

The situation for minorities and women had not improved significantly when the House Subcommittee on Employment Opportunites examined federal employment statistics in 1978. The subcommittee reported that in 1977 minorities and women were still heavily concentrated in the lowest four grade levels. Women still made up over three-quarters of the employees in the GS 1-4 levels and had made slight increases in the GS 13-15 levels. But, "(i)ncreases in the actual number of women in the highest grade level, GS 16-18 . . . virtually did not occur from 1975 to 1977, on a governmentwide basis" (U.S. House 1978, p. 2).

Two basic methods are used by the Civil Service Commission (CSC) for measuring the qualifications of job applicants and for establishing the entry grade level of those applicants. The first is the use of various written tests. The second is evaluation by a CSC specialist of the education, training, and experience of the job applicant. For the most part, women with professional training and experience seeking federal employment would find the second method applied to them. However, both systems permit the CSC to rate job applicants in terms of their skills and abilities and in terms of the CSC assessment of what kinds of qualifications are required to perform certain civil serivce jobs.

The use of any selection test to establish employment eligibility is currently forbidden by law unless the test used is a valid, job related test (*Griggs v. Duke Power Co.*). Both the EEOC and the OFCCP guidelines require that private employers who use tests that disproportionately exclude minorities or women demonstrate that there is a firm relationship between ability to perform on the test and ability to perform on the job for which the test serves as a selection device. When Congress debated the 1972 amendments to the Civil Rights Act, note was made of the use of tests for federal employment that disproportionately excluded women and minorities and that were "replete with artificial requirements" only dubiously related to performance on the job (Legislative History 1972, pp. 84, 423). The Civil Service Commission was directed to review its entire selection process to make sure that it conformed with current law, especially the 1972 Supreme Court decision in *Griggs v. Duke Power Co.*

In spite of congressional instructions, the CSC issued guidelines in 1975 that failed to conform to the requirements of the law set forth in the *Griggs* decision. Instead, the Commission took the position that the *Griggs* standard did not apply since the federal government was not included in the term "employer" as defined in Title VII. In spite of several court rulings to the contrary, the CSC has continued to maintain this position: *Morton v. Mancari* (42 US L.W. 4933,3937, 1974); *Douglas v. Hampton* (338 F. Supp. 18 D.D.C. [1972], *aff'd in part, vacated in part* [No. 72-1376 (D.D. Cir, 1975)]].

The effect of the Civil Service Commission failure was made clear in a 1974 report by the Government Accounting Office. The GAO study concentrated on the rating given applicants for mid-level jobs by civil service specialists who study the applicants' background and qualifications. It revealed that there was little relationship between the point system and merit. CSC staff, when asked to re-rate previously evaluated applicants, often came up with scores significantly different from the original scores. The differences could affect the standing of the job applicant by as much as 50 places on a list of candidates, said the GAO, and could thus substantially affect the candidate's chances of attaining federal employment. Since government officials are required to hire from among only the top three candidates, a system with so much room for variation could clearly prevent the most meritorious candidates from being hired, especially when one remembers that veterans automatically gain additional points merely by being veterans (GAO 1974).

While veterans preference is not a matter of Civil Service Commission control, but rather a legal requirement imposed by Congress, the system came in for major criticism by the Commission on Civil Rights. Veterans preference began after the Civil War when Congress, in an effort to aid the disabled, passed legislation affording them preference for federal employment. Following each war in which the United States has taken part, the veterans preference laws have been expanded in both Congress and in a number of state legislatures. The federal system finally developed to the point where veterans gain extra points when applying for federal jobs or, if they already have such jobs, when applying for transfers within the bureaucracy. In addition, by law, federal officials hiring from outside the bureaucracy must hire according to the "rule of three": the successful job applicant must be selected from only the top three ranked persons on a list submitted by the Civil Service Commission. Veterans preference points increase the likelihood that most, if not all, of the top candidates will be veterans. Since 98.8 percent of the veterans in the United States are male (U.S. Commission on Civil Rights 1975b, p. 30), the system has assured veterans an edge in gaining government jobs and in moving up the federal career ladder.

According to the Commission on Civil Rights, 67 percent of all male employees in the federal government were entitled to veterans preference points, whereas veterans make up only 22 percent of the national workforce as a whole. Only 6 percent of female federal employees were entitled to such treatment. (In certain limited cases, women who have not served in the armed forces qualify, as, for example, if they are spouses of severely disabled veterans who cannot work or mothers of military personnel who died in service.) Veterans also have job tenure rights not enjoyed by other federal employees. When there is a reduction in force, they are passed over, making it likely that women bear the brunt of employment cutbacks. The favored treatment, according to the Commission on Civil Rights, "has an extremely discriminatory effect on employment of women in the Federal Service" (p. 30). (In June 1979, the Supreme Court affirmed the legality of absolute preference for veterans in state employment even though the Court recognized that such preference is discriminatory in its effects on women since, said the Court, it could not be shown that the discrimination was intentional.)

Along with its criticism of Civil Service Commission handling of testing and employment policies, the Commission on Civil Rights severely criticized the discrimination complaint mechanisms that had been set up for federal government workers. The procedure set up before Title VII protection was extended to federal employees was generally unsympathetic to complainants and tended to affirm findings in favor of management. Under Civil Service procedure, the initial findings on discrimination complaints were made within the agency employees accused of discriminating. The Civil Service Commission became involved only if the agency and the complainant had failed to reach settlement and one or the other party wished to appeal. To make matters worse, the Civil Service Commission tended to define discrimination in an outmoded fashion "as primarily a problem of individual bigotry rather than the result of systemic practices" (U.S. Commission of Civil Rights 1975b, p. 61). However, almost three years after the enactment of the Title VII amendments, the complaint procedures "were still fundamentally biased against the employment discrimination complainant . . ." while ". . . interpretations of complainants substantive and procedural rights were in many respects contrary to the requirements of Title VII" (p. 62).

Complaint statistics support the view of the Civil Rights Commission. In fiscal 1974, for example, findings of discrimination were made in only 170 of 2,650 complaints of discrimination filed by federal employees. Approximately 30 percent of the agency findings were appealed by complainants to the Civil Service Appeals Review Board. In 75 percent of the appealed cases, the board confirmed the negative findings of the agencies. In only 5.5 percent of the cases brought before the appeals board did the board reverse agency findings that there had been no discrimination (U.S. Commission on Civil Rights 1975b, pp. 81-82).

In 1976 the staff of the House Subcommittee on Equal Opportunities released a report substantially in agreement with the Commission on Civil

Rights. Women and minorities in federal employment were found to be overrepresented in "non-career, deadend jobs with limited opportunities for advancement." Fifty-five percent of all women and 45 percent of all minority group members in federal white collar jobs were in categories such as file clerk, stenographer, or card punch operator. The committee found no evidence that the Civil Service Commission was taking steps to remedy the situation through strong affirmative action program requirements (U.S. House 1976a, p. 50).

Interestingly—and disturbingly—the House report refrained from joining the Commission on Civil Rights in its stand on the effects of veterans preference on female employment. It merely noted that "(r)epresentatives of national women's organizations testifying before the Subcommittee opposed" the laws, and concluded that "(i)nterest groups have recommended limiting a veteran's use of the preference to a fixed number of times within a set period after discharge" (p. 57).

The subcommittee report concluded:

> The Commission [CSC] has not made agencies accountable for the eradication of employment discrimination in all of its forms. It has not sufficiently asserted its authority to issue rules, regulations, orders, and instructions to agencies in the institution of affirmative programs of equal employment opportunity. . . . Federal EEO programs are not structured to remedy the effects of systemic discrimination through affirmative action. In addition, there is an apparent unwillingness among Federal officials to develop effective methods of identifying discriminatory employment patterns and practices (p. 49).

Exactly how all these failures have affected women in federal employment can best be illustrated by two case histories of women complainants at the Department of Justice—the department charged with the ultimate authority to enforce the law.

   ✿   ✿   ✿   ✿   ✿   ✿   ✿

In April 1971 Lella Smith Candea became the first woman to file a successful sex discrimination complaint against the Department of Justice. Candea had been working as a GS 11 professional staff member in the Department's Community Relations Service—an agency established under Title X of the Civil Rights Act of 1964 to assist communities in coping with problems that might be caused by desegregation efforts. At that time the equal employment obligation of federal agencies amounted to nothing more than a policy statement in the Civil Rights Act of 1964 declaring that the federal government would not discriminate. But the response to Candea's charge, which was based on "years of heavy discrimination" that included failure to promote her, was "instant harass-

ment: my secretary, duties and office were removed and I was relegated
to a broom closet, within 24 hours after I filed my complaint."

Two other women in the small agency filed complaints soon after
Candea. One was a black professional worker, Dr. Dollie Walker, and the
second a Chicana secretary, Consuelo deSchueler. They, too, were
subjected to instant harassment, Candea says.

Due to the pattern of consistent harassment, Candea decided in
February 1972 to file a second EEO complaint through the department's
internal procedures. The response to the harassment charge, however,
was more harassment: Candea was ordered permanently transferred on
one week's notice to a branch office in Columbia, South Carolina. Mary
Eastwood, a Justice Department EEO officer, was able to fight the move
within the department, but no sooner had the order been rescinded than
Candea's agency attempted to transfer her to another building and, later,
to another agency within Justice. When these attempts, too, failed, she
arrived at work one day to find that both her typewriter and her
telephone had been removed during the night.

Since neither of her internal EEO complaints had yet been processed, Candea next went to court. In a class action suit, she and
deSchueler charged the Justice Department with harassing EEO complainants and asked for an immediate end to the illegal activity. In a
precedent setting decision in April 1972, the court issued a consent order
in which the Justice Department agreed that it would not harass EEO
complainants and the two plaintiffs agreed to drop their court suit. The
case, says Candea, was the first in which a government employee was
able to obtain a consent order against the government.

Meanwhile, one of Candea's two internal EEO complaints—the
initial charge of discrimination—had worked its way through the system.
Both the Civil Service Commission and the Justice Department ruled that
Candea had been the victim of discrimination and ordered her immediate
promotion to GS 13 level. The victory was not completely satisfactory,
however. First, according to government regulations then in force,
Candea was not entitled to back pay for the period of time she had been
denied her promotiom. Second, Candea had incurred legal expenses
during the EEO proceedings. Government officials accused of discrimination are represented in EEO hearings by government attorneys. Plaintiffs,
on the other hand, must either pay for their own private attorneys or face
employer attorneys with no legal representation of their own. Third,
Candea felt that she should have been promoted to the GS 14 level.
Candea therefore filed another suit in federal district court, asking for an
award of back pay, legal fees, and an additional promotion.

While the court complaint was awaiting hearings, and in spite of the
consent order forbidding harassment that had already been issued by the

district court, Candea was subjected to still further harassment: her agency supervisors took the first administrative steps leading to her dismissal. "They were obviously keeping book on me—setting things up," she recalls.

Candea decided that the cost of trying to get her position back, once she had been fired, would be impossible to bear. Instead of "fighting my way back in and trying to get a firing off my record" she resigned in August 1972 and filed a third departmental EEO complaint, charging continuing harassment and reprisal and requesting that the case be investigated immediately and that she be reinstated with back pay. Candea was not surprised that the harassment continued in spite of the court order forbidding harassment of EEO complainants. "Even the Justice Department was not going to break its entire 150 year old system of not interfering with its agencies just to save two women," Candea says of the Justice Department attitude toward the order. "Each agency operated as a barony or private fiefdom unto itself." DeSchueler, she says, was also harassed. She failed to win a promotion out of the secretarial ranks and eventually, because of continuing harassment, she, too, resigned.

Candea's first EEO complaint, which had been remedied in a manner far short of satisfactory, eventually bore further fruit: in December 1972, as a result of new government regulations, the Department of Justice awarded Candea one-half of the back pay she had requested to cover the period when she had failed to gain promotion because of discrimination. However, Candea was still out of work and her federal court complaint, requesting full back pay and an additional promotion and legal fees, had not been dropped. In October 1973 the court ruled in Candea's favor on that complaint. It ordered additional back pay for the 1970–72 period when Candea had failed to gain promotion, legal fees, and the further promotion to GS 14 level. This complaint, Candea's second in federal district court, resulted in a second precedent setting decision. It was the first time a federal court had assessed the government legal fees for a successful federal complaint under the 1972 amendments to Title VII. The fees covered both court costs and fees incurred during governmental hearings. However, since Candea had resigned subsequent to filing the complaint and since legal technicalities had prevented the complaint from being amended to cover the harassment that forced her resignation, reinstatement had to wait until Candea's third internal EEO complaint had worked its way through the Justice Department and Civil Service Commission procedures. That did not occur until May 1974.

At that time the Commission and the Justice Department's EEO office released a ruling that found that the Community Relations Service had indeed harassed Candea into her resignation in August 1972. They ordered immediate reinstatement and 22 months of back pay to cover the period since Candea had resigned. If Candea's story ended at this point it would speak eloquently to the horrendous difficulty involved in moving the government's internal EEO mechanisms and it would speak, as well, to the ultimate, if grudging, fairness of those mechanisms. But the story does not end there. When she returned to her job, Candea faced a constant stream of minor harassments. And then, in May 1975, less than a year after her return to the Community Relations Service, she lost her job due to a "reduction in force."

During the time she had been outside the department, Candea explains, there had been a major reduction in force in the Community Relations Service. There was no proof that she might have been included had she been working. But almost a year after she returned to her job the agency attempted to claim that two other people should have been included in the earlier reduction: Candea and "The director's chauffeur, whom he didn't like." Candea once again filed an EEO complaint charging the agency with harassment and with discriminating against its women professional employees as a class.

Candea had been able to gain access to a study of the earlier reduction in force and discovered that it had affected 50 percent of the men in professional positions in the Community Relations Service but 95 percent of the women. About 33 of 35 professional women in the agency had been terminated. She realized that the claim of discrimination would be hard to maintain since, taken individually, each of the women might have been the victim of veterans preference rules. But she also realized that her own case was a strong one: the department attempted to tie her termination to a reduction in force (RIF) that had occurred months earlier but had immediately hired someone else to fill a job Candea had held earlier. "How could they RIF me when at the same time they were hiring for my earlier job?" Candea asks. The new hire, she believes, was the "mistress or girlfriend" of one of the agency administrators.

Once again Candea was out of work, this time for close to one year. She then found a job as coordinator of the Federal Women's Program at the Food and Drug Administration in the Department of Health, Education and Welfare. It is a "woman's job," says Candea, and therefore her series of complaints against the Justice Department did not hurt her. Indeed, she points out, the federal women's program jobs are quite often the "Siberia of complainants" within the federal system.

In July 1976 the Department of Justice offered to settle Candea's fourth EEO complaint. Since her class complaint was not strong so long as veterans preference rules remained a part of civil service employment, she decided to settle. She withdrew her complaint and Justice granted her one-half of the salary she would have earned between her termination at Justice and the beginning of her new job at HEW.

Even now Candea cannot put the experience behind her. The court order forbidding harassment of EEO complainants remains in the record, but she knows of complainants at Justice who continue to experience harassment. Disciplinary action against discriminating officials was not part of the settlement. No example was set indicating that the government will not tolerate such discrimination on the part of its administrators. Therefore, it is not surprising that Candea, in her current job as a women's program coordinator, is continually asked for help by women who are having cases for termination built against them following the filing of EEO complaints. Nor did Candea ever receive full restitution. Although she won more cases, more back pay, and more precedents than any other complainant in federal employment, she has never been completely compensated for the time she was unemployed, she was forced to alter the direction of her career, and had she not experienced discrimination and retaliation for over five years, there is no telling how much further along her career might now be.

Nonetheless, Candea won—not once but several times, not just in the internal EEO procedures but also in federal court, not just in cut and dried areas but in precedent setting areas. The wins were costly and draining for Candea, but they also were expensive for the department in terms of time, allocation of resources, and the approximately $100,000 in back pay and legal fees the department was required to pay. Did the Justice Department learn from its losses? Candea is not too hopeful, although she feels the department at least obtained some idea of its own record: "I think that it made the Justice Department aware that their record was very bad when their record should be the best. They . . . are supposed to be fighting these cases on behalf of [complainants] and they practice discrimination."

❀   ❀   ❀   ❀   ❀   ❀   ❀   ❀

Irene Bowman had been an attorney with the Department of Justice for 20 years and had failed to progress beyond the GS 13 grade level when she decided to file a class action suit in June 1976. Her suit, on behalf of all mid-level female attorneys in the department, contended that women were rarely promoted above the middle levels while men had no difficulty at all in obtaining top GS ratings and even special executive-level posts. Bowman's career had been marked by two lengthy impasses at GS 12 and GS 13 grade level. But the question of excellence seemed to have no relationship whatever to either the earlier impasse or to Bowman's eight years at GS 13 grade level—an impasse that compares with an average time of 16 months at GS 13 level for male attorneys in the department.

Bowman's record is full of praise for her work. In fact, from 1970, when she first became eligible for promotion to GS 14 level in the Antitrust Division in which she worked, to 1976, when she filed suit, evaluations of her work are loaded with such words as "excellent," "diplomatic," "dependable," "reliable," "coperative," and "effective." In 1972 Bowman's supervisor repeated his insistence on her "excellent level of competence" and noted that he intended to recommend her for promotion to GS 14 during the fall 1972 evaluation period. By that fall Bowman had been placed in charge of a major antitrust case. Her supervisor still had nothing but praise for her work and even admitted that she was, in fact, "performing the work of a Grade GS 14 attorney." Yet he failed to make the promised recommendation for promotion to GS 14 since *he* had not yet had "sufficient opportunity to evaluate the quality of her work when it is not being directly supervised."

By March 1974 the supervisor was reporting:

> For more than a year she has been performing the duties of a Grade GS 14 attorney. . . . She has shown exceptional skill in compelling distinguished defense counsel to stipulate to facts sufficient to establish the Government's *prima facie* case. She has also shown an exceptional amount of discretion and tenacity in dealing with opposing counsel and with the Court so that she has been able to arrange for an early trial date. . . . The degree of skill and experience that she has displayed exceeds the normal requirements of a Grade GS 13 trial attorney. It is characteristic of the quality of her work and I expect it will continue.

Nonetheless, her supervisor recommended only an in-grade merit salary increase. He promised, once again, that "this fall, I propose to recommend her for promotion."

Even the modest proposal for a merit salary increase was turned down, however, and Bowman's supervisor in fact waited until March 1975—more than four years after she was eligible for promotion and more than two years after he had himself insisted she was working at GS 14 level—to recommend the promotion to GS 14. But the long overdue recommendation also met with defeat. A promotion committee made up of four male, high-level officials in the antitrust division in which Bowman worked, turned down the recommendation on the grounds that Bowman "needed close supervision." In his promotion recommendation, however, Bowman's supervisor had praised her specifically for not needing close supervision. At least one member of the promotion committee later agreed: "Ms. Bowman probably received less than normal assistance . . . because [her supervisor] was 'spread thin' at the time. . . ." The fact that Bowman's work was both highly praised and admittedly unsupervised did not affect the conclusion that she "required close supervision."

"Patience," says Bowman, "is one of my more unfortunate qualities." But on September 11, 1975, Bowman lost patience and filed a department

EEO complaint. Less than two weeks later a second recommendation that she be promoted to GS 14-level was rejected by the promotion committee. While there is no direct evidence to connect the second promotion denial with Bowman's EEO complaint, it is interesting that the committee in its wisdom now found not one, but four, "strongly" felt reasons for finding Bowman unsuitable for promotion. To the early reason—that she "required close supervision"—they now added the contention that Bowman "has not and never did the work of a GS 14." She was also faulted for failing to demonstrate "antitrust analyitical analysis" and for lacking "cases tried in court."

The rhetoric surrounding the last of these reasons is instructive. At the time Bowman was first recommended for promotion in 1975, she had already taken part in a number of antitrust cases and had just completed a trial as lead attorney in a major case against Air Reduction Corporation (Airco). Her supervisor noted that "expediting techniques" she had used "saved the government a substantial amount of money by completing the trial in two days. . . . In my opinion any qualified Grade 14 attorney would have taken at least a week or more to conclude the same case. . . ." The savings was transformed into a defect by a higher level official on the promotion committee. The Airco case did not impress him because it "was only several days, which is extremely short compared to the average antitrust case." It is also instructive to look at this particular reason for promotion denial in terms of the record of the antitrust division special litigation section. Because of the complexity of antitrust cases, in the five years between 1970 and 1975, the entire section, with approximately 35 attorneys, filed only 10 cases and tried only three. One of the three was Bowman's Airco trial.

The complexity of the Airco case provides further insight. The written record of early Justice Department discussions indicates that the case was viewed as having greater than average complexity. And Bowman's supervisor stated that he would not have given the case to a grade 13 attorney except he felt Bowman was well qualified to take it on. Nonetheless, one promotion committee member dismissed the case in classic catch 22 style: "If it was a difficult case, I suppose [her supervisor] would have assigned it to a Grade 14 or Grade 15." Ergo, if it was assigned to Bowman, it could not have been difficult.

Bowman's complaint was eventually assigned to Mary Eastwood, an attorney in the department's EEO office, who found the pattern at Justice was that women attorneys spend far longer in grade than the median time in grade for men. She concluded that the pattern was so marked that "women will *retrogress* and will not even maintain the status quo in the upper levels unless the promotion rate is substantially increased." Eastwood also found that "not all male attorneys in the Antitrust Division have handled even one trial before being promoted to GS-14. . . . Mrs. Bowman was expected to meet standards that some male attorneys did not have to meet in order to be promoted. . . ."

Eastwood's finding gave antitrust officials an opportunity to exhibit surprising ignorance of Title VII law. She observed that overt discriminatory remarks could not be found in the files and went on to comment that "no one with any sophistication would today make an obvious sex prejudiced remark." In a rebuttal, one antitrust official responded, "as you concede . . . there is no evidence in the complaint file that supports Ms. Bowman's complaint. This should end the matter. . . ." To him, the lack of overt remarks meant nothing less than the lack of discrimination. But, as Bowman points out, "Congress directed the thrust of the Act to the *consequences* of employment practices, not simply the motivation." The same antitrust official went on to insist that there is "no basis in law or logic which supports the shifting of the burden of proof on the discrimination allegations to the Division." But no less an authority than the Supreme Court had long since established that the burden of proof does shift to the employer once a *prima facie* case of discrimination has been established. The official had demonstrated that there was at least one person at the Justice Department—at the level of deputy assistant attorney general—who lacked the sophistication to understand that discrimination is more than "obvious sex prejudiced" remarks or actions. He had also demonstrated that some of the top level attorneys at the Justice Department were unable to find either the "law or logic" of Supreme Court decisions developed over a number of years.

By the time the departmental EEO finding was released, Bowman had invested over a year in attempting to gain equity. She knew, says Bowman, that what "was happening to me . . . was also happening to other women attorneys. . . . I realized we were never going to get any action here unless the department was forced to do it. . . . I felt that once the department gives its own employees equal opportunity it will be in a much better position to give its attention to enforcement of civil rights statutes throughout the country." Bowman therefore filed a class action suit in federal court.

While both court and department actions were pending, Bowman obtained a promotion to GS 14. The rationale used was not that she had earned promotion by her capable legal work but that she had made "an administrative contribution to changes in the antitrust division's promotion procedures." The reason, said Bowman, avoids any admission that my work as an attorney merits such a grade." It is probable that officials in the antitrust division felt that the promotion would silence Bowman. It did not.

In June 1977, a year and a half after he had received the Justice EEO officer's report, the department's complaint adjudications officer released his finding. His review, the officer wrote, supported Bowman's allegation of sex discrimination both in her own case and in the case of mid-level attorneys in general. The remedy ordered by the complaint adjudications officer was to make Bowman's promotion to GS 14 retroactive to April 1975 with "all necessary benefits, back pay, retirement, etc., to put you in the place you would have been had their been no denial." He also ordered remuneration for the salary increase that had been denied in 1974. He did not, however, see any discrimination during the period when Bowman's supervisor admitted she was working at GS 14 level but refrained from recommending her promotion to that level.

The class remedy was less definitive. It included "priority consideration for promotion" for women who had been in grade 13 through 18 for longer than the minimum allowed time and departmental consideration of hiring experienced women attorneys from outside the department at high grade levels. Since evidence submitted by Bowman also suggested that "the problem regarding promotion of female attorneys from grades 13 and above exists Department-wide" the officer also suggested, but did not order, that general affirmative action procedures be set up within the Justice Department.

At that point Justice opted for an out-of-court settlement on Bowman's federal court complaint. Bowman's retroactive GS 14 rating was moved back to March 1973, when her supervisor first stated that she was performing GS 14-level work. Back pay, benefits, and attorney's fees were granted, and a procedure was set up for reviewing the files of all women attorneys at the GS 13 level and above. The department also stipulated that there would be no "reprisal or harassment of plaintiff as a result of her filing."

Shortly after the settlement, in the fall of 1977, Bowman was reviewed for promotion to GS 15 under the procedures set up for review of all GS 13 and above women attorneys in the Justice Department. She was already overdue for the promotion since her GS 14 promotion was made retroactive to 1973. Bowman had a new supervisor at that time—a man who was apparently much in sympathy with the upper level officials who had lost their dispute with her. He recommended against promotion and commented that, because of her litigation against the department, her output had not been as high as he had expected. The assertion, says Bowman, "set up a catch 22 . . . resort to litigation was necessitated by the wrongful withholding of a GS-14 . . . and after having successfully litigated to obtain a GS-14, the section chief is now using that litigation as a basis to deny . . . a GS-15."

Bowman's new chief went out of his way to repeatedly beef up his negative recommendation. And Bowman also learned that he had been

keeping notes on her since March 1977, because, he claimed, he did not
have a good memory. However, he recorded only negative notes, even
though he admitted he had no better memory for positive events. Among
his criticism was the accusation that Bowman had failed to show a memo
she wrote on a pending case to her staff. The supervisor admitted he later
learned that Bowman had no staff at that time. Nonetheless, he did not
remove the note on her "failure" from her record. Bowman was forced
once again to appeal to the courts since the Justice Department had failed
to live up to its obligations in the out of court settlement she had gained
earlier.

❖   ❖   ❖   ❖   ❖   ❖   ❖   ❖

At about the same time as Bowman's original settlement with the
Justice Department, Justice won headlines in Washington papers for a
new "relaxed" position it had supposedly taken in defending government
agencies, including itself, in discrimination suits. The new position had
been worked out between the Civil Rights Division of Justice, which is
charged with representing plaintiffs in employment discrimination suits
against state and local government agencies, and the Civil Division, which
is charged with representing federal officials accused of discriminating
against federal employees. For some time before 1977 there had been
serious legal inconsistencies in the positions taken by Justice in its two
contradictory roles. According to one news article, the change was due
"to a basic policy decision: that the government should not be able, as an
employer, to deny its own workers protection that it seeks for the
employees of private firms or state, county and city government agencies" (Washington Star, October 24, 1977).

Under Title VII law, a worker who is dissatisfied with an EEOC
review of his or her complaint has the right to go to court and be heard in
a completely new review of the complaint. Yet Justice had argued that
federal workers did not have a similar right. If they were dissatisfied with
the agency or Civil Service Commission reviews they could go to court
but the court could do no more than examine these reviews to see whether
or not they were arbitrary. It was not a position that gained much favor
with either government workers or the courts.

The 1977 switch in policy was no small matter since the number of
federal employee civil rights complaints has been sizable. The Civil
Rights Commission reported in 1977 that over 3,000 such cases had been
given to the Civil Division of Justice to defend since 1972, when federal
employees first gained the right to take Title VII cases to court. (U.S.
Commission on Civil Rights 1977a, p. 292). Thus the new "relaxed"
position was welcome news. The Justice Department would no longer
argue that federal workers were not entitled to the same judicial review
that the Justice Department is supposed to gain for other workers.

In his memo announcing the new policy, Attorney General Griffin Bell also acknowledged that "the same kinds of relief should be available [to workers] against the federal government as courts have found appropriate in private sector cases." Thus the government would no longer argue that courts had no right to impose affirmative action on federal agencies, or to award back pay and attorney's fees. Indeed, there was not much point in continuing to insist that the government should be exempted from providing such forms of relief. The courts had already rejected the argument a number of times.

Equally significant, Bell also declared that the government would no longer argue in court that no discrimination exists when the administrative hearing process for federal employees had already found discrimination. Therefore, employees who use the courts to ask for more substantial remedies or findings than those handed down through the administrative procedure would have far less of a burden placed upon them.

Conceivably this part of the new Justice stance could have an enormous positive effect on discrimination complainants who are able to gain findings of discrimination at the administrative level for they would not have the burden of arguing their whole case anew in court. The government, if it argued at all, would not argue that discrimination did not exist but argue only on the degree of discrimination or the nature of a suitable remedy. However, it could also produce additional complications, as it may have in fact done in the Chewning case (see Chapter 11 for details.) There the settlement left to each individual woman in the large class of plaintiffs the chore of establishing that discrimination in fact played a role in her own employment situation.

The change in the official Justice Department attitude toward discrimination complainants was certainly a welcome one, but it does not appear to have translated itself into better treatment of complainants within the department itself. Moreover, there have been virtually no other signs of change in the civil service system handling of discrimination complaints or in government affirmative action efforts. In 1977 the Commission on Civil Rights reported that government hiring and promotion procedures still had a negative impact on minorities and women. Ranking procedures, according to the Commission, continued to be discriminatory and were "not a reliable indicator of successful job performance and may, in fact, screen out qualified candidates" (U.S. Commission on Civil Rights 1977a, p. 25).

The complaint system continued to be stacked in favor of agency defendants and the appeal review procedure continued to uphold agency decisions with embarrassing regularity. Affirmative action remained a particular sore point. In 1976 the Civil Service Commission designed a formula for calculating a "representative employment range" for various federal jobs. Agencies were informed that if their employment levels fell 12.5 percent above or below the range they should take corrective action. However, the range was calculated by examining the current representation of minorities and women in each type of job. Thus, if 20 percent of the persons in a job category were women on a national basis, the acceptable range for any given agency would be from 7.5 percent women to 32.5 percent women in that job category. The effect of the system, if agencies did any affirmative action goal setting at all, was to lock federal hiring into its current level of deficiency.

Interestingly enough, some universities had used a similar system years earlier, setting goals for women and minorities by looking at the percentage of women and minorities already employed by universities on a national basis: goals were set no higher than the national percentage. The system, both in universities and in government, unquestionably implies a belief that there is no underutilization of qualified minorities and women nationally but merely a geographic imbalance. Affirmative action, then, becomes nothing but a matter of redistributing currently employed minorities and women.

Only in the matter of attitude toward enforcement of employment opportunity for minorities and women did the Commission on Civil Rights find any notable change since its earlier report. The new attitude, said the Commission, was displayed in a July 1977 statement by CSC Chairman Allan K. Campbell:

> There is no conflict between affirmative action and merit; in fact, the two are supportive of each other and you can't have one without the other. . . . The breakdown occurs, in my view, when one confuses the word merit with the trappings of merit. As one examines the merit system, one quickly understands that certain practices, regulations, and laws, which in fact comprise the structure of our merit system are sometimes the very ones which simultaneously inhibit the accomplishment of affirmative action goals. . . . A mere look at the numbers is sufficient to illustrate that current selection procedures deny substantial talent to the Federal Government. (1977a, p. 12).

But felicitous statements aside, the seriousness with which the government takes its efforts to assure that federal employment sets an example for the nation seems suspect when measured against the case histories and the findings of the Civil Rights Commission, or when measured against the following additional pieces of information:

- The Government Accounting Office, which investigates agency activity at the behest of Congress, has produced reports critical of the employment enforcement activities of the Office of Federal Contract Compliance Programs, HEW's Office for Civil Rights, the Equal Employment Opportunity Commission, and the Civil·Service Commission. Yet in 1974 the Government Accounting Office set a goal for hiring white women that was so low that if it were filled, it would have produced a *reduced* percentage of women in the agency workforce. The goal considered neither the then current percentage of women at GAO nor the expected turnover rate of employees. Luckily, GAO exceeded its hiring goal for women that year by 4.9 percent. Thus the total percentage of white women at the end of the year had been *reduced* by only .10 percent, to 15 percent of the workforce, rather than reduced several percentage points, as it would have been had the "goal" been met (U.S. Commission on Civil Rights 1975b, p. 113).

- The Equal Employment Opportunity Commission submitted a plan for its own employees in 1974 that failed to analyze current utilization of minorities and women by organizational segment within the agency and only roughly broke out job groupings. Thus the agency judged most rigorous in its expectations for private employers turned in a plan with virtually no means to measure its own accountability (U.S. Commission on Civil Rights 1975b, p. 75).

- The Department of Justice turned in an affirmative action plan in 1974 that contained no useful analysis of its workforce whatsoever and no information about the number of job openings it expected to fill. It listed among its "accomplishments" for the previous year: "Bureau efforts to recruit minorities continue. A variety of special efforts were made during 1973" (U.S. Commission on Civil Rights 1975b, p. 103). The Civil Service Commission approved the department's affirmative action plan.

- In 1974 the Department of the Interior claimed in its affirmative action plan that it was making "slow progress" in hiring members of minority groups. The department presented data in the plan that indicated a total black employment of 3.4 percent. This was 1.5 percent *lower* than the figure for black employment in the department in 1969 and more than one percent lower than the figure for 1972 (U.S. Commission on Civil Rights 1975b, p. 194).

- As of mid-July 1974 the Office of Federal Contract Compliance Programs, which manages the government's executive order program to eliminate discrimination in employment by federal contractors, had a male director, a male deputy director, and five male associate directors. Of the employees at the headquarters office, 56 percent were female (34 women out of 60 employees) but only 8 were employed at GS 11 or above. In field offices, at the end of fiscal 1973, OFCCP had *no* female professional workers (U.S. Commission on Civil Rights 1975b, p. 259).

- A review of selected government agency affirmative action plans in the summer of 1977 revealed that the Department of Justice and EEOC still had not broken down their workforce analyses in a reasonable manner. The Department of Justice had failed to analyze its workforce by GS level and both Justice and EEOC failed to compare their workforce figures with the availability of women and minorities in the workforce at large. Of 12 agency plans analyzed by the Commission on Civil Rights, "none . . . fully complied with the CSC's instructions for affirmative action." Nonetheless, all were approved by the Civil Service Commission (U.S. Commission on Civil Rights 1977a, pp. 47–48).

- In a report released in October 1978, the Department of Justice Task Force on Sex Discrimination revealed that the percent of women working in the four lowest grade levels in the federal government had risen from 75 percent, where it stood in 1975, according to the Commission on Civil Rights, to 76 percent, while government departments were required to maintain affirmative action programs. Women held less than three percent of top paying federal jobs, according to the report, and white males already promoted from within held so many top jobs that "no women or minorities can move into upper level management positions for at least a generation" (Honolulu *Advertiser*, October 4, 1978).

- The Civil Service Commission itself was sued under Title VII by a black woman who claimed discrimination when she was passed over for a position as chair of the Commission's appeals review board—the body that until recently heard appeals from agency findings on discrimination and other employee grievances. Peggy Griffiths, who is an attorney and who served on the board for a number of years, charged that she was denied appointment as deputy chair of the board in 1974 and later denied promotion to chair, both because of sex and race discrimination and because she had a reputation for ruling in favor of employees on a board whose reputation was that of a rubber stamp for agency management. Griffiths became chair of the appeals review board in September 1977 by virtue of a court order rather than as a result of the government "merit system" (Washington *Post*, September 22, 1977).

- Both houses of Congress have traditionally exempted themselves from all laws concerning equal employment opportunity for minorities and women. In 1974 the House of Representatives adopted a Code of Official Conduct that forbids sex and race discrimination, but the code contains no enforcement procedure. A voluntary fair employment practices agreement for House members had been signed by only 107 members as late as January 1978 (Northrop 1978, pp. 57, 60). In April 1978 a bill that would have set up a panel to hear discrimination grievances for Senate employees was still bogged down in Senate committees, even though the proposal provided for no enforced resolution of complaints (Denniston 1978). At the end of 1978, neither the House nor the Senate had voted upon resolutions to protect Capitol Hill employees from discrimination.

- In 1974 Shirley Davis was fired from her job as an aide in the office of then Congressman Otto Passman. The reason offered by Passman was: "On account of the unusually heavy work load in my Washington office, and the diversity of the job, I concluded that it was essential that the understudy to my Administrative Assistant be a man." Davis sued under Title VII and lost in federal district court. The judge found Congress had a right to claim exemption from the civil rights laws and denied Davis a hearing. Davis won her appeal to the Fifth Circuit which ruled in 1977 that Congress' right to exclude itself from laws it passed was not as crucial as Davis' right to the Fifth Amendment guarantee of due process. The appeals court remanded the case for trial. Democratic leaders of Congress then pressured the Carter administration to intervene in Passman's request for a re-hearing before the Court of Appeals. In fact, the pressure occurred even before Passman filed for a re-hearing, and there was evidence that Congress pressured Passman, who had lost a bid for re-election, into filing for the re-hearing. The feeling among congressmen was that there were too many similar cases and that if Davis won, "other women will come forward and start suing their bosses" (Daniloff 1977). The Carter administration succumbed to the pressure and Attorney General Griffin Bell had the Civil Division of the Justice Department submit a "friend of the court" brief arguing that "absolute immunity" was necessary in order for members of Congress to function in their jobs. They must, in other words, be allowed to practice the sex discrimination they prohibit to others. The Fifth Circuit bought the argument and reversed itself, holding in April 1978 that the federal courts could not, after all, consider complaints of sex bias brought against members of Congress. The case has gone on appeal to the Supreme Court (Washington *Star*, April 28, 1979; Washington *Post*, October 31, 1978).

❊   ❊   ❊   ❊   ❊   ❊   ❊   ❊

Private employers and state and local government officials might well ask why they should be expected to conform to equal employment regulations that the federal enforcers themselves seem to regard as a joke. And the federal agencies, in turn, might wonder why they should treat the subject with any seriousness when congressional intent has always been tempered with a strong dose of do-as-we-say-not-as-we-do reality.

Chapter Twelve

SEXUAL HARASSMENT: IS IT DISCRIMINATION?

"What I'm hoping is that as a result of this litigation somebody who comes behind me will be helped. Because it's not going to make me whole—we know that."

Diane R. Williams, Complainant, 1977

Diane Williams began working as a public information specialist in the Community Relations Service of the Department of Justice in 1972. The written record shows that she performed her job well from her hire in early January until mid-July of that year. No complaints can be found concerning her conduct, her professional expertise, or her relationships with other employees in the agency. But from July 17 to September 11, 1972, Williams' personnel file grew fat with written memoranda alleging she arrived at work late, failed to complete assignments in a timely fashion, and sometimes failed to complete them at all. All the memos were written and placed in the file by Williams' immediate supervisor. On September 11, 1972, Williams was told that termination of her employment at the Department of Justice had been proposed. And ten days later, on September 21, "with 25 minutes notice on a Friday afternoon," she was informed that the termination was in effect.

What had happened to a government career that seemed to be off to such a good start? Williams is still reluctant to talk about the events of that year. They were, she says,

> just ungodly. . . . It was a time I don't like to talk about, let alone even recall because it was probably the most humiliating and frustrating time of my whole life. . . . I was 24 years old at the time and a little naive about the world of work . . . and I had always thought and been brought up to believe that if you did well unto other people they would treat you fairly. That was not to be the case.

Shortly after her government service career began, says Williams, she became the object of more than the professional attention of her immediate supervisor.

> It was made very clear to me that if I did not cooperate with my supervisor's sexual advances then I was not going to get the job training opportunities that I was then seeking. I was not going to get the promotion that I was then seeking and my continued employment with the agency would be in jeopardy.
>
> I was given a card by my supervisor that said, "seldom a day goes by without a loving thought of you." There were other things—suggestions, innuendos—and it was not my supervisor alone who was the Romeo of the agency . . . although my supervisor probably had the most notorious reputation for being a womanizer.

Williams first tried to talk with her supervisor, to separate her refusal to comply with his advances from their professional relationship and from her advancement and continued employment within the agency. Her attempts were unsuccessful. She next went to the agency director, who was her supervisor's immediate superior. She had no success in resolving her complaints with the director. She then sought out the assistance of a Justice Department EEO counselor—the first, informal step in the administrative process that is supposed to resolve EEO complaints for federal civil service workers. "The counselor told me that I was not the first person who had been over there to talk about what was going on at the Community Relations Service," Williams says. However, her informal complaint had little effect. The counselor's attempt to talk with Williams' supervisor produced only one result. It alerted him to the fact that she had taken the matter outside the agency.

It was during this period of informal attempts to resolve the problem, first with her supervisor, then with the agency director and the EEO counselor, that her supervisor apparently began keeping a record of Williams' activities. She was informed by a secretary that her incoming and outgoing phone calls were being monitored and that note was being made of all people who still appeared to be friendly toward her in the Community Relations Service. Williams had no recourse at that point but to formalize her EEO complaint.

However, as soon as it became clear that she intended to do so, says Williams, "I was very quickly advised that I had really seriously jeopardized my continued employment with the agency. As a matter of fact, I remember very clearly my supervisor storming into my office and saying, 'If it comes to a showdown between you and me, I'm sure you'll be the loser because I am the director's boy.'"

Williams supervisor next wrote her a letter that contained a collection of charges he apparently believed would lead to a successful adverse action on her employment. The letter stated that Williams had been late from lunch and late to work in the morning, though no specific times or dates were given. Says Williams, "I wonder how he knew if I was late when I got there before he did." In the letter, Williams was also "accused of making false, malicious and slanderous statements against CRS officials," statements that Williams never saw and could not comment on. She was accused of "failing to do assignments he never told me about" and failing to meet deadlines on other assignments, although deadlines had never been established for her work. The letter was almost identical to a letter that had been used earlier against another Community Relations Service employee, Dr. Dollie Walker, who had filed an earlier complaint against the agency. "All you had to do was substitute the name and position," says Williams.

The discrimination complaints of women within the Community Relations Service were particularly ironic to Williams: "This was an agency of the federal government that was dealing in community relations with minority communities primarily. So the top ranking staff was primarily black and chicano. . . ." Her own supervisor was black, Williams points out. "The other irony is that Dr. Dollie Walker and I are both black women. . . . So far most courts have not recognized racial discrimination when both parties are of the same race, although it is very definitely there." Many black men in supervisory positions may discriminate against women in general, but their treatment of black women is far worse than their treatment of white women, Williams believes.

Before she was fired, Williams was able to file a formal request for an EEO investigation and the Justice Department conducted that investigation during the fall of 1972. It found that there was a discriminatory employment pattern within the Community Relations Service and it also found that the changeover from positive to negative reports about Williams' work was too swift to be convincing. The investigator wrote:

During my preliminary review of this case one question immediately became evident. Specifically, how did an employee hired in January suddenly become so bad that during the period from July 17 through September 11, a case was built for her separation. As the investigation progressed, this question became more of an issue. Enough inconsistencies were found to make me curious as to the validity of the allegations against Ms. Williams.

The multiplicity and diversity of the reasons given for the desire to separate Ms. Williams in the letter of proposed separation indicate strongly that a "shotgun" technique was used to justify the separation. None of the charges, standing alone, would have justified the actions taken. Even considering the charges collectively, there is real doubt that separation was warranted under the circumstances.

During the investigation it became clear that Ms. Williams had made an excellent beginning. Her work was acceptable, eliciting favorable comment from several sources. Her conduct and attitude were good. She was cooperative, pleasant and fully accepted as Mr. Brinson's assistant. There are indications of an amicable working relationship between Ms. Williams and Mr. Brinson even though he contends he was having problems with her as early as March. . . . I believe a program of fault-finding, criticism and documentation of minor offenses was undertaken. This program was not successful from the standpoint of obtaining Ms. Williams' voluntary resignation but did develop sufficient data that the proposal to separate was accepted by personnel operations people and she was separated. In my opinion, this separation should be classed as unwarranted and canceled.

The EEO report was next sent to the Justice Department complaints adjudications officer, who rejected the recommendation that Williams be reinstated but ruled that she was entitled to a full, formal hearing on her charge of sex discrimination. The hearing was to be held by the Civil Service Commission. But even though the case was going outside the Justice Department for the first time, Williams had grown skeptical:

The grievance system in federal government is weighted against the complaining party, she says. The complaining party has to find his or her own representative or legal counsel while the alleged discriminating official on the other hand has his or her legal counsel provided by the government which in turn is provided by the taxpayers. The complaining party can be fired or suspended or demoted or whatever during the whole time of the litigation. However, the alleged discriminating official is not reprimanded, there is no mention of this in his or her personnel file whereas it is in the complaining party's file.

What is more, says Williams, even if the Civil Service Commission should find discrimination, it is up to the employing agency to accept or reject the finding and propose a settlement. In her case, Williams points out, the Justice Department complaints adjudication officer followed a pattern of accepting findings when they favored the department and rejecting them when they favored Williams. Thus, the initial EEO finding, which called for Williams' reinstatement, was rejected but the Civil Service Commission finding that no discrimination existed in the Community Relations Service and no remedy was required was accepted.

In January 1974 Williams took her complaint to federal court under Title VII of the Civil Rights Act. Six months later, in August 1974, District Court Judge Charles R. Richey stated "that there was proof suggestive of discrimination in the record and that the defendants had failed to come forward and affirmatively establish the absence of discrimination by the clear weight of the evidence." His order, however, did not demand that Williams be reinstated. Instead, he ordered a second formal hearing within the Civil Service Commission appeal system.

The second hearing was conducted at the end of December 1974, more than two years after Williams' termination. At that hearing the Justice Department called only two witnesses. The first was Williams' former supervisor, who went over the testimony he had previously given regarding her purported employment shortcomings. The second was a woman who had worked for the Community Relations Service for some time and who was apparently brought in, as often happens in sex discrimination cases, to establish that she, as a woman, did not feel the agency discriminated. The woman did testify that Williams' difficulties had nothing to do with sex discrimination. However, her background also revealed that she had progressed in the agency less rapidly than males, that she "found herself generally frustrated and irritated with her superiors, all of whom were males, who gave her no recognition for her work and generally expropriated what she did under their own name." Under questioning, it also became apparent that this woman, too, had wanted to file a sex discrimination complaint against the agency and had sought EEO counseling. Her testimony did little to bolster the department's position, but was heavily relied upon by the federal district court judge in his April 1976 opinion in the *Williams* case to point out a problem of mutual fault-finding between Williams and her supervisor. Part of the problem was a clash between two strong willed individuals, the judge believed.

Following the second hearing, the Civil Service Commission examiner released a finding that Williams "was discriminated against because of sex in the acts of her immediate supervisor in intimidating, harassing, threatening and eventually terminating her." The supervisor was "of a disposition to and did make personal advances toward Appellee and . . . these advances were rejected by Appellee." The examiner recommended immediate restoration of Williams to her position and suggested that the Justice Department take "appropriate corrective action" against her supervisor. Not surprisingly, the Justice Department complaints adjudication officer followed a familiar pattern. Since the finding was in Williams' favor, he rejected it. Williams was therefore forced to go back to court to seek enforcement.

Judge Richey reviewed the record of the second hearing and on April 20, 1976, granted Williams' motion for judgment. He had found that her allegations were accurate and that her termination was the result of her refusal to comply with her supervisor's sexual advances. The relief granted by Judge Richey, however, did not include returning Williams to her job. During the nearly four years of litigation, the Department of Justice had never hinted that Williams would, in any case, have been separated from her job due to a reduction in force. Nevertheless, following his ruling in her favor, Judge Richey allowed the Department to introduce an affidavit, submitted by an employee who had not been with the department in 1973, that stated that Williams would have lost her job in 1973 due to a reduction in force. A similar claim, brought by the Justice Department in the case of Henrietta (Lella) Smith Candea, had already been rejected by the federal court. Judge Richey, however, accepted the claim and concluded that Williams was entitled only to back pay through the time she would allegedly have lost her job in 1973.

"I was merely asking the law to do what it says: make the complaining party who prevails in a discrimination complaint whole. The remedies were nowhere near that," says Williams. The back pay settlement proposed by Justice amounted to little more than $16,000. Nonetheless, "we were going to accept it," Williams says, "merely to get it over and done with because it's dragged on much too long—five years. That's five years out of my life. That's one sixth of my life! And it's still there. It's a recurring nightmare. . . ."

But instead of settling, the Justice Department decided, in its wisdom, to take its case to the U.S. Court of Appeals for the District of Columbia Circuit. The appeal produced several ironies. First, Williams points out, the Department of Justice had initially "vigorously" argued at the district court level that federal employees were not entitled to trial *de novo* and that the hearing should rest on the record developed by the Civil Service Commission. Williams had wanted a new trial but eventually had to settle for resting her case on the record. Meanwhile, the right of federal employees to have *de novo* hearings in federal court was established by the courts in other cases. But the judge ruled in Williams' favor in April 1976 on the basis of the administrative record. Justice having lost in court now decided that she really should have had a trial *de novo* anyway and made this argument a major part of its appeal. Williams, of course, did not want either the pain or expense of going through the entire matter once again and asked only that the appeals court uphold the district court decision.

Second, Justice also argued that sexual harassment is not sex discrimination at all but merely a personal idiosyncrasy that could affect anyone, male or female. The argument was not without precedent. It had been used with partial success by employers in *Tomkins v. Public Service Electric and Gas Co.* et al (422 F. Supp. 553 [D.N.J.1976]). The court in *Tomkins* found that the employer's decision to fire the female involved rather than investigate her complaint might constitute a violation of Title

VII if it could be shown that the action consciously favored the male supervisor over the female employee. However, the judge also found that the sexual harassment complained of was not a violation of Title VII:

> The gender lines might as easily have been reversed, or even not crossed at all. While sexual desire animated the parties, or at least one of them, the gender of each is incidental to the claim of abuse. Similarly, the pleadings in this case aver that the supervisor's advances were spurned. Had they been accepted, however, and the plaintiff thereby preferred, could co-workers be heard to complain in federal court as well? . . . The abuse of authority by supervisors of either sex for personal purposes is an unhappy and recurrent feature of our social experience. . . . It is not, however, sex discrimination within the meaning of Title VII even when the purpose is sexual.

Similarly, in *Corne v. Bausch and Lomb, Inc.* (390 F. Supp. 161 [D. Ariz. 1975]) the court rejected the idea that sexual harassment is sex discrimination.

> In the present case, Mr. Price's conduct appears to be nothing more than a personal proclivity, peculiarity or mannerism. By his alleged sexual advances, Mr. Price was satisfying a personal urge. Certainly no employer policy is here involved; rather than the company being benefited in any way by the conduct of Price, it is obvious it can only be damaged by the very nature of the acts complained of. [The court concluded:] It would be ludicrous to hold that the sort of activity involved here was contemplated by the Act because to do so would mean that if the conduct complained of was directed equally to males there would be no basis for suit. Also, an outgrowth of holding such activity to be actionable under Title VII would be a potential federal lawsuit every time any employee made amorous or sexually oriented advances toward another. The only sure way an employer could avoid such charges would be to have employees who were asexual.

And in *Miller v. Bank of America* (408 F. Supp. 233 [N.D. Cal. 1976]) the court faulted the complaining employee for failing to use company grievance procedures, even though the company had an expressed policy against such harassment. "The attraction of males to females and females to males is a natural sex phenomenon," said the court, "and it is probable that this attraction plays at least a subtle part is most personnel decisions. Such being the case, it would seem wise to refrain from delving into these matters. . . ."

In the *Williams* case, Judge Richy, however, disagreed and found that the Justice Department argument obfuscates the fact that, taking the facts of the plaintiff's complaint as true, the conduct of the plaintiff's supervisor created an artificial barrier to employment which was placed before one gender and not the other. . . .

The reason for this Court's opinion is that it rejects the defendant's narrow view of the prohibition of the statute, which is the result of what this Court perceives as an erroneous analysis of the concept of sex discrimination as found in Title VII, to which the Court now turns. On its face, the statute clearly does not limit discrimination to sex stereotypes. And while there is language in the legislative history of the amendment that indicates that Congress did want to eliminate impediments to employment erected by sex stereotypes, these expressions do not provide a basis for limiting the scope of the statute, particularly since there is ample evidence that Congress' intent was not to limit the scope and effect of Title VII, but rather, to have it broadly construed. Furthermore, the plain meaning of the term "sex discrimination" as used in the statute encompasses discrimination between genders where the discrimination is the result of a well-recognized sex stereotype or for any other reason. It is important in this regard to note that Title VII is applicable to men as well as to women. There therefore can be no question that the statutory prohibitions of SS 2000e-16(a) reaches *all* discrimination affecting employment which is based on gender (413 F. Supp. 654 D.D.C. 1976).

It is entirely possible that the initial insistence of the Justice Department on appealing in part on the grounds that sexual harassment is not sex discrimination has given encouragement to other employers and institutions to attempt the same argument in the federal courts. At Yale University, for example, where several female students and one male professor brought suit for sexual harassment on the part of male faculty and administrators, authorities vowed to fight the action "vigorously" and labeled the complaint a "very reckless and irresponsible action" and a "gimmick to gain publicity" (*Spokeswoman*, April 15, 1978).

Certainly the issue of sexual harassment is no minor one. In June 1978 the Project on the Education and Status of Women released a paper defining sexual harassment and assessing its extent:

Harassment at its extreme occurs when a male in a position to control, influence or affect a woman's job, career or grades uses his authority and power to coerce the woman into sexual relations, or to punish her refusal. It may include: verbal harassment or abuse, subtle pressure for sexual activities, unnecessary touching, patting, or pinching, leering or ogling of a woman's body, constant brushing against a woman's body, demanding sexual favors accompanied by implied or overt threats concerning one's job, grades, letter of recommendation, etc., physical assault" (p. 2).

Few statistics concerning the incidence of sexual harassment existed before 1976, according to the project paper. But since that time a number of surveys indicate that as high a figure as 92 percent of working women have experienced some form of "overt physical harassment, sexual remarks and leering, with the majority regarding this behavior as a serious problem at work" (p. 2). The defense offered in the Williams case and the fact that the Department of Justice raised that defense is most disturbing in view of the widespread nature of the problem.

The issue of sexual harassment is being kept alive for Diane Williams by the Justice Department appeal, as is the pain of having discovered that her career could be nipped so easily by her failure to cooperate with the sexual advances of a supervisor.

> It's just such a widespread problem that we've kind of hushed up and swept under the door and we've just accepted—just like women are expected to take notes at meetings and prepare the coffee [Williams says]. I just didn't happen to see it that way. I thought I had the academic credentials—whatever they may mean. I had the experience, I had the ability, I had the initiative, I had the motivation, I had the will, I had the desire. I thought that was sufficient for me to rely on rather than on how well I looked or how somebody thought I looked or whether I wore my dresses short enough or long enough or whatever they happened to like and it really hadn't occurred to me until that time that you could only be promoted or given job training opportunities or be looked upon favorably or even be hired because somebody liked the way you looked.
>
> And that was a very revealing kind of thing to me. It also hurt me— very much so. I think it's nice that somebody likes the way you look and they say, "Well, that's a nice looking dress or a nice looking suit," or "You look really nice today," or "That makeup looks good on you," or "I like the way you're wearing your hair." But when you are on a job I thought it was supposed to be how well you performed in your given assignment, are you a self starter, are you willing to learn new things, are you flexible? Not "Does Miss Suzie Q cross her legs right?" or "She's got fantastic looking legs," or whatever it is that turns people on. And it hurt me that somebody looked first at the fact that I was physically attractive to him rather than at my paper credentials, my resume or my work performance. It hurt, it really did hurt.
>
> Then I turn it around to the other side . . . how do you deal with an employment setting like that if you're not physically attractive, if you don't wear particularly great looking clothes or you're kind of plump or fat or whatever the euphemism is nowadays? . . . I think any woman who advances through the career ladder simply because she is physically attractive to somebody who is in a position to give her certain advantages is a prostitute. It's white collar prostitution and there is no other way that I can think of that you can define it. So that is part and

parcel of why I took such great offense at what this man was doing to me . . . he was asking me to prostitute myself, and I refused, not only on moral grounds but because I thought I had sufficient qualifications to do the job and had demonstrated that I could do that plus some and was willing to do it. How can you deal with something like that, especially when something as important as a job is concerned . . . I mean, a job is part and parcel of a person's self respect. . . . When you take that self respect, what do you have?

—— *Chapter Thirteen* ——

WHAT THE JUDGES SAY

"We are in a rather bleak period. It's not only the judges on the Supreme Court who reflect the Nixon legacy, but it's also the majority of the judiciary right now. It goes well below the Supreme Court and it will be a period of years before that changes. . . . I think the agencies probably are more of a hope than the courts and even if you don't get as much from the agencies as might be appropriate I think it's still more than anybody would get from the courts."

Howard Glickstein, former Chair,
Presidential Task Force on Civil Rights Reorganization, 1978

The 1978 Supreme Court decision in the case of *Regents of the University of California v. Bakke* (46 L.W. 4896) was perhaps the most discussed court case of recent years. *Bakke* involved a challenge by a white male to a program that reserved 16 of 100 positions for entering medical students at the University of California at Davis for students competing separately in a minority admissions program. (A similar program that reserved five Davis medical school places for students who did not otherwise qualify but whom the dean considered it would be expedient to accept—generally because they had political connections or parents who could be expected to make generous donations to the school—was not even mentioned in the briefs and not faulted as being the possible reason Bakke was denied admission.)

Both before and after the Court's 50,000 word decision, the *Bakke* case and its implications were dissected by virtually every major columnist in every major journal in the country. But with the exception of a few feminist journals, little was said in the commentary about the Court's analysis that distinguished the use of racial classification from gender based classification. Yet, in his passing reference to gender based classification, Justice Lewis F. Powell, Jr. hit upon the essential difficulty faced by women bringing complaints of sex discrimination in the courts:

> More importantly, the perception of racial classifications as inherently odious stems from a lengthy and tragic history that gender-based classifications do not share. In sum, the Court has never viewed such classification as inherently suspect or as comparable to racial or ethnic classifications for the purpose of equal protection analysis.

The intricacies of judicial analysis of sex discrimination have been discussed at great length by others (Babcock et al 1975; Brown et al 1977). We can hardly hope to deal here with every relevant turn of judicial thought or every significant case. We shall try, instead, to provide a framework through which an interested reader can begin to examine cases independently. Most useful to that framework will be two things. First, an idea of the seriousness with which the judiciary cares to examine complaints of discrimination on the basis of sex, and second, a glimpse at the definition of sex discrimination the courts have been willing to accept.

The judicial view of gender based classification provides a starting point. The Supreme Court, over the last few decades, has developed two basic means of examining equal protection issues. In cases where classifications are based on race or ethnicity, and generally in cases where some fundamental constitutional right is at issue, the Court has used the principle of "strict scrutiny" to examine the constitutionality of the law. In other cases it has used a "reasonableless" or "rational relationship" test. In *Sex Discrimination and the Law* (Babcock et al 1975) the difference between the two judicial tests has been excellently outlined. It summarizes as follows:

> With time, it became clear that the Supreme Court would use two tests to determine whether or not a law violated the Equal Protection Clause. In general it applied the reasonableness test. This consisted of asking (1) did the legislature have a constitutionally permissible purpose in view in passing the law in question, and (2) is the classification used reasonably related to accomplishing that purpose? In dealing with legislative distinctions based on race or ethnic origins, the Court began taking a closer look, generally referred to as "strict scrutiny" of the contested law. Strict scrutiny has also been applied to restrictions on certain rights designated "fundamental," such as voting. Scrutinizing strictly, the Court asks (1) did the legislature have a purpose of overriding public importance for passing this law, and (2) were the means chosen by the legislature (the use of a suspect classification or of a classification affecting a fundamental interest) *necessary* to accomplish that purpose? . . .

The difference in outcome, depending on which test is used, is increased by two other factors. These are the requirements under the reasonable test that "if any state of facts reasonably can be conceived that would sustain [the law], the existence of that state of facts at the time the law was enacted must be assumed" and that the person who assails the statutory classification "must carry the burden of showing that it does not rest upon any reasonable basis, but is essentially arbitrary." When the Court uses strict scrutiny, the facts necessary to sustain the law will not be assumed, but must be demonstrated to the Court. Furthermore, the state bears the burden of proof on all issues: whether the legislative purpose is of overwhelming public importance, whether the chosen classification is necessary to accomplish that purpose, and whether less drastic alternatives for accomplishing the purpose are unavailable. Needless to say, the party with the burden of proof is more apt to lose, especially if a factual showing must be made; so the test of reasonableness favors the state, and the strict scrutiny test favors the party challenging the state law (pp. 74-75).

Under strict scrutiny, laws that classify people according to race or ethnicity have been almost inevitably struck down: it is virtually impossible to maintain that they are constitutional. Under the reasonableness test, the opposite situation prevails: it is extremely difficult to maintain that a law is unconstitutional and that it should be struck down. Obviously, cases claiming sex discrimination would benefit from judicial strict scrutiny. And obviously—at least to most feminist thinkers—the parallels between invidious classification based on race and invidious classification based on sex are real and convincing. But despite the continuing efforts by feminist attorneys to bring sex discrimination under the kind of thinking and examination demanded by strict scrutiny, the courts have steadfastly refused to make the break. Reasonableness is, for the most part, the current means for examining issues involving the disparate treatment of women because of their gender.

In a 1948 decision, the Supreme Court provided a classic example of the application of the reasonableness test to a case claiming sex discrimination under a state law. *Goesaert v. Cleary* (335 U.S. 464, 69 S. Ct. 198, 93 L.Ed. 163 [1948]) was brought by four women—a bar owner, the daughter who served as her main employee, a second bar owner, and her female employee—in opposition to a Michigan law that prohibited females from working as bartenders unless they were the wife or daughter of a male bar owner. Women could, however, work as waitresses in a bar. The law had been formulated in postwar 1945 when there was apparently a great deal of pressure from returning veterans for jobs, pressure that often resulted in forcing women from occupations into which they had been welcomed during the war years. A Michigan bartenders' union that prohibited female membership had lobbied extensively for passage of the statute, which seemed motivated by nothing other than the desire to cut competition.

Justice Felix Frankfurter's majority opinion stated that the Michigan legislature unquestionably had the right, if it wished, to prevent *all* women from working as bartenders. But the state did not have the right to "play favorites among women without rhyme or reason." Frankfurter had no problem formulating a reason, however.

> Since bartending by women may, in the allowable legislative judgment, give rise to moral and social problems against which it may devise preventive measures, the legislature need not go to the full length of prohibition if it believes that as to a defined group of females other factors are operating which either eliminate or reduce the moral and social problems otherwise calling for prohibition. Michigan evidently believes that the oversight assured through ownership of a bar by a barmaid's husband or father minimizes hazards that may confront a barmaid without such protecting oversight. . . . Since the line they have drawn is not without a basis in reason, we cannot give ear to the suggestion that the real impulse behind this legislation was an unchivalrous desire of male bartenders to try to monopolize the calling. . . . Nor is it unconstitutional for Michigan to withdraw from women the occupation of bartending because it allows women to serve as waitresses where liquor is dispensed.

In his dissent, Justice Wiley B. Rutledge pointed out:

> The statute arbitrarily discriminates betwen male and female owners of liquor establishments. A male owner, although he himself is always absent from his bar, may employ his wife and daughter as barmaids. A female owner may neither work as a barmaid herself nor employ her daughter in that position, even if a man is always present in the establishment to keep order. This inevitable result of the classification belies the assumption that the statute was motivated by a legislative solicitude for the moral and physical well-being of women who, but for the law, would be employed as barmaids. Since there could be no other conceivable justification for such discrimination against women owners of liquor establishments, the statute should be held invalid as a denial of equal protection.

The dissenters, along with the majority, failed to address the issue of the right of women to seek employment as bartenders, whether or not they were related to bar owners. It would seem that even the dissenters did not object to women who were not related to bar owners being prohibited from working as bartenders. What is more, the Court opinions entirely neglected a central issue: if women must be protected from "moral and social problems" that develop in bars, must the protection consist of prohibiting them from working? Would it not be more logical to take action against the "moral and social" offenders, rather than their victims? (That the Court has continued to buy this peculiarly illogical position is clear from its 1977 decision in *Dothard v. Rawlinson*, discussed in Chapter 2.) Moreover, how, in this case, could the protection of women really be the motive when women were allowed to work as waitresses in bars—positions that obviously placed them in more danger of direct contact with troublesome bar customers?

In 1971 in *Reed v. Reed* (404 U.S. 71 [1971]) the Supreme Court for the first time went beyond the undemanding strictures of the reasonableness test in examining a sex discrimination issue when it wrote:

> To give mandatory preference to members of either sex over members of the other, merely to accomplish the elimination of hearings on the merits, is to make the very kind of arbitrary legislative choice forbidden by the Equal Protection Clause of the Fourteenth Amendment; and whatever may be said as to the positive values of avoiding intrafamily controversy, the choice in this context may not lawfully be mandated solely on the basis of sex. . . .

The case was brought by a woman seeking appointment as administrator of her son's estate. Under an Idaho statute, preference for such appointments went to fathers. The Court ruled that the equal protection clause does permit states to classify people and treat them differently but the basis of that differential treatment must be related to the objective of the legislation. The Idaho law giving preference to males as administrators did have a legitimate purpose, the Court decided, since it did reduce the workload of probate courts by doing away with one class of contestants for the job of estate administrator. However, the Court also held that the purpose, while it had legitimacy, was not forwarded "in a manner consistent with" the equal protection clause.

The case was hailed by feminists as clearing the way for more careful scrutiny by the courts of other sex-based legislative classifications. However, the Court had been careful to avoid the language of strict scrutiny in the *Reed* decision. Instead, Chief Justice Warren E. Burger, who wrote the decision, invoked a kind of intermediate judicial review somewhere between reasonableness and strict scrutiny. The Idaho law that afforded preferential treatment to males, said Burger, "establishes a classification subject to scrutiny under the Equal Protection Clause."

The hopes of feminist attorneys were raised once again in the 1973 Supreme Court term when *Reed* was invoked as precedent in the decision in *Frontiero v. Richardson* (411 U.S. 677 [1973]). The case was brought by Lt. Sharron Frontiero and claimed that the due process clause of the Fifth Amendment was violated by discriminatory statutes that required her to prove her husband was dependent upon her for more than one-half of his support in order to gain housing and other military dependent benefits. Similarly situated men were not required to prove that their wives were dependent upon them for their support in order to gain such benefits. The Court's majority decision, written by Justice William J. Brennan, Jr., was even more promising in its language than *Reed*:

> There can be no doubt that our Nation has had a long and unfortunate history of sex discrimination. Traditionally, such discrimination was rationalized by an attitude of "romantic paternalism" which, in practical effect, put women not on a pedestal, but in a cage. . . .
>
> Moreover, since sex, like race and national origin, is an immutable characteristic determined solely by the accident of birth, the imposition of special disabilities upon members of a particular sex because of their sex would seem to violate "the basic concept of our system that legal burdens should bear some relationship to individual responsibility. . . ." And what differentiates sex from such nonsuspect statutes as intelligence or physical disability, and aligns it with the recognized suspect criteria, is that the sex characteristic frequently bears no relation to ability to perform or contribute to society. As a result, statutory distinctions between the sexes often have the effect of invidiously relegating the entire class of females to inferior legal status without regard to the actual capabilities of its individual members. . . .
>
> With these considerations in mind, we can only conclude that classifications based upon sex, like classifications based upon race, alienage, or national origin, are inherently suspect and must therefore be subjected to strict judicial scrutiny. Applying the analysis mandated by that stricter standard of review it is clear that the statutory scheme now before us is constitutionally invalid.

With *Frontiero* it appeared that the step into strict scrutiny had finally been taken by the Court. But Brennan failed to gain a majority of the Court in support of the strict scrutiny analysis he proclaimed as necessary. Only four justices joined in his opinion. Justice Potter Stewart concurred without addressing the strict scrutiny issue.

In an interesting preview of his 1978 opinion in *Bakke*, Justice Powell wrote in his dissent: "I agree that the challenged statutes constitute an unconstitutional discrimination against service women in violation of the Due Process Clause of the Fifth Amendment, but I cannot join the opinion of Mr. Justice Brennan, which would hold that all classifications based upon sex, 'like classifications based upon race, alienage, and national origin,' are 'inherently suspect and must therefore be subjected to close judicial scrutiny.'"

Powell also provided a display of excessive deference to the legislative branch and to public opinion:

> The Equal Rights Amendment, which if adopted will resolve the substance of this precise question, has been approved by the Congress and submitted for ratification by the States. If this Amendment is duly adopted, it will represent the will of the people accomplished in the manner prescribed by the Constitution. By acting prematurely and unnecessarily, as I view it, the Court has assumed a decisional responsibility at the very time when state legislatures, functioning within the traditional democratic process, are debating the proposed Amendment. It seems to me that this reaching out to pre-empt by judicial action a major political decision which is currently in process of resolution does not reflect appropriate respect for duly prescribed legislative processes.

In 1974 the newly emergent trend begun in *Reed* and *Frontiero* was abruptly halted. *Kahn v. Shevin* (416 U.S. 351 [1974]) involved a Florida law that "provided for some form of property tax exemption for widows." The appellant in the case was a widower who had applied for, and been denied, the same tax exemption automatically granted to widows. The Florida State Supreme Court had found the classification valid and reasonably related to the purpose of the legislation, which was the reduction of "the disparity between the economic capabilities of a man and a woman." The Supreme Court affirmed the decision.

The opinion favoring a sex-based classification was written by Justice William O. Douglas. It read, in part:

> We deal here with a state tax law reasonably designed to further the state policy of cushioning the financial impact of spousal loss upon the sex for whom that loss imposes a disproportionately heavy burden. . . . A state tax law is not arbitrary although it "discriminates in favor of a certain class . . . if the discrimination is founded upon a reasonable distinction, or differences in state policy," not in conflict with the Federal Constitution. . . . The statute before us is well within those limits.

The decision placed sex-based classifications squarely back into the reasonableness test category. The law was found by the Court to be constitutionally permissable and the classification used was judged reasonably related to the purpose of the law.

In 1975 the Supreme Court ruled in a case brought by Navy Lt. Robert C. Ballard, who objected to "up or out" regulations that provided for discharge if male officers were passed over for promotion twice while female officers were not discharged unless they had failed to gain promotion for a full 13 years (Schlesinger v. Ballard, 419 U.S. 498 [1975]). By a five to four majority, the Court ruled that the regulations were acceptable. Writing for the majority, Justice Stewart declared that the Court had overturned rules in *Reed* and *Frontiero* that were "premised on overbroad generalizations that could not be tolerated under the Constitution." In *Ballard*, however, Stewart expanded on the idea of preference arising out of a discriminatory situation. He noted that "the different treatment of men and women naval officers . . . reflects, not archaic and overbroad generalizations, but, instead, the demonstrable fact that male and female line officers in the Navy are *not* similarly situated with respect to opportunities for professional service." Men, said Stewart, were assigned hazardous duty and shipboard duty that provided chances for rapid advancement while women were not.

> Thus, in competing for promotion, female lieutenants will not generally have compiled records of seagoing service comparable to those of male lieutenants. . . . Congress may thus quite rationally have believed that women line officers had less opportunity for promotion than did their male counterparts, and that a longer period of tenure for women officers would, therefore, be consistent with the goal to provide women officers with "fair and equitable career advancement programs."

Stewart's decision also leaned heavily on deference to the legislative branch: "The responsibility for determining how best our Armed Forces shall attend to that business rests with Congress . . . and with the President. . . . We cannot say that in exercising its broad constitutional power here, Congress has violated the Due Process Clause of the Fifth Amendment."

It has been pointed out (Williams 1978, p. 7) that the *Ballard* case has a number of parallels to *Kahn*. In both cases the Court deferred to the legislature and in both it stressed the need to compensate women for some past or current inequity as a rationale for the inequity being challenged in the case.

In his dissent, Justice Brennan stressed the particular irony of the inequity on which the Court majority based its approval of the disparate navy promotion rules:

> I find quite troublesome the notion that gender-based difference in treatment can be justified by another, broader, gender-based difference in treatment imposed by the Navy itself. While it is true that the restrictions upon women officers' opportunities for professional service are not here directly under attack, they are obviously implicated on the

Court's chosen ground for decision and the Court ought at least to consider whether they *may* be valid before sustaining a provision it conceives to be based upon them.

Brennan's point presents an interesting parallel to the earlier *Goesaert* case and the later *Dothard* case. In each case the Court avoids the more general discrimination in the statute under consideration on the presumption that women need some sort of protection—from the moral and social evils present in bars, from the hazards of combat or sea duty in the navy or, in *Dothard*, from the unconstitutionally brutal conditions in a prison. In all three cases the Court has rationalized that it is the women who need protection. Therefore it becomes reasonable, the Court would have us believe, for women to pay the cost of that protection by denying them the right to practice a profession, in *Goeseart* and *Dothard*, or by making their service at lower ranks for longer periods of time inevitable, in *Ballard*.

In two closely parallel social security cases that came before the Court in the mid-1970s the justices seemed more readily to understand the inequities involved. The first case, *Weinberger v. Wiesenfeld* (420 U.S. 636 [1975]) involved a young widower, left with an infant child, who had been told he was not eligible for survivors' benefits because such benefits were reserved for widows only. His child, however, was entitled to social security payments. In a decision written by Justice Brennan, the Court ruled that the social security regulation that prevented Wiesenfeld from gaining survivor's benefits was invalid. It was, said Brennan, based on an

"archaic and overbroad" generalization . . . that male workers' earnings are vital to the support of their families, while the earnings of female wage earners do not significantly contribute to their families' support. . . . Monthly benefits were provided to wives, children, widows, orphans and surviving dependent parents of covered workers. . . . However, children of covered female workers were eligible for survivors' benefits only in limited circumstances, . . . and no benefits whatever were made available to husbands or widowers on the basis of their wives' covered employment. [The regulations, said Brennan,] deprive women of protection for their families which men receive as a result of their employment. . . . Thus, she not only failed to receive for her family the same protection which a similarly situated male worker would have received, but she also was deprived of a portion of her own earnings in order to contribute to the fund out of which benefits would be paid to others.

Califano v. Goldfarb (97 S. Ct. 1021 [1977]) involved a retired widower who sought survivors' benefits based on the earnings of a deceased wife with a lengthy history of working and contributing social security taxes. Goldfarb challenged the provision of the social security regulations that allowed widows to gain survivors' benefits without question while burdening widowers with providing proof of a minimum of one-half dependency of their wives. Quoting his own opinion in *Weisenfeld*, Justice Brennan, writing for the majority, stated that the rule "operates 'to deprive women of protection for their families which men receive as a result of their employment.' . . ."

It is indeed true that gender based inequities were raised in both *Weisenfeld* and *Goldfarb* and that the Court properly recognized and corrected the inequities. And it is indeed true that women workers are entitled to the assurance that their contributions to the social security system will benefit their surviving family members in the same manner as the contributions of male workers benefit their surviving family members. However, the women involved could hardly feel "deprived" since they, and "similarly situated male worker(s)" were dead. The benefits, in these two cases, would seem more realistically to have fallen to the male survivors rather than to their dead mates.

Without faulting the Court as to the outcome of these cases, it should be pointed out that the justices in these decisions and in a number of others have displayed a certain amount of fuzziness in their thinking about benefits and burdens. In *Weisenfeld* and *Goldfarb* genuine benefits are viewed by the Court as accruing to women who are not around to enjoy them rather than to the men who are. In *Ballard*, on the other hand, the somewhat dubious benefit of being allowed to stay at lower rank and pay for longer time periods is showered upon female Navy officers while male officers take home the dubious burden of opportunity for rapid promotion. Even in *Frontiero* the benefit is depicted as accruing to the woman officer who now can unquestionably provide housing for her husband rather than upon the husband, who is now relieved of the burden of contributing to his own housing.

It would be incorrect, of course, to insist that the Court has consistently ruled against equity when the benefit is likely to accrue to females while ruling for equity when the benefit accrues to males. However, there does seem to be a tendency on the part of the male justices to have considerably less difficulty understanding inequity when it is the male who genuinely bears its burden. Since *Reed* and *Frontiero* the Court has ruled in two major disability benefit cases. In both cases the justices again displayed an inability to recognize inequities in benefits received by female workers. The cases also focus sharply on a major difficulty the Court has had in grasping discrimination that is based upon a sex-linked characteristic.

In the 1974 case of *Geduldig v. Aiello* (417 U.S. 484 [1974]), Justice Potter Stewart, writing for the Court majority, rules that a California administered disability insurance plan that covered such sex and race singular disabilities as hemophilia, prostate operations, circumcisions, and sickle cell anemia, but failed to cover pregnancy related disabilities, was not discriminatory. "There is no risk from which men are protected and women are not. Likewise, there is no risk from which women are protected and men are not," wrote Stewart. In a footnote he added: "The California insurance program does not exclude anyone from benefit eligibility because of gender but merely removes one physical condition—pregnancy—from the list of compensable disabilities. While it is true that only women can become pregnant, it does not follow that every legislative classification concerning pregnancy is a sex based classification. . . ."

In his dissenting opinion, Justice Brennan pointed out that the plan covered

> virtually all disabling conditions without regard to cost, voluntariness, uniqueness, predictability, or "normalcy" of the disability. . . . In my view, by singling out for less favorable treatment a gender-linked disability peculiar to women, the State has created a double standard for disability compensation. . . . Such dissimilar treatment of men and women on the basis of physical characteristics inextricably linked to one sex, inevitably constitutes sex discrimination.

Brennan also turned his attention to the new, intermediate standard of scrutiny for gender based classification that had begun to emerge in *Reed* and *Frontiero:*

> In the past, when a legislative classification has turned on gender, the Court has justifiably applied a standard of judicial scrutiny more strict than that generally accorded economic or social welfare programs. . . . Yet, by its decision today, the Court appears willing to abandon that higher standard of review without satisfactorily explaining what differentiates the gender-based classification employed in this case from those found unconstitutional in *Reed* and *Frontiero.* The Court's decision threatens to return men and women to a time when "traditional" equal protection analysis sustained legislative classifications that threated differently members of a particular sex solely because of their sex.

Indeed, as Brennan pointed out, the majority had wholly reverted in *Geduldig* to the old reasonableness test and had concluded that California had a reasonable legislative purpose in excluding pregnancy related benefits from its program and that the exclusion was rationally related to the legislative purpose.

In *General Electric Company v. Gilbert* (429 U.S. 125 [1976]) the Court faced the same issues raised in *Geduldig* except that they had been brought under Title VII of the Civil Rights Act instead of the Fourteenth Amendment. But, again, the Court concluded that the General Electric disability plan did not discriminate, though it covered sports related injuries, injuries incurred while committing a crime, prostate, circumcision, and hair transplants, but excluded pregnancy related disabilities.

Two aspects of the *Gilbert* decision, written by Justice William Rehnquist, are particularly disturbing. First, Rehnquist chose to depend on *Geduldig* for much of his reasoning. He even quotes the *Geduldig* finding that there is "no risk from which men are protected and women are not . . ." and "no risk from which women are protected and men are not." Thus he reinforces the Court majority in its notion that the only possible sex discrimination occurs in instances where men and women are treated differently with respect to a shared situation or characteristic. According to this conceptualization, discrimination based on an immutable characteristic linked to one sex simply cannot exist. In Chapter 2 we developed our own definition of discrimination: it is simply disparate treatment or a disparate impact based on an irrelevant characteristic such as sex. The exclusion from disability coverage in both *Geduldig* and *Gilbert* fits the definition: women are being denied coverage solely bacause of a characteristic that is immutably female. Most of the justices of the Supreme Court have yet to see the point.

Even more alarming, though *Gilbert* was a Title VII case, Rehnquist chose to look to equal protection analysis for a touchstone, thus making explicit a double standard for the analysis of Title VII cases. After noting that Title VII makes it unlawful to discriminate on the basis of "race, color, religion, sex or national origin," Rehnquist writes,

> While there is no necessary inference that Congress, in choosing this language, intended to incorporate into Title VII the concepts of discrimination which have evolved from court decisions construing the Equal Protection Clause of the Fourteenth Amendement, the similarities between the congressional language and some of those decisions surely indicate that the latter are a useful starting point in interpreting the former.

Thus, although Title VII makes no distinction whatever in the requirements of the law when applied to race discrimination as opposed to sex discrimination, Rehnquist has explicitly introduced the two tiered scrutiny of equal protection where strict scrutiny must be used in examining issues of race and ethnic discrimination while the less rigorous reasonableness test is all that is required for sex discrimination. In *Gilbert* he avoids carrying the point further since he first addresses the discrimination issue and finds, as with *Geduldig*, that "(s)ince gender based discrimination has not been shown to exist either by the terms of the plan or by its effect, there was no need to reach the question of what sort of standard would govern our review had there been such a showing." Nonetheless, his analysis introduces the very serious implication that Title VII, though written identically for blacks and women, can be applied more rigorously for blacks and less rigorously for women.

Rehnquist's failure to recognize the possibility of discrimination based on attributes exclusively linked to one sex caused the court to come up with some remarkable hair splitting in two subsequent decisions. In *Nashville Gas v. Satty* (98 S. Ct. 347 [1977]) Rehnquist once again wrote the Court opinion. Here he drew a shaky line between benefits and burdens and between insurance payments for pregnancy related disability and seniority that might be lost when a woman takes pregnancy leave. Nashville Gas maintained a policy that required women to take pregnancy leave during which they received no compensation. Further, they lost all accumulated seniority during such leaves. Seniority rights were retained by employees on all other types of disability leave. Rehnquist's majority opinion confirmed the validity of the imposed, nonpaid maternity leave but rejected the loss of seniority as discriminatory.

Rehnquist pointed out that in *Gilbert*, "there was no showing that General Electric's policy of compensating all non job-related disabilities except pregnancy favored men over women." Similarly, the Nashville Gas policy was neutral and nondiscriminatory on its face. However, in *Griggs v. Duke Power Co.*, the Court recognized that "both intentional discrimination and policies neutral on their face but having a discriminatory effect" may violate Title VII. At this point Rehnquist seems to have gone a step beyond *Gilbert*. In *Gilbert* the failure to pay pregnancy benefits was merely an exclusion of one disability from an insurance plan. Here he insisted that payment would mean women received a benefit "that men cannot and do not receive." On the other hand, to deny seniority rights was to "impose on women a substantial burden that men need not suffer."

Rehnquist went on to insist: "The distinction between benefits and burdens is more than one of semantics." While Title VII does not require that employees of one sex gain greater benefits, neither does it "permit an employer to burden female employees in such a way as to deprive them of employment opportunities because of their different roles.

By insisting that pregnancy related disability payments would constitute an added benefit for women in which men could not share, Rehnquist left himself open to some questions. How, for example, would he characterize disability payments for prostate operations or circumcision? And why should they be allowed to stand merely as sex neutral coverage of certain conditions to the nondiscriminatory exclusion of other conditions such as pregnancy related disabilities?

The absurdity of the arguments produced another turgid bit of reasoning by Justice John P. Stevens in *City of Los Angeles v. Manhart* (46 L.W. 4347 [1978]). The City of Los Angeles Department of Water and Power maintained a retirement plan that, like many similar plans around the country, required women to make larger contributions than men. The differential was based on actuarial tables that show that women, on the average, live longer than men and could thus gain larger accumulated retirement benefits, on average. Stevens distinguished between the pension case and *Gilbert* by asserting that General Electric's disability plan involved two groups of people: pregnant and nonpregnant persons. Since all pregnant persons were female but all nonpregnant persons were not necessarily male, there was no discrimination in leaving pregnancy out of the General Electirc disability plan. In the Los Angeles case, however, all women were required to pay higher pension contributions than all men. The pension plan then "discriminates on the basis of sex whereas the General Electric plan discriminated on the basis of a physical disability." The actuarial tables were an improper means of determining worker contributions since not all women live longer than the average man while some men live longer than the average women.

In his dissenting opinion, Chief Justice Burger insisted that the gender based actuarial tables were a valid basis for pension contributions. While the unequal contributions did have the effect of reducing the compensation paid to females as compared to males, Title VII allows for such reduced pay when there is "a differential based on any factor other than sex. . . ." In this case, said Burger, the other factor was longevity. (We might well ask if Burger would buy the same argument in relation to blacks and whites since it can be shown that whites on average live longer than blacks. Would Burger argue, then, that whites should pay higher pension contributions?)

The two cases, while they did provide significant employment gains for women in the form of fairer pension schemes and improved seniority rights, did nothing to advance or clarify the law. On the contrary, they seem to have given the justices the opportunity to dig themselves further into a hole—a hole apparent to feminist thinkers if not to the justices— from which it is going to require considerable effort to extricate the Court.

The Court, as we might have expected, is making no effort to extricate itself. In two 1978 decisions regarding the rights of students the justices made this clear. *Board of Curators of the University of Missouri v. Horowitz* (46 L.W. 4079) involved a challenge by a woman medical student to her dismissal shortly before graduation. Charlotte Horowitz had been dismissed after compiling an outstanding academic record on the basis of criticism that surrounded her personal appearance and hygiene. Horowitz had been criticized by professors (but not by patients) in her clinical work for wearing dirty lab coats and for inadequately cleaned fingernails. As one medical faculty member put.it in courtroom testimony, "in the eyes of the members of the medical school community, she did not exemplify what they were looking for in terms of personal appearance." According to a student, she was "overweight, unattractive and unkempt, but not uncleanly." And according to Horowitz, "I always wear red nail polish. I don't know how you can see dirt through red nail polish. My lab coats were washed every week, even if they weren't the whitest."

In Horowitz' brief to the Supreme Court, her attorney wrote:

> Finally, the dismissal of Horowitz was arbitrary because it was based in large part upon her sex, female, and her personal appearance . . . because of her sex and appearance she was held to standards of achievement and performance that were not expected of male students. In spite of her brilliant academic record, Horowitz was dismissed from the Medical School because, in large part, she did not meet the appearance standards of the institution, in spite of prior knowledge by school officials that her appearance did not fit the program of the school.

The question that most urgently needed asking in the Horowitz case was: would a similarly situated man—overweight, unkempt, and "unattractive" but academically brilliant—have been similarly treated. For anyone who has even casually observed the appearance of some male M.D.s the answer is obvious. But the Supreme Court did not even bother to ask the question. Instead, in an opinion written by Rehnquist, the court ruled that Horowitz received all the due process to which she was entitled. Even though her academic record was unquestionably excellent and the reasons given for her dismissal concerned her manner and appearance in clinical rotations, Rehnquist characterized the dismissal as "academic" rather than disciplinary and therefore as a dismissal for which the traditional great deference must be allowed to the academic faculty.

In a 1975 case involving a ten day disciplinary suspension of a student from a public school (*Goss v. Lopez*, 419 U.S. 565 [1975]), the Court had ruled that the student had been denied sufficient due process and held "that the student be given oral and written notice of the charges against him and, if he denies them, an explanation of the evidence the authorities have and an opportunity to present his side of the story." In *Horowitz*, where what was at stake was a career rather than a ten day suspension from high school, Rehnquist insisted that "less stringent procedural requirements" were called for because the case involved "an academic dismissal . . . federal courts have recognized that there are distinct differences between decisions to suspend or dismiss a student for disciplinary purposes and similar actions taken for academic reasons which may call for hearings in connection with the former but not the latter."

The sex discrimination charge was apparently of so little consequence that Rehnquist relegated it to a footnote:

> Respondent alleges that the school applied more stringent standards in evaluating her performance than that of other students because of her sex, religion, and physical appearance. The Distirct Court, however, found that "(t)here was no evidence that [respondent] was in any manner evaluated differently from other students because of her sex or because of her religion. With regard to respondent's physical appearance, this in and of itself did not cause [her] to be evaluated any differently than any of the other students."

While sex discrimination was at issue in *Horowitz* and was cursorily dismissed in a footnote, it was not at issue in a second recent case of student rights in professional schools, the *Bakke* case. Nonetheless, Justice Powell, who wrote the opinion for a badly divided court, went out of his way to comment on such discrimination. Since the question raised by *Bakke* involved a racial classification—Bakke had charged that he was excluded because he was a white male—Powell ruled that the case demanded "the most exacting judicial examination." He held that the Davis minority admissions program did not pass muster since it foreclosed consideration for the minority program positions for persons such as Bakke. He therefore ordered that Bakke be admitted to medical school. On the other hand, he held that the goal of achieving minority representation in medical schools was sufficiently important to warrant special affirmative action admissions programs. Such programs, as outlined in the opinion, would involve nothing more than consciously adding race to the existing considerations for medical school admission.

Powell gave considerable attention to his justification for using strict scrutiny in the Bakke case. He traced the evolution of judicial thinking concerning the nature of strict scrutiny. He then pointed out that the notion that strict scrutiny was reserved under the Fourteenth Amendment for blacks and blacks alone had been eliminated by the Court over two decades earlier (*Hernandez v. Texas*, 347 U.S. 475 [1954]). He concluded: "When they touch upon an individual's race or ethnic background he is entitled to a judicial determination that the burden he is asked to bear on that basis is precisely tailored to serve a compelling governmental interest. The Constitution guarantees that right to every person regardless of his background."

But he did not drop the matter there. Instead he gratuitously went on to assure his readers that he did not by any means wish to imply that the rights guaranteed to every person extended to women bringing issues of sex discrimination. The reference to gender based discrimination is worth repeating *in toto*:

> Nor is petitioner's view as to the applicable standard supported by the fact that gender-based classifications are not subject to this level of scrutiny. Gender-based distinctions are less likely to create the analytical and practical problems presented in preferential programs premised on racial or ethnic criteria. With respect to gender there are only two possible classifications. The incidence of the burdens imposed by preferential classification is clear. There are no rival groups who can claim that they, too, are entitled to preferential treatment. Classwide questions as to the group suffering injury and groups which fairly can be burdened are relatively manageable for reviewing courts. The resolution of these same questions in the context of racial and ethnic preferences presents far more complex and more intractable problems than gender-based classifications. More importantly, the perception of racial classifications as inherently odious stems from a lengthy and tragic history that gender-based classifications do not share. In sum, the Court has never viewed such classification as inherently suspect or as comparable to racial or ethnic classifications for the purpose of equal protection analysis.

———— *Chapter Fourteen* ————

REORGANIZATION

"You're talking about merging EEOC with HEW with Labor and if the whole is the sum of its parts, think of the parts you are putting together. . . ."

Lawrence Lorber, former Director,
Office of Federal Contract Compliance Programs, 1976

After taking office in January 1977, President Jimmy Carter authorized the formation of a Task Force on Civil Rights Reorganization within the Office of Management and Budget. The task force mandate was to examine the government's hydra-headed civil rights enforcement scheme—first in employment and then in other areas—and to come up with comprehensive recommendations for overhauling the entire mechanism. The direction the task force was likely to take had already been spelled out by the U.S. Commission on Civil Rights and by the Subcommittee on Equal Opportunities of the House Committee on Education and Labor.

Following its 1975 examination of the major enforcement agencies, the Commission on Civil Rights recommended "that within the next year the president propose and the Congress enact legislation consolidating all federal equal employment enforcement responsibility in a new agency, the National Employment Rights Board, with broad administrative, as well as litigative, authority to eliminate discriminatory employment practices in the United States" (U.S. Commission on Civil Rights 1975b, p. 649).

Eighteen months later the House Subcommitee on Equal Opportunities echoes the Commission and recommended the elimination of multiple enforcement agencies: "Arguments for retaining a many-headed enforcement structure . . . have proven false, and the current structure is both cumbersome and ineffective." The subcommittee staff recommended "consolidating equal employment opportunity enforcement authority in the Equal Employment Opportunity Commission" (U.S. House, 1976a, p. 15).

By 1977 and the advent of a new administration, nothing had been done to further consolidation and the Commission on Civil Rights, in its follow-up report on employment discrimination enforcement, again stressed the need for immediate action:

> In *Volume V*, this Commission reported that the Federal effort to end employment discrimination had "not been equal to the task," and in the year and one half between the publication of that volume and the end of 1976, Federal enforcement of equal employment opportunity laws has not measurably improved. . . . This commission reaffirms its recommendation for the creation of a single agency, enforcing equal employment opportunity under a single law, and notes the growing acceptance of this concept. . . . It is the Commission's view that currently the Government can most effectively achieve its goal of improving equal employment opportunities by reducing the number of Federal agencies to which enforcement responsibilities are assigned, consolidating related equal employment opportunity functions in this cluster of agencies (U.S. Commission on Civil Rights 1977a, p. 333).

By 1977 the Commission had recognized that immediate legislative action to restructure the equal employment opportunity laws and create a single, powerful agency must become a long-range goal. Indeed, the climate in Congress was sufficiently conservative that many believed opening up the equal employment area to congressional scrutiny would lead to a severe weakening of the current laws. The Commission decided it would be better to settle for a reduction in the number of competing agencies that seemed busily engaged in blunting each other's enforcement efforts.

Opposition to consolidation had lessened by 1977. That it had existed at all outside the agencies that were competing to maintain their piece of the action, jobs, and power was the result of years of growing paranoia among civil rights advocates. They had simply become afraid that a single, highly visible agency would make an easy target for a hostile administration or Congress. "We've always feared centralizing all of civil rights enforcement in one place," said HEW Office for Civil Rights official Michael Middleton. Speaking for "civil rights movement people" both inside and outside the government, Middleton expressed doubts about the safety of a single agency.

I mean it's just too easy for a Nixon to come in and grab that and just throw it away. And if you're got it spread around in different little power groups around the government it makes it much more difficult for anybody to dismantle the system. And so there's a serious danger in consolidating everything in one place for that simple reason. Carter may be Mr. Civil Rights, but the next one may not be and that danger certainly exists. . . . Ideally, I'd go for consolidation in one place, but that's a naive approach to take when you recognize that administrations change, that the mood changes.

Howard Glickstein, who headed the presidential task force and whose civil rights advocacy includes serving for several years as staff director of the U.S. Commission on Civil Rights, admits that he, too, had been suspicious of consolidation. He began his task force chores with "a bias for leaving [enforcement] in the agencies, especially in the contract compliance area." The original idea of contract compliance was to place civil rights responsibility on every federal agency involved in acquiring goods and services for the government, he explains. Civil rights groups thought that the system would work if civil rights became a part of every government contract program and if every government official felt she or he had some responsibility to see that the program was carried out. They feared that separating civil rights from other program responsibilities would allow projects to progress to the point where it would be too late to do anything to assure compliance. Building construction, for example, could be near completion before a separate compliance agency became aware of a construction contractor's civil rights failures. Civil rights advocates, Glickstein explains,

felt that every government official had taken an oath to enforce the law and that's where responsibility should be. What changed his mind, says Glickstein, was the realization that it was impractical, that it wasn't going to happen, that there was so much pressure on government officials to see that their programs were carried out that they would always compromise on civil rights, always cut back on civil rights. On the other hand, if it were run centrally, as a law enforcement program with people who had the responsibility for monitoring contracts not being the same people who were responsible to obtain whatever goods were been contracted for it would work more efficiently. By and large the [contracting] companies found that they had very little difficulty with agencies they actually contracted with—they usually could work something out.

The task force, says Glickstein, ultimately concluded that giving a responsibility to the people that sign the contracts to also insure that civil rights obligations are met just presents a conflict of interest that can

never be overcome . . . we've tried doing it for 35 years and it hasn't
worked and it's now time to try something else.

Although a number of civil rights advocates remained suspicious of
placing too much equal employment enforcement power in one place,
opposition to consolidation generally relaxed during Carter's first year in
the White House. Meanwhile, the task force on reorganization moved
toward a series of proposals that would eliminate most of the competing
federal agencies or remove employment enforcement power from them.

By October 1977 the task force had completed its analysis and
compiled preliminary recommendations for approval by the director of
the Office of Management and Budget and for transmittal to the president. The report noted that almost 40 separate laws and executive orders
existed in the equal employment area and that they were enforced by 18
separate departments and agencies—a situation that produced, among
other things, "inconsistent investigative and enforcement efforts," "waste
and inefficiency," "absence of articulated goals and direction," and
"confusion on the part of workers about how and where to seek redress."
It concluded: "It should come as no surprise, therefore, that discrimination in employment on the basis of factors such as race, national origin,
sex, age and handicap is still a pervasive phenomenon in American life"
(Daily Labor Report 1977, p. G-1).

The task force proposed three alternative plans for presidential
consideration. One called for an immediate merger of all equal employment enforcement activities within the federal government into a single
agency. The second called for the consolidation and reorganization of
some equal employment regulatory functions to avoid duplication with
an eye toward later consolidation into a single agency. The third, a band-
aid approach, called for continuing the existing structure with minor
changes, improved coordination and management, and a larger level of
funding.

Over the long range, says Glickstein, the task force recommendation
was that "the president set as a goal a single purpose equal employment
agency and that the EEOC be that agency and that we move toward
consolidating all equal employment opportunity programs in the EEOC
over a period of years. . . . I think we've found in this country that any
time you really want to get something done effectively you put it all in one
place. . . . At least if you have one agency there is more accountability.
You know who you have to put the pressure on. You know who is not
doing the job." However, in recognition of the difficulties of achieving
instant and effective consolidation, the task force recommended the two
step process that would bring major structural changes immediately but
would not integrate equal employment enforcement into a single agency

for several years. The major reason for the alternative selected was the belief of task force members that given the past leadership and management problems of the lead agencies, no agency could be expected to function well immediately if the entire burden were shifted to it.

The task force therefore recommended that major equal employment functions be split between the Office of Federal Contract Compliance Programs of the Department of Labor, which would handle compliance by federal contractors, and the Equal Employment Opportunity Commission, which would take on the bulk of noncontract related enforcement. All authority under executive orders 11246 and 11375 would be taken from the 11 compliance enforcement agencies and transferred to the OFCCP, where it would remain for at least two years. The task force concluded:

> Because of its size and past program deficiencies, transfer of the OFCCP to the EEOC at this time would create enormous management difficulties and interfere with the implementation of other reforms by the EEOC. . . . At the end of two years, after there has been a sufficient opportunity for the consolidated contract compliance program to become operational, the President should determine whether the time is appropriate to transfer the contract compliance program . . . to the EEOC (Daily Labor Report 1977, p. G-1).

Under the consolidation, OFCCP would retain responsibility under Section 503 of the Rehabilitation Act of 1973 and Section 402 of the Vietnam Era Veteran's Readjustment Assistance Act of 1974, since both laws are based on the federal government's contract powers.

EEOC, which the task force recommended should ultimately inherit the contract compliance programs, would, during the first step, take over enforcement of the Age Discrimination in Employment Act of 1967 and the Equal Pay Act of 1963, as amended. Before reorganization, both authorities rested with the Department of Labor. Under the plan, EEOC was also to take over from the Civil Service Commission enforcement of Title VII, the Equal Pay Act, and the Age Discrimination Act as they applied to federal employees. The task force commented:

> The credibility of the Federal equal employment opportunity enforcement effort, as it applies to its own employees, has been and continues to be poor. The record of the Civil Service Commission in this regard has been the subject of harsh criticism. Employees of the Federal Government believe that they are not accorded as much protection from employment discrimination as are their counterparts in private industry. Private employers believe that the Federal Government subjects them

to more stringent requirements than the government is willing to place upon itself (Daily Labor Report 1977, p. G-2).

The task force also recommended abolishing the Equal Employment Opportunity Coordinating Council and transferring its duties to the EEOC. The Council had been established by the 1972 amendments to Title VII in an effort to bring about some interagency cooperation in the equal employment enforcement area. It had, instead, become an arena for constant interagency bickering.

In a major break from its primary philosophy of eventually housing all enforcement within a single agency, the task force recommended that the Department of Justice retain authority to litigate pattern and practice suits under Title VII against state and local government employers "(i)n light of the record and expertise of the Department" (p. G-2). Pattern and practice suits are major actions dealing with company-wide or agency-wide policies or practices deemed to have an adverse impact on women or minorities as a class.

Following its recommendations on procedural change, the task force set out a number of suggestions for changes in Title VII law. The major change proposed was granting cease and desist powers to the EEOC—a change that would enable the agency to establish a system similar to that of the National Labor Relations Board, using administrative law judges with the power to hold hearings and issue orders requiring employers to cease their use of any discriminatory practices the hearings might uncover. Other changes included amending Title VII to prohibit age and handicap discrimination and clarifying the right of the attorney general and of EEOC to bring large scale class actions against industries engaged in discriminatory patterns and practices. The task force also recommended that Title VI of the Civil Rights Act of 1964 be amended to cover employment discrimination. However, the task force was careful to avoid any implication that reorganization required an immediate congressional effort to change existing laws. Such a legislative effort was placed in the vague and indefinite future: "The Task Force further recommends that you [the president] announce that upon completion of the full study of all civil rights programs you intend to propose a comprehensive civil rights bill covering all civil rights areas" (p. G-2).

There were several reasons for the reluctance to rush immediately to Congress, according to Glickstein. One was that some question still remained as to whether or not cease and desist powers would be necessary. There remain civil rights advocates who believe a good litigation strategy can be as useful as a structure based on hearings before administrative law judges leading to cease and desist orders. In light of the present doubts about the judiciary, however, the usefulness of litigation is at least doubtful. But Glickstein points out that the difficulties in creating a smoothly functioning administrative law structure and the difficulties in obtaining cease and desist legislation from Congress are overwhelming. Creating an administrative law capacity within the EEOC would be impossible, he believes, while the agency is attempting to overcome its internal management problems and integrate a large new component of enforcement authority into its current structure. But most important, says Glickstein, is the current mood of Congress toward civil rights legislation. "From a very practical point of view," he says, "I think any equal employment legislation that is proposed now would emerge as the Allan Bakke memorial bill and I think it would be a very, very dangerous thing to do in this Congress. It would just result in affirmative action programs being gutted. There would be nothing left of them after that legislation."

Opposition to the task force reorganization plan came from several quarters, according to Glickstein. Many of the executive order agencies opposed losing their authority to the Office of Federal Contract Compliance Programs. However, the opposition never became serious. There was little in the way of lobbying the compliance agencies were able to do since their authority was a matter of executive order. The Department of Labor strongly opposed the loss of its equal pay authority and gained considerable support for its position in Congress. For a time the AFL/CIO also opposed transfer of the equal pay authority to EEOC. The opposition was blunted, however, when women's groups that had at first expressed concern over the transfer became convinced that equal pay enforcement would not be lost in the wider Title VII effort if the transfer were delayed one year. It became difficult for the labor organization to insist that the authority not be transferred when groups representing those most directly affected agreed to it. The Civil Service Commission, which was very unhappy with the loss of Title VII responsibilities to the EEOC, did lobby successfully in Congress to retain some of its authority.

While no direct opposition to the plan came from presidential advisers, there was, says Glickstein, an antienforcement attitude among some White House staffers:

> There are many people in this country, and many of them on the White House staff, who think we have solved problems of discrimination and that the problems that exist today in this country are very different. They are economic problems. We have to deal with the economy. [They feel] that the civil rights laws are just sort of an archaic bit from the past. They've really done their job and we [should] just let them move along with limited resources and just appease some people. I think there is that general view. . . . There's a group of people at

Harvard who have said that the way to achieve greater equality in this country is not through enforcement of civil rights but through economic initiatives of one sort or another. . . . So I think there are a lot of people who just don't give the enforcement of civil rights laws a very high priority. They don't think it's worth the energy and the aggravation and the hostility that it creates and [they] would just as soon try to bring about change in other ways.

President Carter sent the reorganization proposal to Congress on February 23, 1978. In his message to Congress on the plan—his first major pronouncement on civil rights enforcement since taking office—the president emphasized the importance of the equal employment area to civil rights in general:

Fair employment is too vital for haphazard enforcement. My Administration will aggressively enforce our civil rights laws. Although discrimination in any area has severe consequences, limiting economic opportunity affects access to education, housing and health care. I, therefore, ask you to join with me to reorganize administration of the civil rights laws and to begin that effort by reorganizing the enforcement of those laws which ensure an equal opportunity to a job" (Carter 1978, p. 1).

The first executive order banning job discrimination was issued by President Roosevelt in the 1940s, said Carter. Since that time a number of executive orders have been issued and a number of laws enacted.

But each new prohibition against discrimination unfortunately has brought with it a further dispersal of Federal equal employment opportunity responsibility. This fragmentation of authority among a number of Federal agencies has meant confusion and ineffective enforcement for employees, regulatory duplication and needless expense for employers.

I am proposing today a series of steps to bring coherence to the equal employment enforcement effort. These steps, to be accomplished by the Reorganization Plan and Executive Orders, constitute an important step toward consolidation of equal employment opportunity enforcement.

The timetable announced by the president was: On July 1, 1978, the Equal Employment Opportunity Coordinating Council would be abolished. Its authority to coordinate agencies and set enforcement policy would be transferred to EEOC. On October 1, 1978, the equal employment enforcement authority of the Civil Service Commission would be shifted to the EEOC along with 100 positions and a budget addition of $6.5 million. On July 1, 1979, responsibility for enforcing the Equal Pay

Act and the Age Discrimination in Employment Act would be shifted to the EEOC along with 317 positions and an added $8.8 million. The plan also clarified the authority of the attorney general to file Title VII pattern and practice suits—an authority that had been challenged in the courts due to conflicting language in the 1972 amendments to Title VII. Congress had the authority to disapprove these parts of the President's plan by a two-thirds vote of either house within 60 days of the introduction of the plan.

The rest of the plan concerned contract compliance programs, over which Congress had no authority. The president therefore announced that he would issue an executive order on October 1, 1978, that would eliminate the compliance responsibilities of 11 federal agencies previously handling executive orders 11246 and 11375 and transfer that authority to the Office of Federal Contract Compliance Programs.

His proposal, the president announced, would "reduce from fifteen to three the number of Federal agencies having important equal employment opportunity responsibilities under Title VII of the Civil Rights Act of 1964 and Federal Contract Compliance provisions" (Carter 1978, p. 3). The three agencies were the EEOC, the OFCCP, and the Department of Justice. Carter concluded: "This reorganization will produce consistent agency standards, as well as increased accountability. Combined with the intense commitment of those charged with these responsibilities, it will become possible for us to accelerate this nation's progress in ensuring equal job opportunities for all our people" (p. 6).

As expected, Carter's reorganization plan proved acceptable to Congress and its provisions went into effect on schedule, but not without some changes along the way. In his message, Carter had pointed out that the initial consolidation and the coordinating authority granted to EEOC would "bring overlap and duplication to a minimum" (p. 5). But in at least two major areas of enforcement the promise could not be fulfilled. In both education and federal government employment, the enforcement scheme either remained as complicated as it had been before the consolidation or became more complicated. Roughly 5,170,000 of America's 31,000,000 working women are employed in these two areas. (U.S. Department of Labor 1977, p. 7). Almost one-fifth of all female workers in the United States failed to benefit by the consolidation. What is more, since women professionals are concentrated in these two areas, the effect on enforcement for them is likely to be even more noticeable.

In education the enforcement scheme before consolidation gave Title VII authority to the EEOC. The Equal Pay Act was the province of the Wage and Hour Division of the Department of Labor. And, although the Department of Labor's Office of Federal Contract Compliance Programs maintained minimal supervisory authority, the enforcement of the executive order was left to the Office of Civil Rights of HEW. In addition, Title IX of the Education Amendments of 1972 was the province of HEW's OCR. The Justice Department maintained the right to sue in Title VII cases against public employers.

Under the new scheme, EEOC will retain Title VII authority and gains authority over the Equal Pay Act. The Justice Department retains a major role, on paper at least, since it, rather than EEOC, can litigate in cases against public employers and since most education institutions and school districts are public. Executive order enforcement is transferred to OFCCP. However, HEW's Office for Civil Rights maintains authority to enforce Title IX.

HEW's authority to investigate employment complaints under Title IX has been challenged in the courts on a number of occasions, and in every instance district courts have ruled that the law does not extend to employment. In *Romeo Community Schools v. United States Department of Health, Education and Welfare* (483 F. Supp. [1977]) for example, the small Michigan school district bringing suit readily admitted that its collective bargaining agreement violated certain provisions of Title IX regulations but contended that Title IX does not apply to education employment in any case but only to student affairs.

HEW countered the argument by citing the legislative history of the law, pointing out that it had originally been shaped to parallel Title VI, which has an exclusion for all employment except employment "where a primary objective of the Federal financial assistance is to provide employment." The provision excluding most employment was dropped from Title IX in its Senate version and the compromise bill followed that version. The Senate sponsor for the bill, Birch Bayh, was quoted by HEW in its brief: "More specifically, the heart of this amendment is a provision banning sex discrimination in educational programs receiving Federal funds. The amendment would cover such crucial aspects as admission procedures, scholarships and faculty employment, with limited exceptions" (*Congressional Record*, February 28, 1972). HEW also noted that during the House hearings, Representative Patsy Mink had said:

> the legislative history of Title IX indicates that employment was indeed covered by the broad mandate of the law for non-discrimination on the basis of sex. The original House bill included an exemption for employment patterned after the exemption in Title VI of the Civil Rights Act. The Senate version contained no such exemption, indicating that employment was covered. In conference, the language of the Senate version was adopted.

The basic provision of Title IX is quite simple: "No person in the United States shall, on the basis of sex, be excluded from participation in, be denied the benefits of, or be subjected to discrimination under any education program or activity receiving Federal financial assistance. . . ."

The federal district court judge in *Romeo* however ruled that

> (t)he absence of an explicit provision in Title IX . . . excluding employment discrimination from its coverage does not show a congressional intent to make Title IX broader than Title VI in this respect. Rather, this discrepancy must be traced to the fact that Title IX was enacted as part of a larger legislative program which also included an amendment to Title VII of the Civil Rights Act of 1964, . . . enlarging the scope of *that* provision to include sex discrimination in employment, as well as an amendment to the Equal Pay Act, giving the Secretary of Labor authority to regulate sex discrimination in educational employee compensation.

Perhaps the judge did not say what he meant, but he was clearly in error in respect to Title VII: it had covered sex discrimination from the start, though the 1972 amendments broadened its coverage to include faculty employees of educational institutions. He seemed, in any case, to be reading into Congress motives that were very different from those expressed in the legislative history of the law.

Moreover, common sense would seem to dictate that a law requiring that "no person" be subjected to discrimination in education programs that receive federal assistance would include teachers, who are as much "persons" as are students, and who are clearly affected by the receipt of federal funds by their school districts. The judge, like his fellow judge on the Supreme Court in the *Bakke* decision, seemed to have some difficulty equating "persons" with women. He insisted that the law "is concerned solely and simply with sex discrimination against students." He even insisted that the law covered only *some* but not all programs in districts receiving federal funds. It was written, he said, "not to cover all forms of sex discrimination in education, but only to cover the wide variety of education programs funded by the federal government and the many ways in which sex discrimination against students in those programs can be manifested."

This extremely narrow interpretation of Title IX was one suggested to HEW during preliminary hearings on Title IX regulations. A number of colleges and schools and a number of education administration organizations lobbied for regulations that would place the narrowest possible interpretation on the law. They believed, for example, that athletics should not be covered since most athletic programs did not receive federal funds. Similarly, school busing should be excluded where federal funds did not support transportation. Only the specific program—be it a school lunch program or a program to fund bilingual education—could not discriminate on the basis of sex according to their narrow interpretation.

When HEW promulgated the final regulations for the enforcement of Title IX in 1975, they were, indeed, weaker than many women had hoped they would be. But at least the agency had rejected the narrow theory of applicability that was being touted by some school administrators: it was clear that federal money for one program freed school district funds for other programs and thus indirectly affected those programs. The judge in *Romeo*, however, preferred the narrowest possible theory for Title IX applicability.

If the district court ruling holds an appeal, it would destroy any possibility of employment coverage under Title IX and it could also open the way for a series of challenges to the applicability of the law to numerous student programs not directly funded by the federal government. The loss for student affairs would be severe, should HEW ever manage to bring its compliance program into shape.

But the loss for employment is not nearly so clear. Title IX has produced few positive results (PEER 1977). And the multi-agency approach to employment enforcement has been plagued with problems. All too often in the past, agency findings against complainants have been used by employers to counter findings by other agencies that favor complainants. They have been used, as well, as a means of stifling court complaints of discrimination. In the case brought by Alberta Gilinsky (see Chapter 3), for example, the New York Court of Appeals dismissed the claim of discrimination against Columbia University and gave, as one of its reasons, the fact that "since 1972 Columbia has been operating under an affirmative action program approved by the Department of Health, Education and Welfare." That affirmative action program had indeed been approved and has caused Mary Berry, then chief of the HEW/OCR Higher Education Division, to resign in protest: the plan was, in the view of a number of observers, totally worthless and possibly fraudulent.

HEW has insisted that it will fight in the courts to maintain its right to investigate employment complaints brought under Title IX. And while the court fight continues, the agency is maintaining its Title IX employment program. It is also maintaining its own standards for investigation under Title IX. And despite OCR Director David Tatel's insistence that the agency will cooperate with EEOC in arriving at uniform standards for enforcement, others in the agency continue to hold that the law will be enforced as HEW sees fit since the statutory authority for its enforcement remains with HEW.

One cannot help but speculate whether the decision to fight for continued authority over education employment was honestly made because the agency wished to help women—something it has not shown any inclination to do in the past—or whether it was made to maintain for the agency the widest possible power sphere. Certainly, it would simplify matters if HEW were completely removed from the business of examining employment discrimination.

In federal government enforcement, the second area where presidential reorganization did not serve to simplify or consolidate, the Civil Service Commission previously maintained sole authority over Title VII. The authority was granted the Commission in 1972 when Title VII was extended to cover federal employees. That it never functioned adequately is clear enough. But the presidential reorganization, which was to improve matters by transferring all federal employee Title VII authority to the EEOC, did not pass through Congress unscathed.

On October 13, 1978, Congress passed the Civil Service Reform Act of 1978, and in the process of "reform" dumped a large dose of murky water over the issue of Title VII jurisdiction for federal employees. "Pure" discrimination complaints lodged by federal employees will become the jurisdiction of the EEOC under the new law. However, "mixed cases" will be handled by a complex system that guarantees the cases will be bogged down more severely than ever. "Mixed" complaints are those, according to the law, that involve any action appealable through the newly devised Merit System Protection Board that also include an allegation of unlawful discrimination. Since an allegation of discrimination in employment is always an allegation of the discriminatory use or misuse of some employment practice, almost every action is likely to be considered a "mixed case." The new system requires the agency accused of engaging in the prohibited personnel practice to attempt to review itself within 120 days. The agency decision can then be reviewed by the Merit System Protection Board, should the employee wish to appeal. The decision can also be reviewed by the U.S. Court of Appeals, but this option is unlikely to be used by employees who object to agency decisions since such decisions will most often not be based on a full record of the complaint or on a formal hearing and since the appeals court can only review the already established record.

The Merit System Protection Board is allowed 120 days to decide on both the discrimination issue and the "appealable action"—the language of the law makes it appear that these two items can be separated. At that point, should the employee object to the finding, she or he has the option of judicial review or taking the complaint to EEOC. Again, the option of judicial review, based on what is likely to be an incomplete record, is not tempting. EEOC, should it be petitioned to review a complaint, has 30 days to determine if it will take on the review and, if it decides to do so, has another 60 days to consider the record of proceedings before the Merit System Protection Board and, if necessary, to supplement that record by holding hearings of its own. It also has the option of remanding the entire case back to the merit board for further hearings. If EEOC happens to disagree with the findings of the merit board, the case goes back to that board and it has another 30 days to consider EEOC's findings and accept or reject them. If the merit board rejects the EEOC finding, the case then goes to yet another panel: a three member group with one member from EEOC, one from the merit board, and a chair from outside the government, appointed by the president with "advice and consent" of the Senate. The panel decision will be final.

None of this murky and complicated lawmaking excludes the possibility of a federal employee taking a case directly to federal court under existing Title VII law. Indeed, if one could put aside financial considerations—something it is generally not possible to do—federal court seems the simplest option. Certainly, whether deliberately or not, the Civil Service Reform Act seems designed to force federal employees either to forget about their discrimination complaints or handle them through the courts without troubling the federal complaint-processing bureaucracy.

The structure set up for the processing of federal employee complaints is "a very poor compromise," says EEOC Chair Eleanor Holmes Norton. It is, she believes, "unwieldy and unworkable" and places federal employees in a worse position than ever in comparison to private employees. "Nobody who has looked at it believes that it is anything but awkward and awful," she adds.

In announcing his reorganization plan, President Carter insisted it was "an important step toward consolidation of equal employment opportunity enforcement." It is ironic that it was after, rather than before, "consolidation," in January 1979, that Sears Roebuck and Company decided to sue the government because, according to Sears, the plethora of conflicting equal employment laws has made it impossible for the company to conform. There is a great deal of truth in EEOC's response that the company is using the suit as a device for postponing the implementation of equitable employment practices. Certainly the company's employment statistics leave room for doubt about its sincerity. And certainly there is ample evidence that some employers, if not Sears, have played the conflicting requirements for all they are worth in postponing affirmative action.

In fairness, however, it must be said that there is an equal element of truth in the Sears charge. Government leaders, far from getting their enforcement act together, continue to befuddle complainants, employers, and their own equal employment specialists, if not with conflicting regulations, then with conflicting interpretations of them and with failure to follow through with action when regulations are ignored.

———— *Chapter Fifteen* ————

FOLLOWING UP

"I saw no reason why I should quietly be raped and not scream."
Jenijoy LaBelle, Complainant, 1977

Considerable time has elapsed since most of the women whose cases are reported in this book first filed their complaints of sex discrimination. Yet not one of the women of those I have been able to contact can report that her case is over and done with. Even for those who have used up all legal recourse, the effects of their complaints linger on.

Phoebe Spinrad writes that Barbara Pawlowski obtained a transfer to Norton Air Force Base in California where she is doing the same type of work she performed at Carswell (see Chapter 1 for Spinrad's and Pawlowski's cases). Spinrad's own efforts to find an improved position within the air force have so far been unsuccessful. In January 1978 she applied for a special assignment as an instructor at the Air Force Academy. "This was an exceptionally good job," she writes, "and also included a full year's paid attendance at the university of my choice to finish my master's degree. After all the screening of applications, I was one of the few selected to be interviewed by the Academy staff, and I spent a whole day—at my own travel expense—being interviewed by about fifteen people."

Spinrad was later informed that the department chairman at the Academy had said she was "exceptionally well qualified for the position." But she did not get the job. While at the Academy she was told that her commander would be called for a reference. Her commander, however, told the department chairman that Spinrad's "judgment was poor in filing the lawsuit against the Air Force." "One week later," says Spinrad, "I received a letter from the Academy saying that an instructorship at this point in my career would not be in my own best interests, and therefore they were no longer considering me."

Since that time, Spinrad says,

> I have continued to do my clerical duties in the same squadron, and have continued to get mediocre effectiveness reports—in fact, since one of my two duties (which take about an hour a day) is to monitor the effectiveness reports in the squadron, I happen to know that I consistently receive lower effectiveness reports than any other captain in the squadron. The only recognition I have received since being assigned to the squadron has been a plaque from the junior enlisted members in appreciation for my support of their welfare. My commander apparently did not think that such an award—the only one of its kind ever given to an officer—was worth very much.

Both Spinrad and Pawlowski are working on master's degrees and Spinrad expects to complete hers by December 1979. She has been offered a fellowship for continued work toward her doctorate. Meanwhile, she writes, "we are still waiting for our case to come to court, but we have few illusions left about our Air Force careers."

Mary Lou McEver (see Chapter 1) continued to push for an unbiased review of her case on the University of Florida for some time after her termination. For a while it appeared that she would be successful and a hearing would be conducted by the Academic Freedom and Tenure Committee of the faculty. McEver's former department chair, who remained silent through her battle to forestall termination and who has since retired, finally stepped forward with some information. In July 1977 he wrote of McEver's termination:

> The facts and circumstances seem and sound incredible. It is therefore easy to understand how someone not directly connected with the true situation could conclude that since the facts sound incredible, they must be untrue. This, however, was not the case. Her dismissal was incredible, and the facts, as presented by her to your Panel, were true. [The dean] acted unilaterally without Departmental approval or consultation. In fact, he acted contrary to my recommendation as Department Chairman. Dr. McEver was not given the right to apply for tenure and promotion and be reviewed by the appropriate Department and College Committees. . . .
>
> Regarding Dr. McEver's qualifications, I can truthfully say that she did an excellent job in her position as Assistant Professor of the Field Instruction Unit in Mental Retardation and also in handling the hospital and community practicum program, the internships and other clinical aspects of the departmental program. When called upon to teach some of the more academic coursework in the department, she did this with

equal dexterity and received good evaluations from her students (as good or better than other members of the faculty). She never refused an assignment, nor did she refuse to teach didactic courses. In fact, our practicum or clinical courses had much didactic content and Dr. McEver handled these seminars most successfully. As Department Chairman, I had no reason to offer Dr. McEver anything but praise, a promotion, increase in salary and recommendation for tenure as soon as she served her five years . . . certainly not termination as [the dean] demanded.

Clearly, the letter had been needed three years earlier. But the former chair offered no explanation for his silence during the period when McEver was fighting for academic survival. Instead, he notes that he is writing, in 1977, to "help not only Dr. McEver clear her record but help me reinforce my own integrity as a Department Chairman." Much of his letter is taken up with questioning the integrity of the dean and with indignation at the campus review panel which had asked another faculty member who was "not a functional member of the Department" for its views of McEver rather than asking him.

EEOC has promised a status report to McEver, but so far no such report has materialized. And McEver's attorney has advised her to drop the complaint since he believes there is no way university attorneys will change their minds or drop their support of the dean. To pursue the case further, he pointed out, would require money up front.

McEver has moved from Gainesville to St. Augustine, Florida, where she does some part-time teaching in a community college and is trying real estate. She had recently published several articles about work she did on campus barriers for the handicapped. And, she writes, "I don't consider the case closed!"

Marcia James (Chapter 1) continues her battle to regain her position as a government employee. She notes that her case "has progressed to such a point that it is really entangled in a web of regulations. . . . I am confident that I will win on the merits of my case. . . . I would like to discuss this matter freely and openly with anyone who has an interest, but circumstances being what they are make that situation impossible at the present time."

Iris Carter's Title VII complaint was heard before a federal magistrate in the summer of 1978 (Chapter 1). On February 14, 1979, he released his recommended decision: that the Dayton, Ohio, School Board be found free of discrimination against Carter. The School Board, according to the magistrate, had offered sufficient "legitimate, nondiscriminatory reasons" for passing over Carter for positions as a school principal and for placing her back in the classroom at a $5,000 cut in salary.

In his finding the magistrate showed great receptivity to school administrators' explanations of the manner in which principals were chosen and the criteria for their selection. The criteria included such slippery notions as "leadership," "ability to get along with parents and teachers," "knowledge of the curriculum," "ability to discipline both students and staff," and "ability to supervise extracurricular activities." Somehow, the fact that white males most often proved to have these "abilities" did not strike him as being in the least suspect.

Carter's lawyers have filed objections to the recommended opinion and a federal district court judge has taken them under advisement, along with the magistrate's recommended negative decision. A final decision is expected from the district court judge by summer 1979.

Meanwhile, the Dayton Board ignored HEW's threat to begin proceedings to withhold federal funds since the agency had found discrimination in the district's employment practices under Title IX of the 1972 Education Amendments. The School Board, having informed HEW that Title IX, in its opinion (and in the opinion of some district courts), does not even apply to employment discrimination, left the next move to the agency. HEW, according to Carter, has sent the case to its Chicago office, where the agency may (or may not) decide to pursue it further.

Having gained findings in her favor from the Ohio Civil Rights Commission, the EEOC, and HEW's Office for Civil Rights, Carter remains in the classroom at reduced pay, awaiting a decision from the federal district court. Much of the excitement Carter formerly felt about her career has disappeared. "The joy is gone for me in public education," she comments, "and the economic rewards [are] so small for the emotional and physical energy demanded. . . ." The only positive thing that has happened lately, she says, "has been receiving a Susan B. Anthony award of recognition for fighting sexism . . . from the local women's center here." Carter is one of the few complainants who notes that her case has drawn such recognition from organized feminist groups.

The complaint filed by Shirley Lilge (Chapter 3) is still emeshed in the antidiscrimination bureaucracy. The Wage and Hour Division of the Department of Labor and HEW's Office for Civil Rights both eventually deferred the case to EEOC. But EEOC, writes Lilge, will take jurisdiction only if the Ohio Civil Rights Commission is unable to accomplish anything. The Ohio Commission scheduled hearings for December 1978 but later postponed the hearings to allow further investigation.

One attempt at conciliation was tried, Lilge reports. But Cleveland State's settlement offers left much to be desired: Lilge was offered a salary increase of 4 percent and a chance to once again put her name up for promotion. The offer amounted to nothing whatever: the entire faculty was gaining a 4 percent pay raise at that time and all faculty members had the right, in any case, to place their names in nomination for promotion.

Lilge did request promotion consideration once again in October 1978 and the results were identical to her earlier efforts. Once again the departmental promotion committee voted unanimously in favor of the promotion. Once again the department chair and higher level university officials vetoed the promotion.

Margaret Dobbyn's action was filed in federal district court in March 1975 (Chapter 3). Dobbyn had hoped for rapid action from the court, but it was more than three years before the case was heard. On May 19, 1978, Judge Wesley E. Brown released his decision. Dobbyn was not the victim of sex discrimination, said Brown. To the contrary, it was Dobbyn who was to blame for the whole unpleasant business at the Kansas State University library. Brown, like the judges in the *Johnson* and *Cussler* cases and so many other cases, was all too eager to blame the victim: "Although there was creditable evidence that her action in filing suit was the result of vindictiveness against her peers," he wrote, "we prefer to determine that in this instance, plaintiff's action was a result of an inability to subordinate her considerable ego and correct her abrasive actions. . . ."

Dobbyn's first response was to appeal the case. She advanced her attorney $3,000 to pay for the cost of the trial transcript and another $250 to pay the filing fee. But after the emotions of the trial began to subside, Dobbyn decided, "I could not risk the mental and emotional anguish, or the money that the appeal would require. So I called it off." Although the filing fee had already been expended, transcripts for the appeal had not been prepared. But as of March 1979, almost a year after she decided to cancel the appeal, her attorney had not returned the $3,000 advance.

A second suit filed by Dobbyn in state court, charging that a letter written by a Kansas State library official was libelous, "dragged along" on appeal, says Dobbyn, until "the day after the federal case was over and reported in the paper." The ruling that was then issued was that the letter was "a *privileged* communication." Dobbyn cannot help but feel that the state court was holding back and waiting for the results of the federal case.

After the trial Dobbyn worked for a while for an abstract and title company in Enid, Oklahoma, for a salary of $7,200 a year. In September 1978 she obtained a position as a beginning librarian in the Oklahoma City Metro library at a salary of $9,600 a year. "It has been difficult assuming the status of a beginning librarian," she writes, "but my rent and food depend on doing just that if possible. . . . My relationship with others takes finesse in handling since they have had so much less experience than I, and no matter how careful and submissive I am, it seems to show someplace and intimidates people. Those are real problems to handle daily." The position was not permanent: Dobbyn faced an evaluation in spring 1979. "Should the job end in April," she writes, "I expect the only alternative is secretarial work if possible, or saleslady at the department stores."

Nevertheless, now that the burden of the complaint has ended, Dobbyn has begun to regain her spirits: "I am in much better spirits than for several years, can laugh and sing and accept and enjoy, and I find that is extraordinarily satisfying after a long period of anger and depression. That is good. So much better than I had anticipated in June 1978 that I believe I'll manage to make it the rest of the way."

EEOC gave Alberta Gilinsky (Chapter 3) her right to sue letter and in 1973 a class action suit was filed against Columbia University in federal district court. The case was stayed, however, pending the outcome of Gilinsky's state complaint.

Following her defeat in the New York State Court of Appeals in June 1976, the federal complaint was reactivated, Gilinsky reports. But as of April 1979 the case remained at the district court level awaiting hearing.

Timeliness did become an issue for some of the women who had failed to gain back pay settlements at American Bridge, writes Patricia MacDonald (Chapter 3). Following the settlement of the 1971 "class" complaint for the individual complainant only, a number of women filed their own individual complaints. Three of those women have had their complaints dismissed for lack of timeliness by the National Labor Relations Board, the Pennsylvania Human Relations Commission, and the EEOC. Right to sue letters were issued by EEOC, MacDonald reports, but the women are not going to court: "They said they had enough hassle and lacked time and money to take any action."

MacDonald's own charges, which were filed at an earlier date and therefore considered timely, have not yet been resolved. They are being investigated by yet another member of the Pennsylvania Commission staff. "I have heard nothing from either EEOC or the Pennsylvania Commission official. What needs to be answered is why each time the personnel changes they must begin with 'square one.' The last investigator. . . told me before she left that the case was all wrapped up, tied with a ribbon and ready to calculate dollars."

On April 3, 1977, the Los Angeles Times carried an article headlined: "Woman Professor Wins Caltech Fight." The article reported that Jenijoy LaBelle would be "restored to her teaching position, promoted and granted back pay and benefits" (see Chapter 8).

In February 1976, five months before her termination, LaBelle had filed a complaint with the EEOC. The agency acted with unusual rapidity in the case: in mid-January 1977, less than a year after the complaint was filed, the agency released a finding in favor of LaBelle. In the meantime, she had hired a private attorney. It had become clear to her that EEOC had broadened out its investigation to cover the hiring practices for the entire Caltech campus. Understandably, LaBelle's primary concern was getting back to work. "I could see myself getting lost while they did this huge case. . . . I don't want to spend a lot of time in litigation. I'm interested in literature." EEOC, on the other hand, said the case was "the strongest they had ever seen" and saw it as a major class complaint that could be litigated, if necessary, with excellent prospects for victory.

The agency finding read, in part:

> Respondent's current employment statistics show that out of 481 faculty members there are 35 women [7.3%] . . . these women are clustered in the lower level positions. Further, no females are represented in the two highest job levels—Full Professor and Associate Professor—although 213 males work at those levels. Women are represented in only 5 of the 40 positions at the next highest levels of Assistant Professor and Instructor [11.1%]. In contrast, females are most heavily concentrated in the Faculty category of "other" [e.g. Research Associate; Research Assistant], with 77% of all women working at that level.

EEOC apparently took the position that it was more likely to gain judicial enforcement against an institution that blatantly discriminates against women than one that merely discriminates. Caltech, which EEOC also found had only one black with faculty status "in the lowest faculty salary category," was, by this logic a good candidate for litigation. While the agency was prepared to negotiate a settlement for LaBelle, it seemed clear that she would not be the only, nor necessarily the most central, part of such negotiations.

LaBelle took the EEOC finding to a member of the Caltech Board of Trustees and received a sympathetic hearing. With the support of the board member and her attorney, she managed to negotiate a settlement on her own. She was given a position as associate professor and a promise of an unbiased tenure review two or three years after her return to the campus. Her former tenure rival, although he was hired one year after LaBelle, was by then a tenured associate professor, a position that allowed the university to pay him a higher salary than LaBelle could earn in her untenured position. LaBelle's supporter on the Board of Trustees had made it clear to her she would have to compromise: tenure could not be part of the settlement since he could not interfere to that extent in the peer review process.

The victory announced in the *Los Angeles Times* fell short of equity, but LaBelle had little choice. Her only other options were to file suit in federal court or to wait until EEOC was ready to pursue classwide negotiations and, if those failed, file suit on her behalf. She was unemployed and single and litigation is costly. Private litigation was not a realistic option for her. And, as it later turned out, EEOC never did finish its investigation and never got around to negotiating a classwide settlement with Caltech. In fact, according to one agency official, the Caltech situation was "badly botched" by the agency. LaBelle's choice had clearly been the only one likely to improve her situation, even though she had to return to several more years of insecurity.

In April 1979 LaBelle, on the basis of her extensive scholarly contributions, was given a positive recommendation for tenure by all three of the faculty committees designated to decide tenure cases at Caltech. At that time she became the only tenured woman on the Caltech faculty.

Sharon Johnson was not the only person to experience harassment during the months of her battle against the University of Pittsburgh. Johnson's attorney, Sylvia Roberts, was the victim of a disbarment attempt that was filed by Pitt's attorneys. Grounds for the disbarment were Roberts' supposed "unethical" conduct. As general counsel for the NOW Legal Defense and Education Fund, she had sent out a letter to NOW members, urging them to contribute to the fund, which was helping to support the Johnson case. Although Roberts asked for postponement, a courtesy that is almost automatic between attorneys, she was turned down and therefore forced to prepare briefs in her own defense during the heaviest part of the Johnson hearings. But following the Johnson court defeat, the bar association committee responsible for making a recommendation to the court on the complaint against Roberts wrote: "The committee makes no determination of the merits of the complaint: however consideration of all the circumstances of the case, and *especially the decision of the Court in the Johnson case*, the committee recommends to the Court that the complaint against Silvia [sic] Roberts be dismissed" [emphasis added].

Johnson personally experienced two additional crushing blows following the negative decision by Judge Knox. Immediately after the ruling was announced, the University of Pittsburgh's vice-chancellor, Nathan Stark, wrote Johnson, notifying her that "you ceased to be an employee of the University of Pittsburgh on August 1, 1977." The letter meant instant termination and permanent cutoff from the laboratory Johnson had built up over five years with grants from the National Institutes of Health. And it meant that Johnson could not use her own grant funds for continuing research.

Stark offered Johnson an option, however:

> Nevertheless, if you do not intend to file an appeal from Judge Knox's decision, with the concurrence of the Acting Chairman of your Depart-

ment and the Dean of the Medical School, the University of Pittsburgh is willing to assist you in retaining your grant and to give you sufficient time to seek employment elsewhere by offering you an appointment as a Senior Research Associate at your present salary from August 2, 1977 through June 30, 1978 when the current year's funding on your grant expires or until such earlier date as you may transfer your grant to another institution. This appointment will not be renewed after that date.

The offer was not insubstantial to Johnson and it was contingent upon her not appealing. It was impossible for Johnson to transfer her laboratory to another institution in Pittsburgh. Her laboratory was considered the property of the university and would have been instantly inaccessable to her. She needed the ten months' time to seek out a new institutional home in order to transfer the laboratory and the grant and continue her scientific work.

"I don't know if you know how much time it takes to build a lab," Johnson says. "I've built up three in my lifetime. It takes five years to get all the hardware, to get all the tools, to get everything going, it takes many, many years."

But Stark's letter gave Johnson even further incentive to refrain from appealing the decision:

In addition, since you will be waiving your right of appeal if you accept this offer of employment, the University and all other defendants will be willing to waive the right to seek court costs and attorneys fees, which we understand will be very substantial. If, on the other hand, you decide to appeal, under those circumstances it would be inappropriate for us to continue your employment at the University of Pittsburgh beyond August 1, 1977.

In Title VII cases, successful plaintiffs have the right to collect attorney's fees and costs from defendants. The right of defendants is not as clear, although some recent court cases have held that such a right exists when cases are brought frivolously. Thus the threat of a suit for Pitt's court costs and attorneys' fees in addition to instant termination could not be taken lightly. Johnson had one attorney who was willing to work on a shoestring budget, but the expenses, nonetheless, drained Johnson's personal finances and the NOW Legal Defense Fund. The University of Pittsburgh had four, and sometimes five, highly paid private attorneys on hand through the nearly 80 days of courtroom time, numerous days of depositions, and uncounted days of preparation. Although it would have undoubtedly been difficult for Pittsburgh to prove the suit was frivolous, the threat of being sued for what was clearly a tremendous amount was an effective one. Johnson agreed to the university offer.

The second blow came in September when Dorothy South, one of Johnson's coworkers in the University of Pittsburgh department of biochemistry, commited suicide in her laboratory in the biochemistry department. South had worked as a research assoicate at Pitt. She was one of those many women who appeared in the Johnson suit as statistics. Like many trained women with doctorates in biochemistry and related fields, she had served the university as a researcher on federally funded projects. Her job had come to an end with the end of the federal project. She had sent over 200 applications out in search of other work. None produced employment. Her suicide, which Betty Friedan attributed to sex discrimination, took place five days after her job at Pitt came to an end. South's will left her small savings to "fighting sexism at Pitt." She asked Johnson to serve as her executor. Her suicide note read simply: "Forgive me, I feel rotten and I just don't have it to hassle the world for a way to live." Johnson writes that South was "the *only person* in my department who supported me and came to the hearings. She was not reappointed—and could not get a job ANYWHERE. I have boxes and boxes of her application letters at home. (I still have nightmares about the whole affiar of Dorothy.)"

In the final letter of settlement in which Johnson's attorney spelled out to Pitt attorneys the terms of Johnson's ten months of continued employment, it was made clear that "(i)n the event Dr. Johnson is able to find a place to move her grant, she will be permitted to take with her the equipment which has been purchased under the grant in conformity with regulations of the National Institutes of Health." The terms were acceptable to Pitt. Johnson did find a new home for her grant, at the Polytechnic Institute of New York. But she writes,

> the day I was scheduled to leave from Pitt, a leave which was approved in writing to the NIH by the Dean and Chairman, three armed guards appeared with the mover with the announcement that I was stealing Pitt property if I moved my lab. The guards did not allow students to use the hallway—and created a bad situation with their walkie talkies. This went on all day (while I paid for the movers' time to just sit around). Meanwhile lots of telegrams came to the chancellor's office from eminent scientists, including a Nobel Prize winner, Pitt's science advisors from other schools, etc. After a day of barrage of telegrams, Pitt sent the carpenter to change the locks on the door of my lab.

Late that same day, Pitt's vice-chancellor relented, sent a messenger with a letter, and allowed Johnson to move her lab "as previously planned and approved by the Dean, Chairman, etc."

The continuation of her scientific work was of primary importance to Johnson. It was the main reason she accepted Pitt's offer of ten months' employment and the main reason she accepted employment at New York Polytechnic. But aside from allowing her to continue her research—albeit with the disruption of moving her laboratory with its 20,000 pounds of equipment and setting it up once again hundreds of miles away—the new job did little for Johnson since it placed her once again in a tenuous position: she was hired as an associate research professor without tenure. Johnson now commutes between New York and Pittsburgh, where her husband and children continue to live.

Before the *Williams* appeal (see Chapter 12) was heard by the District of Columbia Circuit Court, a sufficient number of courts had ruled on the issue of sexual harassment that the Justice Department dropped its insistence that such harassment was not sex discrimination. But having accepted that much, Justice continued its appeal. Even though the Civil Service Commission had found discrimination against Williams, even though the Justice Department had declared a new policy of not fighting such administrative decisions but limiting its fight only to the matter of appropriate remedy, and even though the remedy set by the district court in the *Williams* case was an insignificant $16,000 in back pay, Justice persisted.

The Justice Department had initially fought against a trial *de novo* in district court while Williams had wanted such a trial. Justice had won its initial fight and Williams had agreed to allow the lower court decision to be made on the basis of the administrative record. But Justice, having lost in district court on the basis of that record, now argued on appeal that a new trial was in order. And in September 1978 the Circuit Court reversed and remanded the case for a completely new trial.

Williams, who long ago was willing to settle for the small amount of back pay authorized by the district court judge and who would clearly like to put the whole humiliating experience behind her, was forced to gear up for a full district court hearing once again. The new hearing was set for late March 1979, while Williams was completing her second semester of law school. She was forced to spend much of her effort during the spring supplying depositions to the government and trying, after the gap in years, to relocate witnesses. Without the support of Michael D. Hausfeld, who serves as her attorney, Williams believes "the case would have absolutely gone nowhere." It would have been difficult to find anyone

more compassionate or more sympathetic than Michael has been. He has given me hope and inspiration, as well as that all-important "staying power" that EEO complainants so desperately need to withstand years of litigation. When other aspects of the case have bogged down during the past seven years, Michael has always been unequivocal in his support. . . . In addition to being an excellent lawyer, which a good case can always use, he is a very decent human being!

Williams, unlike some other complainants, has been lucky in finding an attorney she can so completely trust. Perhaps that is one reason why, even though she admits that she was very unhappy at the prospect of another trail, she still remains optimistic: "Right eventually triumphs over wrong," she says. "It just takes a while for justice to be done! But, justice will never be done unless we fight for that which we believe in and then fight some more."

Even among the "winners," none can report that her case is at last behind her. At Montana State University, writes Helen Cameron (see Chapter 9), a new affirmative action officer was hired by the administration and it has become clear that she has not adequately grasped the discrimination problem on the campus. She put together a report on the status of women at Montana State that indicated little if any problem. The report did not satisfy any of the women involved in the complaint. "Her comparisons were ridiculous, and frequently violated the carefully developed rules" for assessing the relative salary and position of men and women on the faculty, Cameron says. Because of the inadequate report, the women on campus must once again attempt to gain access to the campus data bank and perform their own analyses—a prospect that is at this point both "time-consuming and aggravating," says Cameron. Once their report is finished, she says, they will present it to the Board of Regents "and if they do nothing, then to the judge." "So," Cameron concludes, "the struggle goes on—forever it seems."

June Chewning (Chapter 10) reports that as of spring 1979 she had received one grade-level promotion "but that is insufficient now!" Full settlement of the class complaint is a long way off. First, says Chewning, the judge had a heart attack. Then he delayed hearings on some complex settlement issues while he attempted to catch up with other cases on his calendar. There is still a dispute over the date from which back pay for the class should be calculated. The government insists it has no obligation for the period prior to the 1972 amendments to Title VII, even if it was discriminating, and Chewning and her attorney insist that government obligations date back to 1966 executive orders that forbid discrimination in federal employment. The earlier date, says Chewning, "really means a great deal for those of us who have been long-term employees." Another issue still to be debated is whether or not the judge will allow the use of a computer to determine the amount of back pay due most of the women in the class.

Following her promotion to GS 14 level, Irene Bowman (Chapter 11) was forced to return to court once more, to ask the district court judge to enforce the stipulation in her settlement agreement that prohibited continuing discrimination or harassment. The Justice Department complaint adjudication officer also took a second look at her classwide complaint and at the efforts the department was supposedly making to correct the discrimination he had previously found. In July 1978 he issued a follow-up letter in which he evaluated the department's progress. "I find," he wrote, "that the Antitrust Division has complied only with that portion of the remedial action requesting retroactive action on your [Bowman's] behalf and that it has failed to comply with the letter and spirit of the bulk of it." The divisional record, he said, "reflects no intent . . . to conform with the requirements of 'priority consideration' for the promotion of women attorneys." Nor did it comply with any other parts of his earlier order. The adjudication officer also found that the negative memoranda on Bowman were "inherently biased and retaliatory. . . . I find that not only did the Antitrust Division fail to provide you with the priority consideration entitled you under our request for remedial action in light of its discriminatory practices, but that the consideration afforded you was of such an unfair and retaliatory nature as to require further action on my part." The adjudication officer then asked that the Justice Department Employment Review Committee, the new departmentwide committee that had been established as a result of the Bowman complaint, review Bowman's file and decide whether she should be promoted to GS 15 level.

Bowman received her promotion to GS 15 in the fall of 1978, but by that time it had become clear to her that she had little future in the Justice Department. None of the discriminating officials in supervisory positions had been reprimanded. Most remained in a position in which they could continue to harass her and hamper her future career. In November 1978 Bowman opted to accept a new federal job as a member of the Civil Service Commission Appeals Review Board. Had she remained at Justice, she believes, no future movement in her career would have been possible without a fight, either through the department's EEO procedures or through the courts. It was clearly not a prospect anyone would relish for a lifetime.

Other women who "won" their battles against sex discrimination report continued harassment. May Hollinshead (Chapter 9) says that she has experienced continued petty harassments, "most of which I've been able to scotch with a memo, copied to the Dean of Medicine and to the Director of the Division on Civil Rights, quoting the terms of the settlement to my reprisal case." More disturbing, she says, is the fact that the one professor who supported her during the reprisal hearings, only to have his own promotion to full professor rescinded, has yet to receive a settlement. A complaint on the incident was filed with the New Jersey

Division, Hollinshead reports, but "we have reason to believe that the school is doing everything it can to muddy the issues with all sorts of extraneous matters. . . ."

Lella Candea (Chapter 11) writes that despite her change of agency, her past complaints continue to haunt her and she has recently undergone still more harassment. She has recently become "heavily occupied in developing innovative new procedures to halt or blunt harassment." The procedures include the use of temporary work assignments and leaves of absence to remove women from the immediate vicinity of the supervisors or coworkers who might be harassing them and to "save women from nervous breakdowns and other illnesses." Candea tells of increased harassment in her own agency and in a number of government agencies— a pattern that seems to indicate that the position of government officials has hardened since the early days of sex discrimination complaints when she was able to win so many victories. At the National Institutes of Health, says Candea, harassment has become so widespread that the director recently set up a task force to study the matter.

Candea tells, as well, of a "leading EEO woman lawyer" who told her "that if the government wished to set up an EEO complaint system for its employees that . . . would inevitably lead to the victory of virtually all the employers and the defeat of the employees, the government would select precisely that system which it now uses." Candea agrees that the current system for government employees is not working to produce equity.

Diana Gutmann (Chapter 10) also finds the government EEO system as frustrating as ever. In September 1977 Gutmann applied for a position in the EEO office of the Naval Air Systems Command. She was the only highly qualified candidate and began her new job as a "race relations/human awareness" specialist in November 1977. "My primary duty is to manage a training program for supervisors and managers called the Shore Equal Opportunity Program which has been mandated by our next higher echelon command. It requires that all supervisors and managers participate. I've been traveling to our field activities as the program is implemented." In spite of the effort to acquaint supervisory personnel with their equal employment duties, Gutmann writes that complaints continue to come in. "I also manage all EEO complaint processing for the command," she says, "which is frustrating when you see people in the same situation as you were in, but often cannot help them."

At the end of February 1979, Valentine Winsey (Chapter 9) was notified that she would once again be passed over for promotion to full professor. She appealed the decision within the university and expected some word before the end of the spring semester.

Winsey notes that since launching her suit in 1970, "to the present, all members of the faculty who testified for the administration have been rewarded with promotion in rank. Among them were four women, all of whom have now been awarded the rank of full professor." She also points out that six of the nine men who served on the core curriculum committee she chaired have been promoted while the other three, who were already full professors, have been given substantial raises.

Daniel Cohen, the lone staff member at Pace who testified on Winsey's behalf, was fired. He placed a retaliation charge with the New York City Commission and within 15 months received a substantial financial settlement.

Meanwhile, Winsey has received none of the back pay the New York Commission and the Courts decided was due to her. In defiance of the agreement executed between Winsey and Pace, the college (by now a university) withheld close to half of the $75,000 settlement, earmarking it as "taxes." An additional third of the settlement remains frozen by a lawyer's lien. "The 'Ordeal of Winning' persists," Winsey writes.

Barbara Clark (Chapter 9) writes that she no longer experiences overt harassment. "Problems continue, of course, as they will in a situation where all the administrators and decision makers are men. Salaries for men rise faster and promotions and tenure come for them almost as a matter of course." Clark is still an associate professor and will become eligible for promotion consideration after she has served at that rank for five years. She comments, appropriately, I believe, for all the women whose cases are related in this book: "When I first read the pages on my case, I thought, 'Well, Oglethorpe is going to get the bad publicity after all.' Some of it sounds so ugly that I had to question whether I wanted my institution so exposed. It quickly dawned on me that it sounded ugly because sexism and discrimination are ugly. So be it."

—— *Chapter Sixteen* ——

DEAR POTENTIAL COMPLAINANT: SOME THOUGHTS BEFORE FILING

"I always tell people, 'Whenever you file a complaint realize that bad things are going to happen to you. People will always believe that whatever happened to you happened because you weren't good enough and people's careers and reputations get destroyed by it.' That doesn't mean they shouldn't complain. It's just that they should know."

HEW executive, 1977

For the women who have filed complaints of sex discrimination in employment, the task they have set for themselves seems incredibly difficult. Almost without exception, they admit that no matter how stern the forewarning and no matter how difficult the anticipated struggle, reality far exceeds their level of expectation. Time for friends, chosen pastimes, and even professional advancement all but disappears or is cut to the bone by the necessity of moving the complaint process or responding to it. In many cases physical health and emotional well being is pushed to the brink. Financial means are often strained to the breaking point. Fewer and fewer lawyers are willing to work on a pro bono or contingency basis. Jobs, if they are not cut off as a direct result of a complaint, become less secure at the same time that the struggle begins to cut more heavily into personal finances.

One of the sorest points raised by complainants is the role of feminist organizations in their struggle. While some (Winsey, Johnson and Carter, for example) have received awards or recognition or even modest funding from such organizations, most women who have pursued complaints of sex discrimination feel they have been left alone in their struggle. What support they have had has come from small groups of coworkers, other complainants, family members, and friends. Some believed the organized women's movement would be their natural ally.

Instead, they found feminist groups indifferent or too busy elsewhere to offer even the small amount of spiritual and moral support that might have left them feeling less alone.

While not universally shared, the reaction is true in the case of too many complainants to ignore. They believe the organized women's movement, if it bothers with them at all, does so in order to take from them rather than to give. They are often made to feel guilty and utterly useless to the movement if they decline to take office in a local chapter or beg off on time-consuming committee work or if they are unable to attend meetings. To venture to excuse themselves by pointing to the time-consuming and draining struggle in which they are engaged or to venture the opinion that the struggle is potentially useful to other women requires more bravery than most complainants have: it is taken, many feel, as an elitist putdown of other projects considered more vital by local chapters.

Diane Williams expresses the feelings of many women complainants about the organized women's movement when she talks of her own ordeal. She still feels alone in her struggle:

> Nobody has come to me and asked me, 'How are you paying your lawyer? Do you need a shoulder to cry on? Do you need somebody to hold your hand while you're sitting in court or sitting at one of those administrative hearings while they are saying such nasty things about you.' And that is an awful thing to sit there and not be able to say anything and listen to somebody tell a lie and then to contradict himself with another lie.

It would be inaccurate to paint a uniformly grim picture of what happens to the complainant's personal and social life, health, and financial security. Many women happily admit they "thrive" on the controversy. Others believe the process has helped them to grow or established closer relationships with friends and family members. Nonetheless, the price they have paid in time, physical and emotional stamina, and money has been enormous.

The victories gained following this huge expenditure have thus far been small. We receive encouraging pieces of information now and then, generally in the form of consent agreements and out of court settlements. The New York *Times*, for example, recently settled a case that had its origins in 1972 when some 90 discrimination complaints were filed against the newspaper. It is to be hoped that the agreement will produce more high-level jobs on the newspaper as well as back pay for the 550 women included in the class complaint. A second suit was recently resolved when Judge John Sirica ruled that the navy was discriminating against its female personel by denying them assignments to shipboard positions.

The navy decided not to appeal the case and women have, of late, been serving in limited numbers on navy ships.

Such settlements are indeed to be celebrated, but they are all too infrequent and those that are completed, on closer examination, often fall short of the anticipated gains. In 1974, for example, the Women's Equity Action League (WEAL) and several other women's organizations filed a major suit against the Departments of Labor and HEW for failure to implement the antidiscrimination laws and executive orders within their charge. In December 1978 the suit was settled with HEW and Labor under court order to take all necessary actions to "end all forms of discrimination at all levels of education which receive federal tax dollars" (*WEAL Washington Report*, February, 1978, p. 1). HEW was committed by the settlement to hire over 800 new enforcement employees and to clean up its complaint backlog by September 1979. But a year later WEAL reported "members who have anticipated significant results from the 1977 Court order to HEW to end education bias will be disappointed by the progress of enforcement of the order during its first year. 'It is deplorable,' said Carol Grossman, WEAL national vice-president and education chair, 'that even with a Court order, enforcement of the law has not been appreciably increased'" (*WEAL News*, December 1978).

For the most part, women who began their struggle years ago are still involved and finding that the estimates of the time it would take them to see· their complaints through were off by many years. A number of women have dropped out along the way. Others have given up only after the losses have become too substantial to continue. And even those who have won victories have found themselves in positions somewhere short of equity.

It would seem from the continuing difficulties faced by these women that employers, supervisors, and managers are discouragingly unable to react constructively to charges of discrimination. Those that have legal counsel generally refuse to comment on the charges that have been made against them. Lawyers, in their wisdom, deem it unwise for clients to say anything whatever when lawyers are not present to control the situation. Yet when these carefully advised employers do talk in administrative or courtroom hearings, their rationale is identical to the rationale of those employers who are free with their opinions at an earlier stage. Almost without exception they insist that the complainant is incompetent or mediocre or that she has unpleasant or divisive personality traits. They insist that they are concerned with merit and excellence and with team spirit and efficiency and nothing more. They certainly bear no prejudice toward women. Deputy Assistant Attorney General Joe Sims, who—surprisingly for an attorney—did comment on the Bowman case (Chapter 11) insisted in typical fashion that he was beyond any suspicion of personal bias. Even though the promotion committee generally gives greater weight to a supervisor's recommendation than to any other factor, the committee felt strongly enough about the Bowman decision to discount that recommendation. There was no discrimination in the antitrust division, he insisted, and no discrimination in the Bowman case. He knew this, he said, because of his own state of mind—"That's of course not provable but I'm comfortable with it"—and because he was convinced that the procedures were fair and that the antitrust division had an excellent record on the promotion of women. When asked why the record did not show up in division statistics, Sims replied that "intelligent people can disagree about the meaning of statistics." Sims, like most of his fellows, would seem to believe that women who do not advance have no one to blame but themselves.

Some of these men will admit that there may be an overall problem and that very few women seem to be advancing in their bureau or business or on their campus. But, they will add—and there is always a "but"—there are good reasons. They have looked and looked but qualified women are in short supply. The women they employ would move faster but they have other interests such as home and family that necessarily delay or stop their professional progress. They are trying to compete for qualified women but other industries are grabbing up all the good women (and many who are not so good) because of the demands of affirmative action. They have hired women in the past but they have been burned because the women left for better jobs or to get married and follow their husbands. They would hire women but women just don't do well with their type of client.

Even those who admit that their own record is shaky always add in any particular instance that it is perfectly plain that the particular woman was not advanced because she did not deserve to be advanced. Never, in the many interviews I have conducted, have I heard an employer or a supervisor, a dean, department chair, or senior colleague admit that perhaps there might be some truth in a particular charge of sex discrimination. Their reactions range from one to five on a continuum of 100, from a militant and angry belief that there is no such thing as sex discrimination to a sincere and apologetic belief that they have not done all that they should to bring women into the mainstream. But one and all they will counter any particular charge of sex discrimination by heaping suspicion upon the woman who has charged it. One corporate president told me that he had *never* seen a case of sex discrimination. There was always, he said, some other, nondiscriminatory reason the woman was in an unfavorable position. He challenged me to describe a case and I responded with the particulars of a woman who had been hired in a dead-end job and who had been praised for her excellent executive ability but told, at the same time, that her job did not prepare her for advancement. That was not sex discrimination, said he; clearly it was the woman's fault. No man would have allowed himself to be hired into such a dead-end position. A far more sympathetic university president admitted that there was discrimination on his campus but said that he was helpless to bring it to an end. Anything he might do to provide incentives for the hiring of females, said he, would be against the law because it would be "preferential treatment" for those woman. When I suggested he might assess his own sizable pool of female lecturers and consider upgrading their positions to regular faculty slots since they were doing the same work as faculty and generally at less than half the pay, he replied that the job had already been done and that only four lecturers (of several hundred) had been up-graded. The result was disappointing because lecturers simply were not doing the same kind of work, he insisted. But didn't most of them have the same degrees and the same training and were they not teaching the same courses? Yes, he admitted, but they had accepted jobs as lecturers and lecturers were discouraged from doing research. It was their own fault, then, for accepting these posts rather than holding out for regular acdemic appointments. Once again, the victim was to blame for her predicament.

In private industry, in government, and on the campus, employers have with no small amount of grumbling learned that they must spend millions to employ affirmative action officers and equal opportunity specialists. Perhaps this is a measurable gain for women and minorities for they have been hired into these jobs in greater proportion than into other professional jobs (although women have consistently been hired into these jobs at lower pay than men). But employers have learned to select well and the best affirmative action officials for them are not necessarily going to be the strongest and most knowledgeable advocates for minori-ties and women. One statewide school district, for example, hired two affirmative action specialists with little background or knowledge in the field and felt, for a time, safe from criticism. But the specialists began learning and then, at a conference, announced to the press that the school district had severe discrimination problems. The two were promptly fired for insubordination. They were reinstated by court order only to be terminated once again. This time school district officials claimed funds had run out for the program (Honolulu *Advertiser*, August 24, 1978).

Employers have also learned that they must spend additional millions to conduct studies and self-evaluations. Here, too, they have learned that studies can be tailored to satisfy the antidiscrimination agencies and demonstrate their "good faith" without effecting any change. They have learned to protest the absurdity of government bureaucratic interference and they have learned to insist with great vigor that government regulations prevent rather than facilitate the achievement of equity. The suit brought by Sears Roebuck and Company is a striking example of just such self-righteous protest. One educator, however, points out: "It is hard to avoid the impression that if bureaucratic complications did not exist, some administrators in higher education would invent them to have something to protest against. It is easier, after all, to denounce the manner in which federal programs are implemented than to propose alternative porgrams or take initiatives at a local level. Sometimes attacks on federal regulation don't quite conceal a disinclination to change" (Birnbaum 1977, p. 226).

Employers, in fact, have become quite comfortable with the terminology and with the financial requirements of affirmative action and equal employment opportunity. The cost is little enough to pay to retain the status quo. Indeed, it has had unexpected side benefits for it has produced the myth of reverse discrimination, a myth that allows them to believe that they are battling discrimination when they continue to hire and promote white males. After all, they can assure themselves and any women or minority group members who may ask, it would be an insult to blacks and women to hire them just because they are balck or female (or both); they wouldn't want to think they had obtained the job for reasons other than their merit. Yet, when a woman or a minority group member *does* get a job, this is exactly what white male associates will often believe. And if the new employee happens to be a minority woman, then her colleagues will believe she needed nothing more than these two immutable characteristics to get her job. Thus the affirmative action stance of employers has produced a most interesting double bind. A woman who does make it in the employment system is viewed with suspicion and there are numerous colleagues who will prefer to believe that she made it because she was a woman and not because she was qualified. A woman who does not make it in the employment system, on the other hand, is dismissed as mediocre or unqualified: had she been qualified she obviously would have made it. In all this, few dare examine the question of whether white males make it in the system because of their qualifications or simply because they are immutably white and male.

The continuing difficulties of women complainants also seem to indicate that we can expect little from the government antidiscrimination agencies. While it might be a little presumptuous to think of these agencies as natural allies, we might reasonably expect that they would serve as objective third party agencies charged with investigating possible violations of the law and with enforcing the law. And we might reasonably expect that they would take action in line with their responsibilities. Those of us who filed complaints of sex discrimination during the Nixon and Ford administrations were disappointed. We found, with few exceptions, that government antidiscrimination bureaucrats, from the top down, possessed a cool sincerity and offered innumerable reasons why it was not possible to make a finding, especially a favorable finding. Lower level bureaucrats would talk about the political pressures they faced and the unfavorable climate and the lack of clear direction from the top. Upper level bureaucrats would talk about the deadwood in the agency and the need for reorganization and the hopes they placed in the latest training program. Bureaucrats at all levels would talk about the need for caution and the way the law bound them to only certain kinds of limited actions. They could not be expected to act rashly or hastily. It would damage the civil rights movement to rush ahead and make findings of discrimination that could not hold up before an administrative law judge or in a federal court. As government officials, after all, they were expected to hold to a very high standard of legal proof.

Those who filed after the Carter administration took power might have found a slightly different situation. Top level bureaucrats appointed by the new president talked warmly and enthusiastically of change. The neglect of the past eight years was about to slip away, they were sure. No one was going to be allowed, any longer, to sit around without doing the job the law required. New training programs were being organized. Internal reorganization of management and staff functions was underway. Directives would be clear. Records would be kept. Accountability would be required at all levels. Employers were going to get the word that the government meant business: the law would be enforced.

Indeed, the new leadership seems remarkably enthusiastic and remarkably sincere. I have walked out of their offices—particularly the office of Eleanor Holmes Norton—dazzled, glassy eyed, and ready to believe. I have had to ask myself why the impressions I gathered in over a year of interviews led me to believe that disappointingly little was going on. How could that be true when one is mesmerized by the enthusiasm of a Norton or by the firmness of a Rougeau?

But at the lower levels one encounters reservations that are not much different from those of the past administrations. In fact, the bureaucrats sometimes sound remarkably like the employers they are legally required to monitor. Not every complaint is legitimate, they will insist. An employer has a right to demonstrate that the woman charging sex discrimination is merely acting out of disappointment. It is difficult for federal bureaucrats to step in and make decisions on qualifications when the employer knows best what his needs are and who can meet them. True enough, all of it, but why is it always the reasons why something cannot be done that are emphasized and never the reasons why something should be done? The regulators echo the regulatees.

It would be unfair to be completely negative. There *is* evidence that more is going on now than in the past. The OFCCP has begun to move toward hearings against some employers. And the EEOC is gaining millions for complainants in quick, predetermination settlements. But there are two vital questions that need to be asked: Is there any evidence of systemic change that will make for permanent improvement in the employment status of minorities and women? And, are the chances for the individual woman in professional employment any better now for gaining a finding of sex discrimination should she file a charge or for gaining equity should she obtain a finding? In both cases the answer at the present time must unfortunately be no.

The courts offer no better solution. The early enthusiasm based on the assumption that decisions regarding sex discrimination would parallel the decisions regarding race discrimination died long ago. The Supreme Court has on occasion made small concessions to women and their rights. But for the most part the justices have had great difficulty understanding that there might be such a thing as sex discrimination and they have found it next to impossible to understand that it might be as serious a problem as race discrimination. Discrimination based on sex-singular characteristics is totally out of their range of understanding. In lower courts the results of Title VII litigation for women have been mixed. In individual cases they have been disastrous. One unpublished study revealed that of all individual claims of discrimination involving hire, promotion, and discharge issues at both the district and appellate court levels between 1973 and 1975, plaintiffs prevailed in only slightly more than one-third of the cases. Either there is very little discrimination or the courts are not helping people any more than the administrative agencies.

The next question must by "Why?" With so much good will at the top of the two most crucial agencies, why is there so little indication that enforcement will turn into a meaningful process or that discriminatory employment practices will be brought to an end?

EEOC theorist Peter Robertson gives us a clue. The goal of federal antidiscrimination legislation, says Robertson, "is to change unnecessary employment systems which have an adverse impact" (1978, p. 25). By this measure, stepping up the pace of predetermination settlements that give small or even moderate sums of money to complaining parties while leaving the employer free from a stigma of guilt are nice for the complainants involved but irrelevant in terms of the goal. They do nothing to change the system that produced the alleged discrimination in the first place. They do not even assure the complainant that she will not be returning to the same discriminatory situation or perhaps even a worse one.

This is so, Robertson points out, because a charge of discrimination is, by its very nature, a class charge. When one individual is complaining that she or he is being treated inequitably because of sex or race, she or he is charging that all similarly situated individuals are also being treated inequitably because of sex or race. The payment of back wages, the promotion or reinstatement of one individual is, in itself, not going to change the system that produced the damage. The only remedy that will prevent future damage is a change in that system. According to Robertson, Congress underscored this approach to discrimination when it expanded EEOC's powers in 1972. And indeed the legislative history of the 1972 amendments does indicate that a number of senators and congressmen made statements about the systemic nature of discrimination and the need to change business practices that had exclusionary consequences.

The motive behind the "across the board attack on discrimination" Congress intended, according to Robertson, "is that there is a public interest in eliminating discrimination" (1978, p. 27). He finds backing for his assertion about congressional intent in the Seventh Circuit Court opinion in *Sprogis v. United Airlines* (444 F. 2d 1201 [1971]): "The vindication of the public interest expressed by the Civil Rights Act constitutes an important facet of private litigation under Title VII . . . and the court has a special responsibility in the public interest to devise remedies which effectuate the policies of the Act as well as afford private relief to the individual employee instituting the complaint." Yet there is very little evidence at this time that EEOC has been able to gear up its systemic program into a mechanism for effecting major change and, at the same time, the agency has stopped entirely using individual complaints as a tool for triggering systemic actions. One is forced to ask why a national goal, if that is what existing antidiscrimination laws can be called, is so difficult to meet.

In one of his papers, Robertson (1976) analyzes the tasks EEOC is charged with in terms of Congress as the ultimate "customer." The agency, he points out, has a number of "customers"—complainants, civil rights groups, women and minority group members, employers, labor unions, and taxpayers, for example, might also be considered "customers" for EEOC services. In discussing the idea, Robertson adds,

> ultimately if you draw a United States government paycheck the United States Congress, under the constitution is [composed of] the people who tell you what to do and what not to do. Now there are some constitutional limits on what they can tell you to do and not to do. They cannot tell you to go out and limit everybody's freedom of speech. They cannot tell you to go out and search everybody without a warrant. But within those constitutional limits ultimately Congress grades your paper. . . .

For Robertson, considering Congress as the ultimate customer provides a framework for discussing legislative intent and for analyzing exactly what it is that Congress wanted accomplished when it passed antidiscrimination laws. But if we think for a moment about Congress as the ultimate customer of antidiscrimination agencies rather than the complainants who may wish to have their own grievances explored, we open up a new perspective and we are forced to ask a new set of questions.

Does congressional intent, as spelled out in the antidiscrimination laws, represent the will of the people or at least the will of the majority? Does it even represent the will of Congress, as Robertson believes? Does Congress, as primary "customer" for the equal employment laws, really want what it says it wants: a change in the basic American employment system that has for so long excluded women and members of minority groups or limited them to the classes of jobs and salary levels that nobody else wants? Or are the laws merely a means of mollifying certain elements among the constituency? Does Congress really want enforcement of the antidiscrimination laws?

The questions may seem cynical. But many women who have become frustrated with the antidiscrimination agencies have written their senators or congressmen. They have received help: generally the congressmen have been willing to write forceful letters to agency heads demanding explanations. Generally the explanations have been unsatisfactory. And generally they have been accepted. The congressman merely sends the explanation along to his constituent with a note of his own assuring her that should the need arise he will gladly help out once again. For these women the questions are legitimate.

Among the handful of blacks and women who have achieved high level positions in the Carter administration, as among complainants, there are those who believe that Congress never intended any real systemic change as a result of the laws Congress passed that require such change. For these people, as well, the questions are legitimate. A conversation with one such leader, a black woman, is revealing:

"I have a general philosophical point of view about government enforcement agencies . . . and that is that women and minorities have to understand that government agencies are not likely to enforce any rights that they might think they have, especially when it brings them into economic conflict with men and majority groups. That's the nature of all kinds of economic systems." White males, she insists, are not going to give up economic power to people who have none. Yet that is exactly what civil rights enforcement is all about.

How, then, is progress possible? "Beginning with the Civil Rights Act of 1964, there was a time, from then until about 1970 that people thought there was enough to go around for everybody and that you really could do all kinds of things that were what we call liberal and bring people into the so-called mainstream and it wouldn't hurt you if you did it, you know, it would be fine, there was enough so you could do this." During boom times "people forget about what happens when you're really in direct competition with somebody else." About 1970, she continues, people began to realize that there was not enough to go around. Opening the doors to women and minorities increased the competition unnecessarily. "It doesn't surprise me that you get in the '70s people talking about reverse discrimination. I mean it's just finding another reasons for saying that you don't want to happen what all of human history leads us to believe people would not want to happen. It doesn't surprise me."

But what role does the government antidiscrimination bureaucracy play in this?

> Government agencies are designed to see to it that those people who have power in the society keep the power they've got. Sometimes in order to keep the power you've got to give up a little bit of it to people. It's like FDR and the New Deal: in order to maintain the system he gave a little here and there . . . but he really didn't change the system. What happened in the '60's was giving up a little bit because it seemed like you could and it maintained the status quo and you wouldn't have riots and it wouldn't hurt you anyway. What happened in the '70's then was the notion that all the power that can conceivably be given up for this purpose had been given up and people were lulled into sort of a notion that the problems of disorder were no longer as serious and that they could manage to deal with them.

The women's movement, unfortunately, came along when economic conditions were not the best; when those in power resisted the notion that there was any more that could be given up to mollify those on the outside. "The bureaucracy will do what it's told to do," she explains. During the early 1970s "they knew that if they [brought] one of those issues up to the Secretary there wasn't going to be any enforcement." For a while, she explains, they sent things up again and again, believing the rhetoric of top level government officials about the need to enforce the antidiscrimination laws. "But nothing happened and it became clear to them that nothing would happen. So you get people who are lulled into not doing their jobs because their job is to do something that you're not supposed to do. So then their job becomes to find reasons why you can't do [anything] and to take as long as possible to do it so that it never gets done."

When the administration changed, some people believed that the job of the bureaucracy would change as well and that real enforcement would begin. There was, she says, a burst of enthusiasm with the new administration.

> But what we're all faced with now is that it still is not possible to make room—given the current economic system as it exists—to make room

for everybody. And white males have to give up something. This department, at its top, is run by white males just like almost everything else and they're not about to give up what they have. And they are not about to give it up for all the other white males either. It's not politically feasible. So what you get under these circumstances is very small gains if any at all.

There is, in our society, a tendency to believe that if an issue is public for long enough it will have been resolved.

We have a sloganistic society, our interviewee continues, [and people like to say] we've been talking about employment opportunity for ten years so we must be finished with it—let's talk about something else. If you keep saying, "from now on I'm going to stop all fraud and abuse" and you say that enough times, in five years people think you've stopped all fraud and abuse and it doesn't really matter that you've never stopped it, you get the reputation for having stopped it just because you kept saying it.

Thus we find that among certain close advisors to the president there are those who believe that the time for employment equity enforcement is past—we have already done that—and we should now move on to new programs that focus on "economic incentives" for blacks and women. Thus we find among magazine and newspaper editors a decline in interest in articles that claim that nothing has been done to improve the status of minorities and women: they simply do not believe that this is possible. After all, we have, as a society, been "working on" the issue for almost two decades. And thus we find that even feminist magazines such as *Ms.* have become impatient with the same old depressing stories: the editors search instead for "uppers" to cheer the readers along.

Our interviewee's views may seem harsh to some people, but rarely to people who have attempted to push complaints of discrimination. There are those both inside and outside the antidiscrimination bureaucracy—perhaps many more than those who would agree with out interviewee—who insist that the failure of the antidiscrimination efforts is a result of nothing more than bureaucratic ineptitude. The antidiscrimination agencies, the entire government system, and the courts as well, they insist, are examples of the Peter Principle gone berserk. Nothing works anymore. We are being drowned in a sea of ineptitude. As one observer put it, "The police can't even catch a cold, so what can you expect?"

The two theories are not incompatible, however, and the results are the same: little if any progress for women and members of minority groups. Yet we all know that even with its bureaucratic ineptitude and bumbling and extravagence, our society does get some things done. I think, somewhat dramatically perhaps, of John Kennedy's declared national goal of reaching the moon in the 1960s. We reached the moon.

We declared another national goal in the 1960s—the goal of employment equity for minorities and women. We have not achieved the goal. We are not yet such a society of bunglers that we fail to achieve national goals we wish to achieve. The laws by which we claim equity as a national goal serve a purpose. They pacify those who believe in equity or, when they no longer pacify, they engage those people in prolonged and confusing entanglements with the bureaucracy and with the courts. They lull us into believing that something eventually will be done, that justice in the long run will somehow prevail. Like the Moslem husband who can declare, "I divorce thee," three times and accomplish his divorce, some in our society are willing to concede that equity must be so because it has been declared a legal goal. Let us be blunt: we have not achieved equity because we do not, as a nation, want equity. We will not achieve it until it truly becomes a national goal.

What hope is there, then? "The only way you get change is incrementally," claims our interviewee. "You get small amounts in particularly good times." And, she adds, you get only as much as is necessary to maintain the system. If the economy is on the upswing, small gains are possible. But now it is going down and "white males are not about to give up something. . . . Unless the economic system in this country changes— and I don't think it is going to—to get any more change than that is just not possible."

During one of the final interviews I conducted for this book the complainant I was questioning told me that the antidiscrimination complaint system was not worth using. "Life is much to short for it—mine is much to short," she said. "I don't think it's machinery that a significant number of people are going to use. You have to be crazy. We got involved and we didn't know what we were getting involved in. . . . I wouldn't dream of undertaking a thing like that again."

She was not alone. Said another, "I just feel fortunate that I got through this without breaking down physically or mentally, however, if anybody asked me should they complain, should they file with EEOC, should they go to court, I'd almost have to tell them it's not worth it. The mental anguish you go through is not worth it."

Others express considerable ambivalence. "You have to evaluate the whole picture," said one. "I can win and I know I am going to win. But what have you won? When you get through, you've lost."

But many more believe that one can, with the right attitude, gain from the experience. Writing for the *Federal Times* after her initial win in federal court, June Chewning pointed out:

My first and highest hurdle was stripping away all of my emotional reactions to the situation which had brought me to the point of contemplating filing a complaint—anger, humiliation, vindictiveness, disgust, hurt—so that I could view the situation objectively and decide what was the proper, moral course of action . . . such an undertaking must be toward a positive end, one beyond selfish gain. Otherwise, it would be better if I just took my talents elsewhere and removed myself from the situation" (Chewning 1979).

Chewning believes her attitude helped her survive the complaint process. She concludes: "By aiming for the final objective, all of the petty things that happened in between were just stepping stones to the goal. In fact, many things were so ridiculous that they were humorous. Once one can laugh at the pettiness of a huge government agency, the battle is half won."

Many complainants, knowing everything they have learned through their years of battling the system, insist that they would file again and would encourage other women to do so. "Some people just have to fight, regardless," says one. "I would have filed anyway, even if everybody ahead of me had lost," adds another. A third urges, "Don't be too negative because you will scare off everybody and they won't ever do something. You know, somebody's got to encourage them to keep up the good fight."

Many, like Jenijoy LaBelle, believe they had no choice but to file: they had nothing left to lose. It might have been easier not to fight, LaBelle admits. But, she says, "I didn't see how I could be ruined any more. My scholarship had been besmirched, my teaching had been besmirched. And they said I hadn't served on any committees. It turns out the chairman appoints everyone and he wouldn't appoint me even though I went in and asked him several times to be appointed. Then they held it against me that I didn't serve on committees. I felt I had nothing to lose."

To some it may appear that these women are engaged in an effort as futile as that of Sisyphus, condemned forever to rolling a stone uphill, only to have it slip from his grasp each time he reaches the top. But is it not possible that these women, and hundreds like them who are fighting sex discrimination, are the only ones who are, by their enormous effort, keeping the situation from becoming worse? Pushing a stone uphill, after all, beats lying down at the bottom and allowing the stone to pin you down.

I do not believe "you have to be crazy" to complain and I find these women quite admirable and remarkable. I find nothing sad or self-righteous about them. They have become justifiably angered at the system and they have decided that there are times when fighting injustice is better than silent suffering, even when one grasps the fact that the world is not always just.

Our high level government interviewee pointed out that "we might be worse off if it didn't happen. . . . You could argue that if nobody pushed at all there wouldn't be any women or minorities who would get to do anything . . . at least some people get something and that can't be all bad either."

I began my first book on employment discrimination by quoting the Red Queen in *Through the Looking Glass*. Now, four years later, it seems a fitting way to end my second book on the subject: "Now *here*, you see, it takes all the running *you* can do, to keep in the same place. If you want to get somewhere else, you must run at least twice as fast as that!" This may be, after all, the perfect paradigm for the position of women in the workforce today. And if it is, the message must be that there is no way to stop running and remain in place.

BIBLIOGRAPHY

BOOKS AND ARTICLES

Abramson, Joan. 1977. "Measuring Success or What Ever Happened to Affirmative Action?" *Civil Rights Digest*, Winter, pp. 14-27.

——. 1975. *The Invisible Woman: Discrimination in the Academic Profession.* San Francisco: Jossey-Bass.

Aiken, Ray J. 1976. "Legal Liabilities in Higher Education: Their Scope and Management." *The Journal of College and University Law* 3, nos. 2, 3, 4: 3-214.

Astin, Alexander W. 1977. "Academic Administration: The Hard Core of Sexism in Academe." *UCLA Educator*, Spring, pp. 60-66.

Babcock, Barbara; Ann Freedman; Eleanor Holmes Norton; and Susan C. Ross. 1975. *Sex Discrimination and the Law: Causes and Remedies.* Boston: Little, Brown.

Baker, Curtis O. 1977. *Students Enrolled for Advanced Degrees, Fall 1975 Summary Data.* Washington, D.C.: National Center for Education Statistics, HEW.

Beazley, Richard M. 1977. *Salaries, Tenure, and Fringe Benefits of Full Time Instructional Faculty in Institutions of Higher Education, 1975–76.* Washington, D.C.: National Center for Education Statistics, HEW.

——. 1976. *Salaries and Tenure of Instructional Faculty in Institutions of Higher Education, 1974–75.* Washington, D.C.: National Center for Education Statistics. HEW.

Beazley, Richard M., and George Toolan. 1976. *Higher Education Salaries and Fringe Benefits, 1971-72 and 1972-73.* Washington, D.C.: National Center for Education Statistics, HEW.

Bell, Griffin B. 1977. "Memorandum for United States Attorneys and Agency General Counsels Re: Title VII Litigation." Department of Justice, August 31, Xeroxed.

Bethell, Tom. 1977. "My Turn: Anti-Discrimination Run Amuck." *Newsweek*, January 17, p. 11.

Birnbaum, Norman. 1977. "Higher Education and the Federal Government." *Educational Record* 57 no. 4: 225-31.

Abbreviations used in this bibliography are the same as those used in the text: EEOC for the Equal Employment Opportunity Commission, GAO for the Government Accounting Office, HEW for the Department of Health, Education and Welfare, OFCCP for the Office of Federal Contract Compliance Programs, OCR for the Office for Civil Rights of HEW, OMB for the Office of Management and Budget.

Blumrosen, Alfred W. 1977. "Toward Effective Administration of New Regulatory Statutes." *Administrative Law Review* 29: 87-114, 209-37.

——. 1972. "Strangers in Paradise: Griggs v. Duke Power Co. and the Concept of Employment Discrimination." *Michigan Law Review*, November, pp. 59-110.

Boring, Phyllis Zatlin. N.D. "The Double Use of Availability Data." Washington, D.C.: Women's Equity Action League, Xeroxed.

Bowen, William G. 1975. "Affirmative Action: Purpose, Concepts, Methodologies." In *Affirmative Action 1975: Higher Education Testimony Before the Department of Labor.* Washington, D.C.: American Council on Education, September 30, pp. 6-27.

Brown, Barbara; Ann Freedman; Harriet Katz; and Alice Price. 1977. *Women's Rights and the Law.* New York: Praeger.

Business Week. 1976. "A New Boss Breathes Life into Affirmative Action," May 10, p. 98.

Carter, Jimmy. 1978. "Address to Congress." From press package on civil rights reorganization. Washington, D.C., February 23.

Chewning, June S. 1979. "Forum: Surviving a Class Action Suit: A Matter of Attitude." *Federal Times*, January 15, p. 12

Cilliton, Barbara J. 1975. "Weinberger on Affirmative Action." *Science*, August 22, p. 618.

Daily Labor Report. 1977. "White House Views Expanded EEOC Role." Bureau of National Affairs, October 9, pp. 1-2, G1-G2.

Daniloff, Ruth. 1977. "A 'Shabby Farce' About Women's Rights." Los Angeles *Times*, April 14.

Denniston, Lyle. 1978. "Senate Senses a Hot Potato in Bias Safeguards for Own Employees." Washington *Star*. April 29.

Dorfman, Robert. 1977. "No Progress This Year: Report on the Economic Status of the Profession, 1976–1977." *AAUP Bulletin*, August, pp. 146-228.

——. 1975. "Two Steps Backward: Report on the Economic Status of the Profession, 1974–75." *AAUP Bulletin*, August, pp. 118-99.

Dorfman, Robert, and Donald C. Cell. 1976. "Nearly Keeping Up: Report on the Economic Status of the Profession, 1975–76." *AAUP Bulletin*, August, pp. 195-284.

Eiden, Leo J. 1977. "Salaries of Selected College Administrators." *American Education*, November, back cover.

Frank, Charlotte, and Brook Trent. "Equal Employment Opportunity Commission Model Offices, Summary Progress Report: September 26, 1977–August 28, 1978." Washington, D.C.: EEOC, Xeroxed.

EEOC. 1978a. "Background on Internal Reorganization of the U.S. Equal Employment Opportunity Commission."

EEOC. 1978b. "EEOC: The Transformation of an Agency," July.

EEOC. 1977. "Background on New Charge Processing Procedures of the U.S. Equal Employment Opportunity Commission."

EEOC. 1976. *Tenth Annual Report.*

EEOC. 1975. *Ninth Annual Report.*

EEOC. 1974. *Eight Annual Report.*

EEOC. 1973. *Seventh Annual Report.*

EEOC. 1972. *Sixth Annual Report.*

EEOC. 1971. *Fifth Annual Report.*

EEOC. 1970. *Fourth Annual Report.*

Eynomerie, Maryse. 1978. "Report on the Annual Survey of Faculty Compensation, 1977–78." *AAUP Bulletin*, September, pp. 193-266.

GAO. 1978. *The Affirmative Action Programs in Three Bureaus of The Department of Justice Should be Improved*, July 7.

GAO. 1975a. *The Equal Employment Opportunity Program for Federal Nonconstruction Contractors Can be Improved: Department of Labor*, April 29.

GAO. 1975b. *More Assurances Needed that Colleges and Universities With Government Contracts Provide Equal Employment Opportunity: Departments of Labor and Health, Education and Welfare*, August 25.

GAO. 1974. *Improvements Needed in Examining and Selecting Applicants for Federal Employment*, July 22.

Ginsburg, Ruth Bader. "Women, Equality, and the Bakke Case." *Civil Liberties Review*, November-December, pp. 8-16.

Glickstein, Howard, and Miro Todorovich. 1975. "Discrimination in Higher Education: A Debate on Faculty Employment." *Civil Rights Digest*, Spring.

Golladay, Mary A., and Jay Noell, eds. 1978. *The Condition of Education: 1978 Edition.* Washington, D.C.: National Center for Education Statistics, HEW.

Goodman, Ellen. 1978. "Women's Work." Honolulu *Advertiser*, October 12.

Grant, W. Vance, and C. George Lind. 1978. *Digest of Education Statistics, 1977–78.* Washington, D.C.: National Center for Education Statistics, HEW.

————. 1977. *Digest of Education Statistics, 1976 Edition.* Washington, D.C.: National Center for Education Statistics. HEW.

Hager, Philip. 1975. "'Quota Mentality' in Seeking Equality Rapped by Educator." Los Angeles *Times,* Feburary 15.

Heyns, Roger W. 1975. "Statement." In *Affirmative Action 1975: Higher Education Testimony Before the Department of Labor.* Washington, D.C.: American Council on Education, September 30, pp. 2-4.

Honolulu *Advertiser.* 1978a. "Study raps sex bias in government hiring," October 4.

————. 1978b. "2 DOE rights workers return to court in battle to keep jobs," August 24.

Kashket, Eva Ruth; Mary Louise Robbins; Loretta Leive; and Alice S. Huang. 1974. "Status of Women Microbiologists." *Science,* February 8, pp. 488, 494.

Kilpatrick, James. "Fighting Job Bias Red Tape." Honolulu *Star Bulletin,* January 31.

Legislative History. 1972. *Legislative History of the Equal Employment Opportunity Act of 1972, amending Title VII of the Civil Rights Act of 1964.* Washington, D.C.: U.S. Government Printing Office, 74-699-0.

Los Angeles *Times.* "U.S. Antibias Agency Found Guilty of Bias," January 6.

Maxfield, Betty D.; Nancy C. Ahern; and Andrew Spisak. 1976. *Employment Status of Ph.D. Scientists and Engineers: 1973 and 1975.* Washington, D.C.: National Research Council, National Academy of Sciences.

National Research Council. 1976. *Doctoral Scientists and Engineers in the United States: 1975 Profile.* Washington, D.C. National Academy of Sciences.

National Science Foundation. 1978. *Employment Patterns of Recent Entrants into Science and Engineering: Reviews of Data on Science Resources.* Washington, D.C.: National Science Foundation, June.

————. 1977. *Women and Minorities in Science and Engineering.* Washington, D.C.: National Science Foundation.

Newsweek. 1974. "Quality or Quotas?" July 15.

Northrup, Ann. 1978. "Why the Justice Department Doesn't Want You to Know What Happened Between Otto Passman and Shirley Davis. *Ms.,* January, pp. 57-59.

Norton, Eleanor Holmes. 1978a. "Before the Committee on Governmental Operations, Subcommittee on Legislation and National Security, U.S. House of Representatives, March 2, 1978," EEOC.

————. 1978b. "Remarks at National IMAGE Convention, June 8, EEOC.

————. 1977a. "Testimony Before the Subcommittee on Employment Opportunities, U.S. House of Representatives, July 27, 1977," EEOC.

——. 1977b. "Speech Before the Washington Press Club, December 1", EEOC.

OCR. 1972. *Higher Education Guidelines, Executive Order 11246*. Department of HEW.

OFCCP. 1977. *Preliminary Report on the Revitalization of the Federal Contract Compliance Program*. Department of Labor.

OMB. 1978. *Special Analyses: Budget of the United States Government, Fiscal Year 1979*. Washington, D.C.: U.S. Government Printing Office.

Ott, Mary Diederich. 1977. *Analysis of Doctor's Degrees Awarded to Men and to Women 1970-71 Through 1974-75*. Washington, D.C.: National Center for Education Statistics, HEW.

Panetta, Leon and Peter Gall. 1971. *Bring Us Together*. Philadelphia: J. B. Lippincott.

PEER. 1977. *Stalled at the Start: Government Action on Sex Bias in the Schools*. Washington, D.C.: Project on Equal Education Rights, NOW Legal Defense and Education Fund.

Project on the Status and Education of Women. 1978. "Sexual Harassment: A Hidden Issue." Washington, D.C.: Association of American Colleges, June.

Robertson, Peter C. 1978. "A Discussion of Recent Proposed Guidelines Dealing with Discrimination," EEOC, mimeographed preliminary rough draft.

——. 1976. "What is the Business of the Equal Employment Opportunity Commission? A Paper Submitted to the Carter/Mondale Transition Team," EEOC, December 20.

——. 1975. "Statement on Behalf of the Equal Employment Opportunity Commission Before the Office of Federal Contract Compliance Programs," EEOC, October 7 and November 2.

Sawyer, Kathy. 1977. "Black Woman Wins Fight for $43,592 Federal Job." Washington *Post*, September 22.

Seligman, Daniel. 1973. "How 'Equal Opportunity' Turned into Employment Quotas." *Fortune*, March, pp. 160-68.

Siena, James V. 1975. "Before the Department of Labor: Hearings on Proposed Revisions of Revised Order #4 As it Applies to Institutions of Higher Education." In *Affirmative Action 1975: Higher Education Testimony Before the Department of Labor*. American Council on Education, September 30, pp. 68-92.

Spokeswoman. 1978. "New York Times Women Win." December 15, p. 1.

U.S. Commission on Civil Rights. 1978a. *Social Indicators of Equality for Minorities and Women*, August.

——. 1978b. *The State of Civil Rights: 1977*, February.

——. 1977a. *The Federal Civil Rights Enforcement Effort—1977: To Eliminate Employment Discrimination: A Sequel*.

——. 1977b. *The Federal Civil Rights Enforcement Effort—1974: Volume VII: To Preserve, Protect, and Defend the Constitution*, June.

——. 1975a. *The Federal Civil Rights Enforcement Effort—1974: Volume III: To Ensure Equal Educational Opportunity*, January.

——. 1975b. *The Federal Civil Rights Enforcement Effort—1974: Volume V: To Eliminate Employment Discrimination*.

US Department of Commerce. 1976. *A Statistical Portrait of Women in the U.S.* Current Population Reports, Bureau of the Census.

US. Department of HEW. 1977a. *Selected Statistics on Salaries Paid to Administrators in Colleges and Universities, 1976-77*. Washington, D.C.: National Center for Education Statistics, July.

——. 1977b. *Selected Statistics on Salaries and Tenure of Full-Time Instructional Faculty, 1976-77*. Washington, D.C.: National Center for Education Statistics, April.

——. 1975a. *Final Title IX Regulations Implementing Education Amendments of 1972 Prohibiting Sex Discrimination in Education*.

——. 1975b. *Manual for Investigation of Allegations of Employment Discrimination at Institutions of Higher Education*. Chicago: Commerce Clearing House.

——. 1972. *Higher Education Guidelines, Executive Order 11246*. Office for Civil Rights.

U.S. Department of Labor. 1977. *Minority Women Workers: A Statistical Overview*. Employment Standards Administration, Women's Bureau.

——. 1977a. *Women and Work*. Employment and Training Administration.

——. 1977b. *U.S. Working Women: A Databook*. Bureau of Labor Statistics.

——. 1977c. *Women with Low Incomes*. Women's Bureau, Employment Standards Division.

——. 1976a. *Trends in Women's Employment and Training in Selected Professions*. Women's Bureau, Employment Standards Division.

——. 1976b. *The Earnings Gap Between Women and Men*. Women's Bureau, Employment Standards Administration.

U.S. House. 1978. *Staff Report Comparing Figures for Minority and Female Employment in the Federal Government, 1975 and 1977, and in Forty-Four Selected Agencies, 1977*. Subcommittee on Equal Employment Opportunities, Committee on Education and Labor. Washington, D.C.: U.S. Government Printing Office.

——. 1976a. *Staff Report on Oversight Investigation of Federal Enforcement of Equal Employment Opportunity Laws, Subcommittee on Equal Opportunities, Committee on Education and Labor*. Washington, D.C.: U.S. Government Printing Office.

———. 1976b. *Hearings Before a Subcommittee of the Committee on Appropriations, House of Representatives, Ninety-fourth Congress, Second Session, Part 6: Department of Health, Education and Welfare.* Washington, D.C.: U.S. Government Printing Office.

United States Law Week. 1978. "Review of Supreme Court's Term: Individual Rights." August 22, pp. 47 LW 3081-88.

US News and World Report. 1976. "'Reverse Discrimination' Has it Gone Too Far?" March 29, pp. 26-29.

U.S. Senate. 1976. *Hearings Before a Subcommittee of the Committee on Appropriations, United States Senate, Ninety-Fourth Congress, Second Session, Part 5: Department of Health, Education and Welfare.* Washington, D.C.: U.S. Government Printing Office.

Van Alstyne, Carol; R. Frank Mensel; Jullie S. Withers; and F. Stephen Malott. 1977. *1975-76 Administrative Compensation Survey: Women and Minorities in Administration of Higher Education Institutions: Employment Patterns and Salary Comparisons.* Washington, D.C.: College and University Personnel Association.

Vetter, Betty M.; Eleanor L. Babco; and Judith E. McIntirc. 1978. *Professional Women and Minorities—A Manpower Data Resource Service,* 2d ed. Washington, D.C.: Scientific Manpower Commission.

Vladeck, Judith P., and Margaret M. Young. 1978. "Sex Discrimination in Higher Education: It's Not Academic." *Women's Rights Law Reporter,* Winter, pp. 59-78.

Wall Street Journal. 1978. "Sauce for the Gander," October 9.

Westervelt, Esther Manning. 1975. *Barriers to Women's Participation in Postsecondary Education: A Review of Research and Commentary as of 1973-74.* Washington, D.C.: National Center for Education Statistics.

Williams, Wendy. 1978. *Babcock, Freedman, Norton, Ross's Sex Discrimination and the Law: 1978 Supplement.* Boston: Little, Brown.

WEAL National Newsletter, 1978. "WEAL Suit Responsible for Landmark Result: HEW Agrees to End Bias," March, p. 1.

WEAL News. 1978. "HEW Education Suit: First Year Proves Disappointing," December, p. 1.

WEAL Washington Report, 1978. "WEAL Wins Education Suit: Court Orders U.S. to End Bias," February.

———. 1977. "Veterans' Preference and Affirmative Action Incompatability in the Civil Service," October.

Women's Representative. 1978. "New Study Shows Continued Gap in Men and Women's Earnings," September 30.

INTERVIEWS

Ahmed, Marianne. Office for Civil Rights, HEW. November 17, 1977. Washington, D.C.

Anderson, Barry. Office for Civil Rights, HEW. July 16, 1976. Washington, D.C.

Bailiff, Lynn. Statistician, University of California at Berkeley. September 8, 1976. Berkeley, California.

Bierman, Leonard. Assistant Director, Office of Federal Contract Compliance Programs. July 19, 1976. Washington, D.C.

Bittenbender, Virginia. Administrator, Antitrust Division, Department of Justice. July 19, 1976. Telephone interview.

Blackwell, Ann. Office of Federal Contract Compliance Programs. June 1, 1978 and November 2, 1978. Washington, D.C.

Blumrosen, Alfred. Equal Employment Opportunity Commission. March 1, 1978. Washington, D.C.

Bowker, Albert. Chancellor, University of California at Berkeley. September 1, 1976. Berkeley, California.

Bowman, Irene. Attorney, Antitrust Division, Department of Justice. July 13, 1976, November 28, 1977, and November 2, 1978. Washington, D.C.

Braden, Ina. Former University of Pittsburgh faculty member. December 4, 1977. Pittsburgh, Pennsylvania.

Brown, Cindy. Chief of Operations, Office for Civil Rights, HEW. November 17, 1977 and November 3, 1978. Washington, D.C.

Cameron, Helen. Associate Professor, Montana State University. May 3 and 4, 1978. Bozeman, Montana.

Candea, Henrietta (Lella) Smith. Women's Program Coordinator, Food and Drug Administration, HEW. February 27, 1978. Washington, D.C.

Carter, Iris. Teacher, Dayton School District. May 2, 1978. Dayton, Ohio.

Chandler, Joanne. Attorney, Public Advocates, Inc. April 1, 1974, San Francisco, California.

Chewning, June. Manpower analyst, Department of Energy. December 1, 1977. Washington, D.C.

The following is a list of the persons who were interviewed for this book who had no objection to the use of their names. The office or position of each interviewee at the time of the interview, date of interview, and place of interview follow each name.

Clark, Barbara. Associate Professor, Oglethorpe University. February 11, 1978. Atlanta, Georgia.

Clutts, Alva. Faculty member, Southern Methodist University. November 22, 1977. Dallas, Texas.

Cohen, Herbert. Administrator, Wage and Hour Division, Department of Labor. April 25, 1978. Washington, D.C.

Cole, Ursula. President's Task Force on Civil Rights Reorganization. April 28, 1978. Washington, D.C.

Cussler, Margaret. Associate Professor, University of Maryland. November 29, 1977. College Park, Maryland.

Dinnerstein, Dorothy. Professor, Rutgers University Newark Campus. November 6, 1978. Telephone interview.

Dobbs, Julia. Office of Federal Contract Compliance Programs. November 2, 1978. Washington, D.C.

Dobbyn, Margaret. Former librarian, University of Kansas. November 23, 1977. Oklahoma City, Oklahoma.

Donovan, Joe. Statistician, Office for Civil Rights, HEW. November 17, 1977. Washington, D.C.

Eastwood, Mary. EEO officer, Department of Justice. November 30, 1977. Washington, D.C.

Ervin-Tripp, Susan. Professor, University of California at Berkeley. September 2, 1976. Berkeley, California.

Fitzgerald, Ernest. Cost analyst, Department of Defense. February 19, 1978. Washington, D.C.

Gerry, Martin. Director, Office for Civil Rights, HEW. September 9, 1976. Telephone interview.

Gilinsky, Alberta. Professor, Bridgeport University. November 25, 1977. Scarborough, Connecticut.

Gilinsky, Armand. Attorney. November 25, 1977. Scarborough, Connecticut.

Glickstein, Howard. Director, Task force on Civil Rights Reorganization. November 29, 1977. Washington, D.C. April 25, 1978 and November 2, 1978. Telephone interviews.

Goodwin, James. Office of the Vice-President, University of California. September 6, 1976. Telephone interview.

Green, Lola Beth. Former associate professor, Texas Tech University. February 5, 1978. Telephone interview.

Gregory, Gwendolyn. Public Relations, Office for Civil Rights, HEW. August 23, 1976. Honolulu, Hawaii.

Gutmann, Diana. Naval Air Systems Command. February 27, 1978. Arlington, Virginia.

Hennigan, John. Director, Office for Civil Rights, Maritime Commission, Department of Commerce. February 24, 1978. Washington, D.C.

Heyman, Ira. Vice-Chancellor, University of California at Berkeley. September 1, 1976. Berkeley, California.

Hitch, Charles. Former President, University of California. September 9, 1976. Telephone interview.

Hodgdon, John. Former acting director, Higher Education Division, Office for Civil Rights. July 15, 1976 and February 23, 1978. Washington, D.C.

Hollinshead, May. Professor, New Jersey College of Medicine and Dentistry. May 26, 1978. Newark, New Jersey.

Holmes, Peter. Former Director, Office for Civil Rights. HEW. July 20, 1976. Washington, D.C.

Huessy, Paula. Legal Coordination Division, Equal Employment Opportunity Commission. February 22, 1978. Washington, D.C.

Idelson, Evylyn. Equal Employment Opportunity Commission. February 27, 1978. Washington, D.C.

Johnson, Sharon. Senior Research Associate, University of Pittsburgh Medical School. December 3, 1977. Pittsburgh, Pennsylvania.

LaBelle, Jenijoy. Associate professor, California Institute of Technology. November 10, 1977. Los Angeles, California.

Lau, Sharon Lim. Former affirmative action officer, University of California at Berkeley. September 7, 1976. San Francisco, California.

Lilge, Shirley. Assistant professor, Cleveland State University. May 1, 1978. Cleveland, Ohio.

Lorber, Laurence. Director, Office of Federal Contract Compliance Programs. July 15, 1976. Washington, D.C.

Lowery, Bette. Professor, Montana State University. May 4, 1978. Bozeman, Montana.

King, Patricia. Office for Civil Rights, HEW. September 3, 1976. San Francisco.

Lepper, Mary. Former Director, Higher Education Division, Office for Civil Rights, HEW. July 12, 1976. Chapel Hill, North Carolina.

Leventhal, Mel. Office for Civil Rights, HEW. April 25, 1978. Washington, D.C.

MacDonald, Patricia. Personnel specialist, American Bridge Company. December 4, 1977. Pittsburgh, Pennsylvania.

Madison, Waite, Jr. Office for Civil Rights, HEW. September 3, 1976. San Francisco, California.

Maslack, George. Provost, University of California at Berkeley. September 2, 1976. Berkeley, California.

McEver, Mary Lou. Former assistant professor, University of Florida. February 11, 1978. Atlanta, Georgia.

McGowan, Francis. Administrator, Wage and Hour Division, Department of Labor. April 25, 1978. Washington, D.C.

McKinney, Roy. Office for Civil Rights, HEW. July 17, 1976. Washington, D.C.

Middleton, Mike. Office for Civil Rights, HEW. April 25, 1978. Washington, D.C.

Norton, Eleanor Holmes. Chair, Equal Employment Opportunity Commission. November 3, 1978. Washington, D.C.

Panetta, Leon. Former Director, Office for Civil Rights. September 8, 1976. Telephone Interview. February 22, 1978. Washington, D.C.

Park, Roderick. Provost, University of California at Berkeley. September 2, 1976. Berkeley, California.

Parr, Carol. WEAL Legal Defense and Education Fund. November 30, 1977. Washington, D.C.

Pawlowsky, Barbara. Lieutenant, U.S. Air Force. November 22, 1977. Ft. Worth, Texas.

Pierce, Floyd. Director, Region IX, Office for Civil Rights, HEW. September 3, 1976. San Francisco, California.

Pottinger, Stanley. Assistant Attorney General for Civil Rights, Department of Justice. July 16, 1976. Telephone interview.

Pratt, Eleanor. Affirmative action officer, Montana State University. May 3, 1978. Bozeman, Montana.

Pritchard, Isabel. Graduate student, University of California at Berkeley. August 31, 1976. Berkeley, California.

Rayburn, John. Coordinator, Technical Guidance, Equal Employment Opportunity Commission. February 22, 1978. Washington, D.C.

Robertson, Peter, Director, Program and Policy Planning, Equal Employment Opportunity Commission. June 1, 1978 and June 13, 1978. Washington, D.C.

Rougeau, Weldon. Director, Office of Federal Contract Compliance Programs. April 27, 1978 and May 31, 1978. Washington, D.C.

Sims, Joe. Deputy Assistant Attorney General, Antitrust Division, Department of Justice. July 13, 1976. Telephone interview.

Slavin, Laurie. Attorney, Equal Employment Opportunity Commission. February 27, 1978. Washington D.C.

Solomon, Samuel. Assistant to Assistant Secretary of HEW for Education. December 1, 1977. Washington, D.C.

Spinrad, Phoebe. Captain, U.S. Air Force. November 22, 1977. Ft. Worth, Texas.

St. Lawrence, Patricia. Professor, University of California at Berkeley. September 2, 1976. Berkeley, California.

Suhre, John. Equal Employment Opportunity Commission. April 24, 1978. Washington, D.C.

Tate, Carla. Former EEO specialist, Office for Civil Rights, HEW. March 7, 1978. San Francisco, California.

Tatel, David. Director. Office for Civil Rights, HEW. June 2, 1978. Washington, D.C.

Taylor, Louise. Affirmative action statistician, University of California at Berkeley. November 9, 1977. Berkeley, California.

Trout, Yvonne. Department of the Navy. November 30, 1977. Washington, D.C.

Wego, James. Director, Higher Education Division, Office for Civil Rights. April 25, 1978. Washington, D.C.

Weinberg, Stewart. Carter Campaign policy staff. September 19, 1976. Telephone interview.

Weinberger, Caspar. Former Secreatry of HEW. September 9, 1976. Telephone interview.

White, Barbara. Computer specialist, Office for Civil Rights, HEW. February 23, 1978. Washington, D.C.

Wiener, Rosa. Office for Civil Rights, HEW. February 28, 1978. Washington, D.C.

Williams, Diane. Former assistant to the public relations director, Community Relations Service, Department of Justice. December 2, 1977. Arlington, Virginia.

Wilson, Olly. Professor, University of California at Berkeley. September 2, 1976.

Winsey, Valentine Rossili. Associate Professor, Pace College. November 27, 1977. New York, New York.

Wolinsky, Sid. Attorney, Public Advocates, Inc. September 3, 1976. San Francisco, California.

OTHER SOURCE MATERIALS

In addition to the materials listed in the bibliography and the interviews, I have used a wealth of material that is not generally available to the public. A number of the complainants I interviewed, for example, were kind enough to provide me with unpublished manuscripts detailing their complaints, as well as with letters and memoranda exchanged with employers and agencies and findings by the various agencies. Some material was also gathered from the various agencies through the Freedom of Information Act and through my own sources inside the agencies. Material for the chapter on statistical manipulations was gathered from the various university affirmative action submissions to the government as well as from the HEW computerized case following system and from later hand-tabulated HEW statistics.

INDEX

ABOUT THE AUTHOR

JOAN ABRAMSON is a writer and consultant in the area of affirmative action and equal employment opportunity. She has a master's degree in journalism from the University of California at Los Angeles and has worked as a newspaper and magazine writer and editor for various publications, including the Palo Alto *Times*, the Redwood City *Tribune*, *Time* Magazine, *Life* Magazine, and the Time-Life Book Division.

Abramson taught for six years at the University of Hawaii in the Department of English and at New College. She served as assistant director of New College in 1972–73 and was elected director of New College and chair of the University of Hawaii faculty senate in 1973. Currently Abramson is the plaintiff in a sex discrimination suit against the University of Hawaii.

Abramson has published six books, including two in the area of Hawaiiana (*Mark Twain's Letters From the Sandwich Islands* and *Photographers of Old Hawaii*) and one concerning discrimination against women in the academic world (*The Invisible Woman: Discrimination in the Academic Profession*). She has also written a number of magazine articles on employment equity.